About the Author

Albert Ellis holds M.A. and Ph.D. degrees in clinical psychology from Columbia University and has been Adjunct Professor of Psychology at Rutgers, at United States International University, and at Pittsburg State College. He has served as Chief Psychologist of the New Jersey State Diagnostic Center and Chief Psychologist of the New Jersey Department of Institutions and Agencies, as well as a Consultant in Clinical Psychology to the New York City Board of Education and to the Veterans Administration. He currently is Executive Director of the Institute for Rational-Emotive Therapy. He has practiced psychotherapy, marriage and family therapy, and sex therapy for over forty years and continues this practice at the Psychological Clinic of the Institute at 45 East 65th Street, New York, N.Y. 10021-6593.

Dr. Ellis is a Fellow of many psychological associations; has been President of the Society for the Scientific Study of Sex, Vice President of the American Academy of Psychotherapists, and an officer of the American Association of Marital and Family Therapists, the American Association of Sex Educators, Counselors and Therapists, and of several other professional societies. He is a Diplomate in Clinical Psychology of the American Board of Professional Psychology, a Diplomate in Clinical Hypnosis, and a Diplomate of the American Board of Psychotherapy.

Several professional societies have honored Dr. Ellis, including the Humanist of the Year Award of the American Humanist Association, the Distinguished Psychologist Award of the Academy of Psychologists in Marital and Family Therapy, the Distinguished Practitioner Award of the Division of Psychotherapy of the American Psychological Association, the Distinguished Professional Contributions to Knowledge Award of the American Psychological Association, and Membership in the National Academy of Practice in Psychology.

Dr. Ellis has served as Counsulting or Associate Editor of many psychological and sociological journals. He has published over six hundred papers and one hundred cassettes; and has authored or edited more than fifty books and monographs, including *Sex Without Guilt, How to Live with a "Neurotic," Reason and Emotion in Psychotherapy, Humanistic Psychotherapy: The Rational-Emotive Approach, A New Guide to Rational Living, Overcoming Procrastination, A Handbook of Rational-Emotive Therapy, A Guide to Personal Happiness, Rational-Emotive Approaches to the Problems of Childhood,* and *Overcoming Resistance: Rational-Emotive Therapy with Difficult Clients.*

Books by Albert Ellis, Ph.D.

HOW TO LIVE WITH A NEUROTIC
THE AMERICAN SEXUAL TRAGEDY
THE ART AND SCIENCE OF LOVE
CREATIVE MARRIAGE
ENCYCLOPEDIA OF SEXUAL BEHAVIOR
A GUIDE TO RATIONAL LIVING
SEX AND THE SINGLE MAN
SEX WITHOUT GUILT
REASON AND EMOTION IN PSYCHOTHERAPY
and others

How to Raise An Emotionally Healthy, Happy Child

Albert Ellis, Ph. D.
with Sandra Moseley & Janet L. Wolfe

formerly titled:
How to Prevent Your Child From Becoming a Neurotic Adult

Melvin Powers
Wilshire Book Company

12015 Sherman Road, No. Hollywood, CA 91605

Published by arrangement with Crown Publishers, Inc.

Contents

1

Neurotics Are Born As Well As Made

In spite of the popularity of the scads of authoritative works on child care that now exist, no drastic drop in the rate of neurosis in our society seems to have been wrought since our grandmothers' day. It is estimated that one out of four Americans seeks psychotherapy or counseling of one type or another each year; and this is probably only a fraction of those who should receive help. The most intensive study ever done of a large segment of the population in New York City concluded that more than eight out of ten of the individuals who were investigated were quite seriously emotionally disturbed. Similar studies tend to show that people in other parts of the country are equally neurotic.

The present book takes a radically different stand from most of the existing literature in the field. It stoutly combats the orthodox Freudian and behaviorist view that neurotic behavior is strictly a matter of upbringing, and that early environment so completely determines a child's life that he is bound to be either emotionally stable or aberrated. Not that this view is entirely false; for there is no doubt, as we shall show later in this volume, that early teaching and training do have some specific and significant effects on behavior in childhood, adolescence, and adulthood. But this is only part of the story!

The rest of the story, as Sigmund Freud was careful to note, but as most of his followers have unfortunately forgotten, is that man is a biologically rooted animal. While he has virtually no strict instincts, in the sense that most of the lower animals do, he has a great many inborn propensities, or what Abraham Maslow calls "instinctoid" tendencies; and the various kinds of things which he can easily be trained or conditioned to do are closely related to these innate biological trends. The rewards or "reinforcers" that psychologists and parents employ to induce him to go to bed early, or to refrain from hitting other children, or to feel safe when he is riding in an automobile are things which he innately *likes,* such as to eat lollipops or to be caressed. If inherently noxious or dislikable things are used to "reward" his good behavior, they will rarely work; but these same innately disliked things—such as spanking or isolation—may readily be used to train him not to indulge in various kinds of poor behavior.

More important, perhaps, children (as well as adults) have inborn tendencies which make it much easier for them to behave badly or neurotically than for them to behave well or sanely. This does not mean that they are born with specific neurotic symptoms, such as shyness, hostility, or a tendency to bed-wetting. They rarely, if ever, are. But they do seem to inherit tendencies toward irritability, perfectionism, and short-range hedonism which make it much easier for them to become shy, hostile, and bed-wetting than for them to avoid these behaviors. This means that although they are not irrevocably imprinted, at birth, with specific neurotic characteristics, they are biologically prejudiced to acquire and retain some of these traits; and unless something is actively, directly, and consistently done by their parents and by themselves to counter and thwart these inborn tendencies, they will probably be troubled for the rest of their days.

Peculiarly enough, although I first practiced psychoanalysis for several years, and was biased by my psychological training to believe in the all-important effects of environment on human behavior, I found that my clinical observations contradicted this hypothesis, and I began to believe more and more that hereditary factors also play an enormous role in emotional disturbance. For years, I received virtually no support for my theories from other psychotherapists; but recently experimental and clinical studies seem to have caught up with my thinking.

Thus, recent studies at the National Institutes of Health show that, from birth onward, children exhibit clear-cut temperamental differences. When subjected in their cribs to such stimuli as cold discs, one child bawls vociferously while another calmly shifts an inch or two. Long-term studies have also demonstrated that the child who is inhibited at birth and in childhood continues to act in a similar fashion into adulthood, while the energetic, assertive child becomes an equally energetic and assertive adult. The old theories which hold that there are definite stages of development for all children, whereby a child passes through a nasty phase at age four and then emerges into sunniness and tractability at age five, are being made obsolescent by scientists who now find that a child's unique and largely inherited reaction pattern is the chief determinant of his behavior at each age level.

It has also recently been found that, just as a mother may influence the development of her child by her own behavior, so may a baby be born with certain traits that directly influence his own development and direct the way his mother responds to him. Dr. Leon Yarrow, a noted research psychologist, says in this respect: "Most of the research on parent-child relationships has been designed to consider one-way effects—the influence of the mother on the child's behavior. The major reorientation required in our thinking is to accept the fact that the infant is a potent set of stimuli." In one of his studies, Dr. Yarrow reports that one infant placed with foster parents was an exceptionally cuddly baby, whose foster mother and her entire family found that holding and feeding him was "a mutually gratifying experience," while another infant was "tense, restless and apparently uncomfortable in being held," so that his foster parents did not treat him very warmly.

Whereas psychoanalytic theorists are always insisting that the rejecting behavior of parents drives their children into isolation, Dr. Yarrow contends that many of the infants he observed literally drove their parents (or foster parents) into rejecting attitudes because of their own poor behavior. With one of his negative infants, Potter, Yarrow reports that "This pattern of isolation, deprivation, and rejection started very early with Potter and became accentuated. The differences in handling and the differences in feeling toward the two infants [that is, Potter and the cuddly child mentioned in the previous paragraph] were apparent before they were three months of age."

Drs. Stella Chess, Alexander Thomas, and Herbert G. Birch have been conducting studies of infants, including long-term follow-up observations, for several years, and they fully confirm the fact that all children are unique, and that they are born with very definite physiological tendencies which often predispose them to react in certain psychological ways. They note, for example, that the way in which a child responds to new situations is most important, since it may determine how quickly or slowly he adjusts to a new person, place, or thing and may influence his attitude when he anticipates a novel experience. They report:

"It may make a big difference in the way other people react to him. The child who can meet the new and unfamiliar easily and cheerfully has a decided advantage. The toddler who bounces into a roomful of new people bursting with curiosity and zest gets a smiling welcome. This adventurous, outgoing type meets with few brush-offs. As a result, he usually views the world as a delightful place full of friendly, helpful people. Successive good experiences fortify this attitude. He makes friends sooner. Life with him is easy for his parents, and this inevitably makes life pleasant for him.

"At the other extreme is the child who has a tantrum when he has to deal with the strange and new. He can't seem to adjust quickly to a change of scene. He usually shies away from a new face. He is distressed at the prospect of trying anything different, from skates to arithmetic. Grownups and children, too, have a hard time getting interested in a youngster who stays on the sidelines, answers questions in monosyllables, and rejects their first efforts to make him happy.

"In our study we have been able to gather information on the different ways in which children react to the new. The differences have been evident in the first months of life. Most of the children have retained their characteristic pattern as they have grown older."

Related evidence shows that the old behavioral and psychoanalytic theories of how parents absolutely influence and determine the behavior of their children are sadly misleading. Thus, according to psychoanalysis, babies who are weaned early from their mothers' breasts and are forced to drink from a bottle or cup should exhibit great signs of frustration and restlessness. But an actual study conducted at the University of Iowa, in the course of which three groups of young children were fed with breast, bottle, and cup, showed that all three groups were equally restless and frustrated. Moreover, longer-term studies showed that fifteen-year-old youngsters who were cup-fed as babies were not different in personality from children of the same age who were allowed to breast-feed for a much longer time during their infancy.

The concept of the utter perniciousness of maternal deprivation, which again was almost undisputed twenty years ago, has also been seriously challenged today. Harry Harlow's famous studies of monkeys have shown that offspring nurtured by a warm, terry-cloth mother-substitute grow up to be as healthful as those nurtured by animal mothers; and that it is more important for the monkey's mental and physical health for him to receive ample stimulation from playing with his siblings than it is for him to have much intimate contact with his own mother during his infanthood. More to the point, it has recently been shown that human children with constantly attendant mothers who gave them considerable attention and love were not mentally healthier than infants who were communally cared for in a nursery for the greater part of the day because their mothers were working.

Still another kind of recent study has tended to undermine the undue importance that has previously been placed on the role of early influences in traumatizing children. Some researchers have wisely studied the case histories of normal children and adults, to discover what kinds of traumas they encountered during their early childhoods. In one such study of one hundred individuals, who were diagnosed as being psychologically normal at the time they were studied, it was found that their childhood histories contained as many traumatic events and other tensions and hazards as did the histories of disabled psychotic patients. No significant differences were found between the normals and the psychotics in regard to family tension, excessively rigid or indulgent patterns of discipline, oedipal anxieties, unresolved sibling rivalries, or repressed sexuality.

On the other side of this same fence, Dr. Aaron Beck of Philadelphia has been intensively studying depressed patients for the last several years, and he finds that when the so-called traumatic events of these patients' early lives are investigated in detail, it appears that these events were really minor upsets and frustrations, which the patients *viewed* as being terribly catastrophic, and hence actually *made* traumatic. I have consistently found the same thing in my severely neurotic and borderline psychotic patients: Frequently, their early lives were no more traumatic than those experienced by the rest of us, but they were apparently predisposed, from birth onward, to interpret the common frustrations and disappointments of existence as being catastrophic. They therefore *invented* most of the traumas that they claimed to have experienced.

So much evidence of various kinds has been accumulating in the last decade, indicating that environment is not all-important in sensitizing the child to emotional upsets, that even such a dyed-in-the-wool psychoanalyst as Edmund Bergler finally concluded, just before his death, that it is not the parents' attitudes and the psychological climate they provide that create automatic changes in the child's unconscious attitudes toward himself and others; rather, it is the child's unique and largely inborn way of viewing the world and the people around him that importantly contributes to what happens to him. The best that his parents can do if they are to rear him with few disturbances is to provide a climate where he will have minimal opportunities to display his own tendencies to get into serious conflicts with reality.

Bergler also embraced a semibiological view by pointing out that seriously neurotic children tend to perpetuate their misery, whether the abuses that occur to them are real or imagined, while the truly abused but non-neurotically predisposed child tends to correct his situation and his view of the world later in life, so that he is not continually miserable even when unpleasant events occur.

It should not be thought for a moment that just because we realistically keep pointing out in the pages of this book the biological underpinnings of all human behavior, including what are usually termed emotional disturbances, that we take a fatalistic view about what parents can do to educate their children to stave off or to minimize neurosis. On the contrary, we take the opposite view, for several reasons:

(1) The mere fact that a tendency, or even a specific human trait, is inborn hardly means that nothing can be done about changing it. Pronounced tendencies toward curvature of the spine, teeth malformations, poor muscle development, and a host of other physical defects are distinctly inherited (or else acquired through pathological influences when a child is in his mother's uterus); yet most of these inborn predispositions can be appropriately corrected through proper treatment, diet, exercise, and other therapeutic measures. Similarly, children who have inborn mental proclivities—such as those toward slow reading, doing poorly in arithmetic, and having huge temper tantrums—can definitely be trained so that they are minimally handicapped in these respects by the time they reach adolescence or adulthood.

(2) Man not only has the power to correct his innate defects, he also has the ability, if he is willing to put in much work and practice, to add in an almost superhuman fashion to his inborn talents. Thus, although he is born with a mild ability to do gymnastics, he can train himself to be such a fine gymnast that he can learn to swing from trees better than, say, monkeys, who are born with a natural propensity for that kind of activity.

(3) Man is the one animal who *can* change his inherited

characteristics. His behavior is invariably the result of both hereditary and environmental influences, and by modifying the latter he can seriously modify the effects of the former. Unlike lower animals, he has a large cerebral cortex, which gives him the power to re-evaluate and reassess his own perceptions and hypotheses and to change himself significantly in various directions. Although he hardly has unlimited power to change—for example, he cannot flap his hands and fly, no matter how often he tries—he does have considerable ability to do so. Man, moreover, is a uniquely acculturated animal; his cultural heredity is just as important as his physiological heredity; and that cultural aspect of his life he can significantly—and even greatly—change. Finally, man is now beginning to understand his hereditary apparatus, and he is getting more and more in the position of being able to modify it. He can already selectively breed certain propensities into or out of himself if he wishes to do so; and by surgical, drug, and other physical procedures he may soon be able to change his chromosomal structure and modify his heredity directly.

(4) If man acknowledges his hereditary defects and disadvantages, he can then do much more to change his physical and emotional ways than if he refuses, in an ostrich-like manner, to admit their existence. The more we face the fact that our children often are born with very strong predispositions to be emotionally disturbed in various ways, the less we shall tend to blame them for their behavior, the less we shall condemn ourselves for making them the way they are, and the more we shall be able to show them that persistent hard work to overcome their biologically predisposed handicaps will be rewarding. To become truly minimally neurotic, we have to admit that it *is* very difficult for us to fight against our inborn tendencies to be disturbed, but that we can still greatly prevail if our battle is hard and continuous.

(5) Sometimes genetic endowments, though in some ways handicapping, can be put to good use when fully accepted. The "difficult child" who cries and screams from the moment his umbilical cord is cut may be helped to utilize some of his special sensitivity and may become a brilliant, if high-strung, artist. The

withdrawn baby whose parents calmly accept his tendency toward shyness, and who do not insist that he be molded into a bubbling, assertive youngster, may be helped to emerge into a persevering scholar who may never fully enjoy people but who may do remarkably well with books and writing materials.

It is one of the main functions of this book, then, to stress the full scope of psychological heredity *and* environment. If I didn't believe in the power of environmental conditioning, I would hardly write a book on child-rearing, for unless parents can have a highly important influence on their children, why should they bother to learn any child-care practices over and above taking good care of their physical needs? I do believe strongly in environmental influence. Even though, as Lois Murphy points out, the child's environment is filtered by his own perceptual and conceptual tendencies, this environment also interacts importantly with these tendencies, and in its turn helps modify them. Thus, a child may feel that his mildly arguing parents are very angry at each other; but their real anger may also tend to be unpleasing to him, make him look for signs of its breaking out again, and thereby help him interpret what are actually mild arguments as great hostile outbursts.

An empirical example of the interaction of environment and heredity was found by Dr. Charles A. Malone in his study of the influence of external danger in the lives of children of disorganized families. Dr. Malone found that the children he investigated "are reared by mothers who are limited in their capacity to give and frustrate excessively; on the other hand, the children are overindulged and infertilized. They grow up in a world of general apathy, inactivity, and 'depression' in a derelict, normless society." Because these mothers probably couldn't and wouldn't give the children realistic norms to live by, Dr. Malone found that "under the pressures of outer danger and the need to grow up fast, these children grow up too fast and relinquish their childhoods too early. Their early independence and premature coping and defensive ability do not lead to later full independence. It is our impression that the children's premature capacity to adjust leads to early closure of their development whereby genuine mastery and flexible adaptability are forfeited."

In another study of environmental conditioning, by Dr. Robert G. Wahler and his associates, a stubborn child was treated with behavior therapy by having his mother ignore his oppositional behavior and respond enthusiastically and with a smile to his cooperative behavior. After a short while, his oppositional behavior declined sharply in rate, while his rate of cooperative behavior increased markedly. In this and other cases of difficult children it was found that the mothers were unwittingly provided social reinforcement for their children's behavior, and when the experimenters induced the mothers to ignore the poor conduct and to provide rewards for opposing kinds of behavior, this differential reinforcement procedure was quite effective in helping improve the children's conduct.

So environmental manipulation can certainly help; but only within realistic limits, which are partly formed by the child's heredity. It is my aim in this book to recognize these limits and at the same time to suggest to parents actions which may aid a child to grow emotionally, so that, achieving the best that he can from his inborn potential, he will become a happy, confident person.

Although the points made in this book apply to children from infancy onward, there is a special emphasis on procedures that are useful with those above the age of five. This emphasis on the emotional training and educating of children upwards of five is made for several reasons. For one thing, it is exceptionally difficult to tell whether a child really has an emotional problem or is predisposed to neurotic behavior during his first four years because so much of his behavior during that time is, at least from an adult standpoint, relatively bizarre and "childish" that it is still too early to see very clearly whether he is headed in a truly aberrant direction. There are certain modes of behavior, such as autistic schizophrenia, where a child withdraws completely and silently into a world of his own for months at a time, that clearly indicate serious disturbance. Also, in the case of children who later turn out to be very disturbed, motor behavior of a bizarre nature, such as head hanging and tic-like movements, may frequently be observed during their first few years. But in children who become moderately neurotic adults, these signs may be totally lacking; and much of what appears to be utterly "crazy" activity on the part of a very young child, including jumping up and down and rolling his eyes, may be fairly normal or else is soon outgrown.

By the same token, certain doings of children become problems only when the children have reached a sufficiently advanced age. Bed-wetting, for example, is quite normal for three-year-olds. But when a six- or seven-year-old child is continually enuretic, it is obvious that he has a distinct problem.

Although very young children may display bizarre behavior and may be said to be indicating evidences of disturbance, what we usually call *neurosis* is largely a matter of disrupted communication, with the individual's not being able to communicate effectively with himself and others. Another way of stating this is to say that neurotic behavior stems from the individual's tendency to evaluate himself and others in an exaggerated, distorted manner; and since children are not too effective at making evaluations, generalizations, or conceptions until they are around five years of age, it is difficult to tell how neurotically trended they are until they become that old.

Another point is that children, partly because of their increased mobility, tend to become much more socialized after the age of five than previously; they tend to interact more steadily with other children and adults. At this age, their neurotic thinking becomes much more important to their effective performance and therefore begins to show itself more conspicuously.

Finally, and perhaps most importantly, I disagree with the Freudian hypothesis that children can best be helped to become relatively unneurotic adults by emphasizing their very early emotional training and education, and particularly by stressing the proper breast weaning, toilet training, and eating habits. There is no real evidence that faulty bowel training traumatizes a child for the rest of his life, and much evidence that this is not true. There is much more evidence that good thinking and healthy living habits can more logically be taught to most children when they are five years of age or older than when they are considerably younger. For they then can be *persuaded* rather than merely *conditioned* to think and act more rationally, can become problem-solving rather than merely auto-suggestive individuals.

I am convinced, in other words, that although tendencies to be disturbed are to some extent inborn in a child, and although these tendencies may distinctly be exacerbated by the ways in which his parents relate to him when he is very young, the alleviation and removal of these tendencies is not very practicable until the child learns to use language. He can then be shown what his basic attitudes toward himself and others are, and he can be taught how to change these attitudes for the better. Once he begins to verbalize to himself his attitudes toward himself and the world, the adults around him can effectively show him by their teachings and their own behavior how to modify and improve his internalized "philosophies" of life, so that he can become, while still a child, much less neurotic, and so that he can grow into a relatively healthy adult.

This book will consequently attempt to show parents how to assess their child's unique genetic endowment, as evinced by the behavioral patterns that emerge in his first five years or so of life, and how to see the child's temperament producing a reaction in themselves—a reaction that they then tend to feed back to the child, influencing his personality growth or maldevelopment. It will try to teach parents how to be alert to the weaknesses of even an irritable and whiny youngster; how to firmly teach him the differences between his desires and his needs; and how to reduce his threshold of frustration to a level where he can accept the perpetual disappointments of life.

More specifically, this book will show parents how to teach their child the far greater efficacy of his realistically accepting rather than grandiosely making himself angry about a harsh world; and the virtue of his refusing to catastrophize about the dangers rather than making himself needlessly anxious over them.

It will indicate methods by which the child can be taught to accept himself as a worth-while human being even when he fails, so that he will be able to go forth into adolescence and adulthood with maximum self-acceptance and full ability to overcome the innumerable stresses of modern life.

2

What Is a Neurotic Child?

What is a neurotic child?

A perfectly honest answer to this question might well be: every child. For if an adult neurotic is an individual who consistently acts illogically, irrationally, inappropriately, and childishly, the question may well be asked: What child doesn't? A child, naturally, is childish.

A youngster, moreover, has a mental age which is low, no matter what his Intelligence Quotient, or I. Q., may be. Thus, if a child of six has an I. Q. of 150—which is exceptionally high, since it places him in the upper one per cent of the populace in intelligence—his mental age is still only nine; and at that age, what human being would behave with consistent rationality and sanity?

Even bright children, we must also admit, are abysmally inexperienced in many essential ways. I am presently seeing for psychotherapy a remarkably sharp lass of twelve, who is far better able to enter into philosophical discussions with me than is her reasonably intelligent mother. But she knows hardly a thing about sex, dieting, or social intercourse. So, naturally, she behaves very stupidly in these (and several other) areas. Is she, then, truly neurotic or emotionally disturbed? Or is she mainly (and, I hope, understandably) ignorant?

"But doesn't that depend on her behavior?" you ask. Yes, to some extent it does. And her behavior, admittedly, is execrable: She continually masturbates in school; stuffs herself to a fare-thee-well during and in between meals; and is inordinately insulting to many other children.

"Well?" you demand. "Doesn't that show that this child is emotionally disturbed?"

It could, I respond. But let's make sure, first, that it does before we put the girl in a special class for disturbed children or cart her off to the psychotherapist's office. For—lest we forget—she is a child; and children do almost routinely make false conclusions about themselves and the universe. That's the way their thinking apparatuses are constructed. Maturation (meaning, increased chronological age and concomitant growth) alone often turns them from howling demons into quite well-behaved adolescents or young adults; while the same can often *not* be said for certain other children who may behave angelically only to manifest (ten or twenty years later) serious behaviorial and emotional problems.

"Why, then, are you seeing this twelve-year-old monster, if you don't think that she's disturbed enough to merit psychotherapeutic attention?"

Oh, I didn't quite say that. I merely noted the possibility that, with her presenting symptoms, she was not so much disturbed as she was the victim of inexperience and ignorance. Actually, several sessions of psychotherapy with this youngster have revealed a substratum of self-hate a mile deep, along with an inordinate intolerance of others. Much of her time spent in trying to put other children down, hoping thereby to elevate herself, consists of vain attempts to compensate for the low esteem she has for herself. Her self-defeating and antisocial behavior is itself not remarkably different from that of many other children—but her general philosophy of life is addled: a philosophy which tells her that either she must be utterly superior to all her associates, or else she is worthless. As a result of this self-defeating view of herself and others, she has acquired the narcissistic, overeating, and hostile behavior for which she was sent for therapy; and unless she changes this view, she will doubtless acquire many other unpleasant symptoms. It is this attitude, then, which makes her emotionally disturbed; and it is not just her dysfunctional behavior—which could well stem from ignorance, intrinsic stupidity, the specific teachings of her parents or peers, or from various other sources.

"Is neurosis, then, strictly a matter of attitude and philosophy of life?" you may ask.

Pretty much so, say I. It is an unrealistic, immature, and usually self-immolating way of looking at oneself and the world. It is a perfectionistic or grandiose demand (rather than a reasonable enough preference) that things occur and people act in a certain way; it is *over*-concern about and *over*-reactivity to the things that may or do happen in life; and it is usually a determined, pigheaded *refusal* to accept oneself and the world as they are and an asinine insistence that things *should,* or *ought,* or *must* be different from the way they are.

"Well, that may be," you note. "But—and now I'm beginning to see the wisdom of what you said right at the start—if neurosis consists of being demanding, or being overconcerned and overreactive, and of stupidly insisting that things should, ought, or must be a certain way (when it is obvious to any thinking person that they often are not that way), aren't these kinds of thinking patterns or attitudinal ways indigenous to practically every child? Isn't it practically the very essence of childhood for the youngster to be consistently demanding, overreactive, and moralistic?"

No, not consistently. Here lies one of the main distinctions between the states of mental health and emotional disturbance. The disturbed child—much like the emotionally upset adult—consistently, rigidly, and bigotedly sticks to his view that things aren't the way they ought to be, either with himself or his fellows; and, by George, they should be the way they are not. The

normal child (or the normal but somewhat childish adult) sometimes is reasonable about his demands—and sometimes is not.

"So the real neurotics are nothing but bigots—is that it?"

Yes, that's pretty much it. All human beings tend to be born
and raised in such a manner that they very easily and surprisingly
often act in a foolish, self-sabotaging, and socially inappropriate
way. They are therefore all, and this includes even the most
intelligent among us, genetically predisposed to be what we might
call "normal neurotics," or occasional self-destroyers. Thus—if
you would like some proof of this thesis—just look around you.
How many people do you know who do not, at one time or another, overeat, oversmoke, overimbibe alcohol, or otherwise
abuse their health? And how many do not fairly regularly put
off their homework or other assignments until the very last minute, and consequently do them poorly; or do not stay too long
at a party, when they have faithfully promised themselves to get
to bed early that night; or do not cravenly go along with what
their friends or neighbors want them to do, instead of firmly
standing up for their own desires and interests? Incredibly few!

"True. But these 'normal neurotics' are not the bigots you
mentioned a few paragraphs back, are they?"

No, that's exactly the point. These ordinary, fallible, and therefore frequently self-destructive, people are still only intermit-
tently and unrigidly disturbed. But the true neurotic is a Jehovian
or Hitlerian moralist who really believes that right is right and
wrong is wrong and that there are no two ways about it. He is
what Eric Hoffer has termed a "true believer"—one who absolutely and inalterably knows the Truth with a capital T, and who
is not going to permit himself to be talked out of this Truth no
matter what contradictory evidence is presented against it. My
twelve-year-old patient, for example, dogmatically believes that
she must obtain 100 per cent on every spelling test—or else she
cannot spell at all. She thinks that if her friends, even on a single
occasion, behave badly, they deserve to be immediately pulver-
ized. She feels that if she has a single "impure" sex thought, she
should roast forever in Hell. And yet, this is an exceptionally
bright girl, who does remarkably well in mathematics and his-

tory, and who is thought by several of her teachers to be almost a genius.

"I see what you mean. She's pretty rigid."

Yes; and so, I contend, are nearly all serious neurotics or psychotics. Not only do they fail to think straight about themselves and the world (which is true of just about all of us on innumerable occasions), but it's almost as if they *can't* cogitate in a flexible, error-checking manner, especially when it comes to gauging their reactions toward others. Actually, as I think I have shown in my psychotherapeutic practice during the last twenty years, these severely disturbed individuals can, with much prodding and guidance, think considerably better about themselves and their surroundings than they usually do; but they seem to have great difficulty in doing so; and are almost allergic to continuing to think straight for any period of time. Given proper guidelines, and practically being *forced* to follow them for a while, they can gradually be trained to become more consistent straight-thinkers. But what a job it is to teach them! And how they usually resist!

"Is that the answer, then, to the problem of neurosis—training in straight thinking?"

Definitely yes, in my way of looking at things. But more of that later. What we're trying to determine, at this point, is exactly what serious emotional disturbance, especially in children, is. Later on in this book we'll get around to more of the details of how to treat it.

"Fair enough. I take it, then, that your twelve-year-old patient is overdeterminedly moralistic, both about herself and about others; and that is why you think that she is more than "childish" and why you differentiate her from other children who may have similar behavioral traits, but who are so endowed for other reasons."

Exactly. And that's the way it is, I contend, with practically all severely neurotic, borderline psychotic, or outright psychotic children. All these terms, incidentally, are somewhat interchangeable, depending on who is doing the diagnosing. If a psychologist or a psychiatrist is something of a "do-gooder" and does not believe in labeling people negatively, he tends to call highly disturbed individuals *behavior problems* or *emotionally confused* or perhaps *neurotic*. If he is more hardheaded, and does not believe that overreactive and consistently self-defeating individuals should be personally condemned and punished for their peculiarities (as, alas, they often are excoriated and penalized in our society), he may call these same people *sick* or *schizoid* or *autistic* or *psychotic*.

Theoretically, a child may be deemed to be *neurotic* when he is moderately but not too encompassingly disturbed, while he may be said to be *borderline psychotic* or *psychotic* when he is more severely aberrated. However, terminology in this area is so confused and unstandardized, and usage is so inconsistent, that the word neurotic may well cover any kind of emotional upsetness, from the relatively light to the extremely heavy. We shall try to use the term in this book to refer to a child who is pretty severely disturbed, rather than to one who has some mild or moderate manifestations of upsettability, and who may well, if left to his own devices, fairly easily straighten himself out and begin acting within the normal range of youthful behavior.

Let us now list some of the results of childhood neurosis: the behavior problems which result from an unduly narrow, rigid way of viewing oneself and the world.

Self-depreciation

The vast majority of neurotics feel that they are quite worthless. They perfectionistically demand that they achieve mightily; and many of them believe that they must do practically everything better than everyone else in the world. Consequently, they spend their time comparing, comparing, comparing themselves to others; and when there is even the slightest possibility that they may not measure up to others—that others may surpass them in some significant area that they have chosen to excel in —they become woefully self-depreciating and depressed, and tend to evaluate themselves as worth absolutely nothing.

Neurotic children, in other words, often subscribe to two of the main irrational ideas leading to emotional disturbance that I outline in my book, *Reason and Emotion in Psychotherapy* and in my other writings on rational-emotive therapy. The first of these is *the idea that it is a dire necessity for a human being to be loved or approved by virtually every significant person in his life.* A good case can be made for the point—and has been made in most of the contemporary psychological texts—that young children need to be loved; or, at least, that they have to be taken care of properly and not severely castigated and punished for their everyday behavior, if they are to grow up to be emotionally sound. This is because they tend to be imitative and other-directed, and they tend to use as their evaluation of themselves the estimations and values that their parents and significant others place on them. It is possible that children may somehow edit out the negative criticisms of others and like themselves even when the adults and peers around them do not like them; but, statistically, speaking, most of them do not. Therefore, the safest way to raise a child is to show him that you love or accept him even when he does not behave too well; that even when you dislike his behavior you do not abhor *him* for performing in a certain way; and that you think that he has a right to live and enjoy himself even though he is a most fallible human being who will continually make one kind of error or another.

Granting, however, that most children have to be helped and approved to some considerable degree before they begin to accept and value themselves even when they have done many wrong deeds, there is certainly no evidence that youngsters have to be greatly loved if they are to get along reasonably well. To the contrary, studies of children, communally attended and seen only a few hours a day by their parents, have shown no significant differences in emotional disturbances from similar groups of children reared at home by mothers who were always around.

Actually, most children can hardly be given love and adoration by all their associates and relatives; and since only a small percentage of children seem to turn out to be exceedingly self-hating as a result of this dearth of unalloyed approval, we may justifiably conclude that this kind of total acceptance is hardly a requisite for mental health, and that the lack of it does not automatically send each "deprived" youngster into the doldrums.

Common observation shows, however, that a minority of children *are* highly traumatized by almost any criticism or rejection on the part of their peers or adult caretakers. These few are supersensitive to even the slightest signs of withdrawal of affection or disapproval on the part of others; and they most strongly —and inflexibly—believe that they are insignificant without near-total approbation.

A similar group of youngsters dogmatically believes one of the other irrational ideas which are emphasized in rational-emotive psychotherapy: namely, *the idea that one should be thoroughly competent, adequate, and achieving in all possible respects if one is to consider oneself worth-while.* If anything, this idea is often more pernicious than the idea that the child needs to be thoroughly approved by others in order to prove to himself his own intrinsic value. For where it is quite possible, by fortunate accident, for a youngster to have a set of parents, and perhaps even some aunts, uncles, and grandparents, who continually dote on him, and who consistently tell him that he is the greatest child in the world, it is infinitely less likely that this same child will keep proving himself to be thoroughly competent, adequate, and achieving. For it is the very nature of a young person, no matter how superior to other children he may be, to be far less achieving than the storybook, movie, television, and other heroes that he will inevitably idealize and wish to emulate. And even if most of the people around him care for him and even if he is unusually competent, he will still tend to worry about the continuance of this desirable (or, rather, demanded) state of affairs. So he has virtually no chance whatever of being truly and irrevocably calm and uncatastrophizing once he sets up these premises and distinctly believes them.

Emotionally disturbed people usually feel that they are inadequate, worthless, and wicked in general or specific ways. They think that they are worthless if they handle a problem in such-and-such a manner, and that they should have handled it another way. They do not merely recognize their own faults; they inordinately magnify and catastrophize them. And, above all, they think it is wrong for them to have any failing; they blame themselves incessantly for having it. Like neurotic adults, neurotic children make mistakes (which we all do) and then absolutely refuse to give themselves *the right to be wrong*. It may seem absurd that human beings have to give themselves this right, if they are to remain truly healthy and mature; but, let's face it, they do. For all humans are fallible and consequently will continually keep making mistakes. That is not good; it is too bad. But that is all it is—too bad—and not horrendous and unforgivable. When a child recognizes first, that he is definitely wrong about something, and second, that he has *a right to be wrong* (however unfortunate it may be that he is), he will truly be sane. But lamentably few are in this class.

It is most difficult for even intelligent adults to figure out the lack of contradiction between the two sentences: (a) "It is wrong for you to do this"; and (b) "You have a right to be wrong." "But if it is wrong for me to do a thing," they will object, "how can I possibly have a right to do that same thing?"

Perhaps the best way to explain this seeming contradiction is to emphasize the difference between the pronouns "it" and "you." As Dr. Haim Ginott, an authority on child care and the psychotherapy of children, puts it to the parents of the children he is trying to help, when a youngster spills some milk at the dinner table, you may say to him either (a) "You spilled the milk"; or (b) "The milk (or it) spilled." If you make the first statement, then the child is likely to say to himself: "I spilled the milk; it is wrong to spill milk; therefore I am a wrong or bad child." If you make the second statement, the child is more likely to say to himself: "It spilled; it is unfortunate that the milk spilled; now let me see what I can do to mop up the spilled milk and see if I can't prevent it from spilling next time."

The pronoun "I," then, when used in conjunction with a wrong or mistaken or unfortunate act, tends to give the child the impression that because *he* performed the act, *he* is as wrong or bad as the act is. The prounoun "it," when used in connection with the same act, is more likely to give him the impression that although the deed is unfortunate, it is somehow remediable, and *he* is not a louse for doing it. This does not mean that the child is not responsible for his poor (or, for that matter, good) deeds; for, of course, he is. But *he* is not his *performance;* and the kind of language that we generally employ to show him that his performance was mistaken or erroneous tends to help him to identify himself with his act and to condemn himself for a poor deed and glorify himself for a bad one. It is this self-condemnation or self-glorification which constitutes much of his neurosis.

Strictly speaking, no person is either good, bad, or indifferent, although his acts may justifiably be judged in these terms. For, as Robert Hartman, an unusual modern philosopher, has pointed out in several of his recent writings, it is not accurate for us to measure ourselves with the same kind of standards that we use to measure our deeds. Our *deeds* may be rated from good to bad: our racing, for example, may be timed; our piano playing judged by experts; and our character compared to that of others. But our *selves* cannot be evaluated in the same way as can objects and performances. One reason we may not evaluate the self in terms of our performances is that there seems to be no accurate way of measuring it. Thus, suppose a child is good at ball-playing, reading, and behaving himself in class, but he is poor at skipping rope, arithmetic, and behaving himself outside of class. Can we evaluate *him,* him*self,* as either a "good" or a "bad" child? Or suppose he is a fine performer in a variety of ways—in fact, in almost every way imaginable—but he has one very serious defect of character: for example, he continually tortures other children. Again, is he, as a whole, "good" or "bad"?

And self-evaluation leads down this paradoxical path: If you like or respect or love your *self* when you do good deeds, then you must logically dislike or disrespect or hate this same *self* when you do bad deeds. What is more, the very self that you are evaluating positively or negatively seems to be doing part of the evaluating itself.

People's performances, reflecting their fallibility, fluctuate from good to bad: measuring your self as bad or good, according to your performances, will ultimately lead you to a distinctly negative, disrespectful evaluation of this *self*. And, finally, because your evaluation of yourself normally has direct or indirect results on your deeds (that is, self-confidence helps you to perform relatively well and self-hate relatively poorly), evaluating your *self* in relation to your performances almost always results in a vicious circle: Because you blame yourself for poor achievement, you lose confidence, perform badly, and then blame yourself still more.

For many reasons such as these, it should be obvious that if a child insists that he achieve perfectly well—or even that he consistently do pretty well—he will sooner or later end up by considering himself worthless and will make himself distinctly neurotic. Only by deeming himself essentially worth-while just because he is alive (and therefore *self*-perpetuating); or, better, yet, only by refusing to evaluate his *self* at all and sticking to objective evaluations of his performances, is he likely to have basic feelings of self-respect and worth.

The neurotic child is one who almost invariably defines himself and his intrinsic worth in terms of how much other significant people in his life approve and accept him and how well he does in his performances. On either or both of these counts he tends to be perfectionistic and to wind up by depreciating himself enormously. His basic problem is not his competence in attaining love or achieving success but in his vigorous, perpetual *negative assessment* of whatever competence he may or may not have in these areas. He is either a relatively adequate person who over-conscientiously considers himself inadequate; or he is an ungifted individual who deems himself a bum. In either case, he is unrealistically self-denigrating.

Low Frustration Tolerance

It may seem odd to note, in one breath, that the emotionally disturbed child is self-depreciating and overwhelmed by feelings of inadequacy, and yet to note, in the next breath, that he is frequently self-grandiose and conceited. Yet this is true. Part of this seeming paradox is resolved if we understand that feelings of worthlessness and grandiosity are, in some respects, different sides of the same coin. For if a child is perfectionistic in his aims, he will first insist that he be King of the May and do everything remarkably well, and he will then conclude that he is utterly worthless if he is not the glorious person that he is determined that he *must* be. By the same token, if this same youngster begins by thinking that he is no good unless he is loved by everyone and does remarkably well in all things, he will usually become so depressed by his inevitable failures that he will have to do *something* in his own defense to pull himself out of the slough of despondency. Consequently, he may self-protectively imagine that he is the greatest of the great, often denigrating others so as to elevate his own stature.

This is not to say that grandiosity is *always* the other side of the coin of self-denigration; for it is probable that it often has independent roots. Almost every healthy child seems to have a distinct tendency to think of himself as the center of the world, to insist that everything go his way, and to be ruthless in his dealings with those who frustrate him. He is normally self-centered and has a difficult time accepting the fact that others have as much right to the good things of the world as he has, and that he would do well to respect their rights.

Every child, moreover, seems to have a tendency toward anger, temper tantrums, and injustice-collecting. When something goes wrong in his world, and particularly when other people treat him badly, he tends to tell himself, first, a sane sentence, and then an insane one. It is this second, insane, and invariably grandiose sentence that brings on his hostility toward the world around him. The sane sentence that the child tells himself when he is either fairly or unfairly frustrated is, "I don't like this situation; I wish it did not exist; and I hope it soon changes for the better." Or: "I think your behavior toward me is unfair and unethical, and I strongly hope that you quickly change it and act more fairly in the future." These kinds of sane sentences cause the child to experience feelings of frustration, annoyance, irritation, or displeasure and in themselves lead to no unusual difficulties.

The insane sentences that a child also tells himself when he has experienced serious frustration are of a quite different order. They consist of: "Because this poor situation exists, and I do not like its existence, it is awful, terrible, and horrible; and I can't for a single moment *stand* it!" Or: "Since your behavior toward me is unfair and unethical, I cannot see how you could possibly act that way, and I utterly hate you because you *should* not behave the way you are behaving toward me." Or: "How can the world possibly be the miserable way that it is; I *demand* that it cease being this way!"

The neurotic (and, even more so, the psychotic) child, then, is usually to some degree grandiose. He has a considerable amount of what psychologists call low frustration tolerance—which stems from his erroneous perception that because things *could* be different, they *should* be different. He is essentially a little Hitler—and he either rules the world around him in a tyrannical manner or (much more often!) makes himself completely miserable because his tyrannical demands are unheeded.

The stable and well-adjusted child, who keeps confronting grim reality as he grows older, gradually learns to surrender his grandiosity and to accept the fact that, although many frustrating things in life can be changed, many other things and people are the way they are, and that is that. Consequently, when he is seriously impeded from doing what he wants to do, or when he is forced to perform acts which he would much rather not perform, he learns to tell himself: "Even though this sorry situation exists, that's too bad! I can still stand it." And: "Although your behavior toward me is unfair and unethical, I can well see how you could behave that way (since you *are* the way you are), and I can also see that there is no real reason why you *should* act as fairly as I would like you to act." And: "It is obvious that the world is the miserable way it is, even though I very much would like it to be otherwise. Tough! I would prefer it to change, but there's no point in *demanding* what I prefer."

Shyness and Inhibition

Most—though hardly all—disturbed children who have low feelings of self-esteem tend to be shy and withdrawn. Because they think it absolutely essential that others view them favorably, and because they are terribly afraid that they will not be accepted in the manner they demand, they have an enormous fear of failure, and especially of social failure. They are afraid to do the wrong thing, make social *faux pas,* be laughed at by others, or in any way be deemed less than ideal. Quite logically, therefore, considering their irrational major premises in this connection, they withdraw almost completely from competition (which they view as full of potential threats), refuse to participate in many activities, and act shyly and inhibitedly when they are forced to participate in some social sphere. Then, of course, because they refrain from participating in various activities, they do not give themselves the opportunity of practicing these performances, and they soon turn out to be just as inept at dancing, conversing, ice-skating, and other pastimes as they were originally terrified of being. Finally, they illogically deduce that they cannot engage successfully in various ventures—when they actually mean that as yet they have not impelled themselves to do so—and they withdraw even more. The usual vicious circle of anxiety leading to inactivity, which in turn leads to more anxiety, which in turn leads to more withdrawal, is then established.

In extreme instances, neurotic children, as they withdraw from various activities of which they are abnormally afraid, become listless, depressed, anhedonic, and uninterested in practically everything. The prototype here is the child like Jim D. A bright and good-looking ten-year-old, Jim seemed to excel in music and in his relations with girls. He was an excellent pianist and composer for his age; and he had a series of almost continual "dates" with young female classmates, who would keep calling him up to insist that he see them. One day, however, a music critic, who had been asked by Jim's parents to listen to his piano playing and to review some of his compositions, made some very disparaging remarks about young prodigies and how badly they usually turned out later in life. Jim soon began playing and composing only occasionally; within a year he seemed to have lost all interest in music and was trying, instead, to excel at drawing (at which he actually seemed to have little talent). At the same time, he appeared to lose confidence in himself, to believe that the girls who liked him were themselves silly and worthless, and he began to behave ineptly with the few girls whom he still admired. After a while, he stopped almost all his dating activities, began to be attracted to rough boys, and made great strides toward adopting a homosexual absorption. As a result of several months of intensive psychotherapy, in the course of which he was shown that his fear of failure was leading him to withdraw from the kinds of participation that he had previously enjoyed, and during which he was convinced that the purpose of life is full commitment and enjoyment rather than mere success, he resumed his musical and his dating activities and seemed more interested in them than he had previously been.

Children who are shy and withdrawn also tend to be supersensitive and oversuspicious. Believing that they are inadequate and worthless, they project their own view of themselves onto others and think that these others see them in an equally bad light. Then, because of their false perceptions of how others respond to them, they sometimes behave hostilely or poorly with them—and thus bring about a self-fulfilling prophecy, since the others soon *do* see them in a negative light. The usual vicious circle sets up: Severe feelings of worthlessness lead to oversuspiciousness of others, which in turn results in condemnation by these others, finally culminating in more feelings of worthlessness. Supersensitiveness, then, is one of the main cores of severe emotional disturbance in children; and it is a rare neurotic or psychotic child who doesn't, on some level, demand that he be nigh-perfect, and denigrate himself mightily when he makes mistakes.

Underachievement and Ineptness

A large percentage of neurotic children behave inefficiently, stupidly, and underachievingly. This is not because they are innately stupid, since many of them are exceptionally bright judging from results of intelligence tests and other reliable indices of cognitive performance. Neurosis, in fact, I would define as stupid behavior by a *non*-stupid person. It should not be confused with mental deficiency, brain injury, and other states in which the child acts incompetently because he really *is* incompetent.

Emotionally disturbed children frequently behave idiotically because they are so terrorized at the thought of their failing at some problem-solving task that they practically *force* themselves to fail at it. They are obsessively absorbed, sometimes almost every minute of the day, with the thought, "Wouldn't it be awful if I did poorly!" that they leave themselves little time or energy to concentrate on the task at hand and to do reasonably well on it.

Susan D., for example, a nine-year-old girl with a tested Intelligence Quotient of 133, did remarkably well in arithmetic, but was failing most of her other subjects, largely because she read very poorly and found it painful to do any kind of homework except arithmetic. Her younger brother, William, was something of a reading wizard, and was wading through stories and plays during kindergarten. Susan, who had to excel at almost everything if she was going to permit herself to be happy, was perpetually petrified that she would not be able to keep her reading pace up with William's. Consequently, whenever she did try to read, she focused on anything but the subject matter of the material before her; she catastrophized mightily if she missed a word, had to read a sentence over, or got the gist of what she was reading but took more time to do so than she thought she *ought* to take. She therefore found reading increasingly painful, did less and less of it, and fell behind in most of her studies.

Children like Susan seem to have an inborn need to be perfectionistic and to demand that they outdo practically all others in virtually every possible field of endeavor. Sometimes, at great cost, they "succeed," in that they get good marks in class or on tests, but remain supertense and compulsive. More often, especially in some specific area, they fall on their faces, do much worse than they are capable of doing, worry endlessly over doing so poorly, and frequently "cop out" by giving up entirely on this specialty.

As David C. McClelland and Robert White have noted in recent writings, and as Dr. Robert A. Harper and I emphasize in *A Guide to Rational Living*, the mastery impulse is an integral part of healthy human behavior, and bright and talented people in particular find it almost impossible to lead a thoroughly enjoyable life unless they find some vital task with which to occupy themselves a good deal of the time. Emotionally unhealthy children, on the other hand, often become so addicted to fear of failure, and so convinced that they cannot possibly get anywhere with their chosen goals, that they give up completely, loll around day after day, and feel (and overtly tell anyone who wants to hear) that they don't really know what they want to do and have no important goals.

It is incredible how even some of the most talented of these children can vegetate for long periods of time. A fifteen-year-old girl whom I saw some time ago wrote high-level poetry, was a superb ballet dancer, and beat most of her father's chess-club members at their own game. But when left to herself during the school vacation months, she idled away most of her time playing solitaire and was as bored as she could possibly be. What she really seemed to want was a guarantee that the book of poems she planned to do would be grabbed up by a large publisher and quickly promoted (as, of course, books of poetry almost never are) to the best-seller list. Sensing that no such guarantee could be had, she wrote less than a handful of poems during that summer, polished up a few more that she had previously written, and then went back to her perennial solitaire game. There, at least, she had little to lose—and whatever losses she did have would remain mercifully secret.

Escapism and Avoidism

These practices are sometimes special forms of laziness and inertia. Instead of *frankly* doing practically nothing, in order to maintain his perfectionism and to circumvent his fear of failing, the neurotic child mightily preoccupies himself with some pursuit—but in a form that is viewed as being much less commiting and risky. Thus, he may daydream incessantly; or playact when he is around others; or build up a long series of pathological lies;

or become obsessively attached to athletic pursuits when he is afraid he will do poorly at intellectual activities; or otherwise manage to keep "busy" with the kind of work which is easy but not too rewarding. He may even, in extreme cases, make this activity rewarding by creatively building it into fetishistic proportions. At the same time, he may tend to make his other life participations seem mild and uninteresting by comparison and may give most of them up.

Ronald T. was a thirteen-year-old child who used tranvestism, or cross-dressing, as a fetishistic form of escapism. At the age of six, he found that his parents and relatives considered it very "cute" if he dressed as a girl and mimicked female manners in an ostentatious way; so he continued this practice for a number of years and gained a good deal of approval thereby. Immediately after puberty, however, when he began to get sex kicks from wearing girls' underwear, he became fetishistically attached to this kind of cross-dressing, and engaged in it constantly—but then in secret—while to others he gave the appearance of a rather rough-and-tumble boy's boy. His new-found fetishistic devotion to cross-dressing did not stem merely from its new connection with sexual titillation but also from his semiconscious realization that if he worked at getting this kind of thrill, he could take his mind off his schoolwork, at which he was doing badly and for which he appeared to have only a mediocre aptitude. He was so concerned with being cock of the walk, and had had so much prior experience successfully getting the center of attention, that when his childish tricks no longer bore such good fruit, and he was expected to buckle down to more serious activities (including good grades, which his parents particularly began to emphasize), he felt that he couldn't face the outside world any longer. In order to effectively keep from facing some of the adolescent, academic, and other unpleasant realities that he was supposed to tackle and conquer, he developed a secret form of transvestism that led to immediate orgasmic pleasure, and he clung to it almost for dear life. Ronald was a difficult patient to treat—since, like most fetishists, he derived a great deal of direct, sensuous satisfaction from his escapist proclivity, and he was loathe to give this up—but when I was able to help him to accept himself more fully even when he did not perform very well academically, he was gradually able to return to the real world, resorting only occasionally to his secret transvestite pursuits.

Still another form of avoidism is excitement-seeking. It is quite probable that some of us, as Abraham Maslow has theorized, are even born with a greater tendency toward pursuing danger, thrills, variety, and psychophysical excitation than is the average individual. Whether or not this is so, it is certain that many children somehow have powerful inclinations in these directions. They seem literally to irritate themselves and their elders until a real blowup takes place. They often get into fights and riots; ride their bicycles at breakneck speeds; spend much time with older, rather dangerous companions; practically dare their teachers to punish them for their brash behavior; and otherwise keep themselves, and their poor suffering parents, incessantly on their toes. Yet, far from being happily absorbed in their excitement-creating pursuits, they are frequently morose, irritable, and even severely depressed.

Afraid that if he really works at anything, he will not do it well enough, and recognizing that if he escapes merely by inertia and being lazy, he is liable to boredom, the disturbed child looks for bigger and better ways to escape from his feelings of irritability and depression. Not having the adult paths of alcohol or drugs to resort to (though in some instances, he is even able to become addicted to these), and not having the full escapist resources that may be at his disposal in later years, he does the best he can to create exciting *divertissements* for himself. In many instances, delinquent pursuits are particularly attractive to such a child, especially if he lives in a poor neighborhood and there are some fellow malcontents among his friends. Stealing cars, robbing candy stores, assaulting drunks, engaging in gang warfare—acts which bring him into rebellion against society and the minions of the law (and thus provide both danger and false ego enhancement)—may easily be his lot.

In more sedate ways—especially if the child happens to be a girl and lives in a more respectable kind of milieu—excitement-seeking can also be found by children who want to look outwardly rather than inwardly, and thus avoid facing their own anxieties and self-depreciations. Girls, for example, can use "improper" words; sass their teachers; be sexually promiscuous; go out with older boys and play the dangerous game of sexual teasing; spend a considerable portion of their time in the bohemian section of their town; and otherwise be pseudononconformists—since, like most "beatniks," they are actually conforming to an unconventional minority, or are arousing the interest and envy of a more conventional majority.

Anxiety and Tenseness

Tension actually is a good and healthy trait, since a completely relaxed human being would be, in the long run, empty and passive. *Hyper*tension, or tenseness, however, is undesirable. For where the normal human being is appropriately vigilant as he plows through a life-space where small and large dangers incessantly lurk, the severely disturbed person is inappropriately *overvigilant*. He finds dangers where there are none; or he exaggerates them when they do exist; or he thinks that the penalties that risks involve are much too great; or he keeps worrying, worrying about what may occur in the future, though there is little likelihood that the event he fears actually will occur, and still less that it will be truly catastrophic if and when it does. The exaggeratedly fearful or hypertense individual, therefore, spends enormous amounts of time and energy keeping himself in a perpetual emergency-oriented state, when there is little likelihood that his real-life ventures are proportionately that hazardous. In consequence, he often has relatively few remaining resources to meet the dangers that do exist, and he may be unable to constructively plan his life on the assumption that he will probably survive everyday affairs.

The prototype of the terribly anxious child is one who has a phobia of school. John Z. is a case in point. When I first saw him he was eleven, and he had spent perhaps thirty days—and partial ones at that—in the classroom. He resisted going to kindergarten in the first place and refused to stay there without his mother, so that he finally had to be removed; when he was later placed in the first grade, he ran out of class within fifteen minutes and somehow found his way home across twenty city blocks; thereafter he only spent a day here and there, and no more than two at a time, in the regular classroom. Tutored privately, he did well in his academic work; and when allowed to play in his own neighborhood, he did manage to acquire a few friends and to get along tolerably well with them. But the mere mention of his going to school would throw him into a fit; he would raise such a fuss that the idea would quickly have to be abandoned.

At first blush, John's school phobia appeared to be a specific terror of going to school, since he seemed to get along in several other aspects of life. However, having seen school phobiacs before, and having talked to them about their general attitudes toward life, I suspected that John, like the others, might have a generally fearful attitude to his environment; and that was exactly what I soon found to be the case. He was exceptionally afraid of making almost *any* mistake; of doing the wrong thing in front of others; and of possibly being laughed at by those others. Moreover, he was afraid of numerous physical dangers: of being assaulted by other boys, of becoming ill, of cutting himself with a knife, and the like.

The illusion of general emotional health in John's case stemmed from the fact that on several occasions—as instanced by his relations with the other boys in his neighborhood—he had started out by being terribly fearful of what people might think of him if he happened to do the wrong thing. But he had fortuitously discovered that either he did not do the wrong thing, and was consequently accepted by the group, or that he did make what he considered to be a fairly serious error, but that nonetheless things turned out all right and he was still accepted by those who witnessed the error. Whenever either of these eventualities occurred, John saw that making a mistake in *this* particular area wasn't so bad. And he gradually overcame his extreme anxiety in this regard.

Unfortunately, alas, John had a general tendency to find new fields of endeavor (or nonendeavor) in which to imagine catastrophe. If he managed to get along with the boys in his own neighborhood, he then created for himself a terror of the boys a few blocks away. If he started off with a fear of doing spelling, and eventually conquered that, he would turn up the next week with a fear of learning geography—and then had to work hard at overcoming that. Whatever victories over anxiety he won, he soon began to lose the battle all over again in a somewhat new or different area.

Under these circumstances, John's school phobia was quite understandable. For school is an unusually large area of a youngster's life, including a plethora of possible hazards. Almost from the first day he attended school, John knew that he would have to adjust himself to (a) going a distance to the school; (b) being without his mother for a considerable period of the day; (c) adjusting to his teacher; (d) doing the classroom work properly; (e) making friends with a new batch of boys and girls; and so on. If he had been presented with *one* of these problems at a time, he might possibly have buckled down, sweated out his discomfort, and finally made his peace with each one in turn. But he could see no possibility of successfully meeting *all* these great "dangers" simultaneously. Consequently, he didn't want to stay in school even for a single day; and he became so upset and obstreperous that he managed to have his negative desires (impelled by his fears) realized.

John's case epitomizes the fact that certain children are enormous catastrophizers who actively seek conditions to worry and fret about. Some do so mutedly and manage to get through the normal happenings of their existence with too much tenseness, but without dramatic upheavals. Others, like John, seek such conditions dramatically and wind up by having school phobias, excruciating nightmares, withdrawals from social groupings, psychosomatic upsets, and various other manifestations of intense, irrational fear. Most children, of course, are much more afraid of various people, things, and events than are average adults. But a minority of youngsters are pathologically afraid of innumerable things or immensely afraid of a few; and these children have to be somehow disabused of their anxiety-creating philosophies of life if they are to live comfortably and if they are to give their parents peace.

A somewhat specialized form of anxiety is that involving indecision, doubt, and conflict. Because the disturbed child feels that it would be the greatest sin in the world to make a blunder and then to be roundly criticized for making it, he soon begins to find it "easier" to put off making any major decisions. This is notably true when conditions are so arranged—which they repeatedly are in the course of his life—that distinct disadvantages will accrue no matter what decision he makes.

For instance, the child may have to choose between being noisy, thereby bothering his parents, and remaining prim and quiet, thereby spending a relatively boring afternoon. If he chooses the first course, he will incur criticism and perhaps penalization from his parents; if he chooses the second course, he will hardly have a pleasant day. Commonly, faced with such a grim choice, he will think that the world is entirely unfair, make himself unduly frustrated because of its unfairness, and fret and sulk. His childish grandiosity simply refuses to accept the fact that things are the way they are, and he spends most of his time angrily insisting that they shouldn't be that way—that his choice should be between two good things instead of between two evils.

Equally, or more often, however, he will blame himself for not being able to find a more satisfactory way out of his dilemma —for he cannot quite see that there simply is no perfect way out of it—and he will keep wavering between the main choices that he can envision. Thus, he will be noisy for a while, until his parents give him clear indications that he is being an utter nuisance; and then he will be very quiet for a while, until he perceives that his freedom of action is severely restricted and that he is not having much fun. When he is at either of these poles, and no solution to his dilemma presents itself, he may blame himself for taking the wrong path—largely because he still insists that there must be an undeniably right one. After enough of this kind of self-condemnation, he becomes convinced that he just cannot handle the problem at all; and after enough of his "poor" handling of these kinds of problems, he is practically sure that he cannot handle any such choice and that he had better avoid making decisions in the future.

Usually, once the child reaches this stage of conflict and doubt, he tends to excoriate himself for being indecisive, and thereby he enhances his self-depreciation and anxiety. Then, as a result of his being still more anxious—and afraid, of course, of making the "wrong" move—he finishes by becoming more indecisive, more self-hating, still more anxious, still more indecisive, and so on. As time goes on, the number of conflicts about which he hesitates to make a choice tends to increase; and eventually there is hardly any alternative that he can consider without getting himself into trouble.

Another specialized form of anxiety—and one that is highly dramatic and causes perhaps the most acute form of mental anguish—is that state of emotional upset which we label *guilt*. This feeling can sometimes (though probably not always) be rather clearly differentiated from its common companion-feeling, *shame*. Shame is mainly a form of anxiety or self-depreciation that is concerned with incompetence. The child wants very much to do certain things well, particularly so that others will approve of him and look up to him for these performances; and when, in fact, he does these things badly, he censures himself and brings on feelings of inadequacy, which constitute the emotion of shame. Thus, he is ashamed of getting poor marks in school, being a subaverage ball player, wearing thick glasses, and seeming inefficient or substandard in various other ways.

The child's feelings of guilt, on the other hand, are more likely to be felt in terms of the moral proscriptions of his community, particularly when his misconduct involves other people. If he lies to his parents, or beats up another child, or feels so ashamed at the prospect of doing poorly on an exam that he has to resort to cheating—under these conditions, he tends to denigrate himself morally, to feel that his entire being is worthless, and therefore to feel guilty or sinful. This latter feeling is usually even more intense and self-destructive than is the feeling of shame, since the child who believes that he is a sinner commonly is convinced that he is rotten to the core and that there is no possible redemption for him. Although some god or older person may conceivably forgive and thereby redeem him, there is little he can do to help himself in this connection. Even future good deeds seem somehow palliative rather than curative; and for the rest of his life he may well have to suffer whenever he recalls the terribly immoral deed he has committed.

Shame, on the other hand, is much more correctable in terms of future performances. For if a child shamefully strikes out one day every time he gets up to bat in the baseball game, he may well redeem his atrocious performance the next day by hitting three home runs in a row. If he performs well, his sense of incompetence and shame is likely to be banished; and even if he fails miserably in the next few games, his feelings of adequacy may remain intact, since he now knows that he can perform well, and may wait confidently for the time when his home-run hitting potential once again becomes kinetic. Once, however, he performs an unmitigatedly heinous antisocial act, he also knows that he may repeat a similar act anytime in the future; and this knowledge of his past and possible future immorality may keep him conceiving of himself as an arrant failure (or sinner) who is *hopelessly* immersed in failure (or iniquity).

Although guilt is usually a more intense and more self-castigating emotion than shame, the latter tends to be more widespread in our society. The main reason for this probably is that a child almost always has more control over his sins than his incompetencies, and he can also set up better defenses in the case of the former rather than in the case of the latter. Thus, if Jimmie knows that it is immoral for him to belt Willie, he has an excellent chance of refraining from doing so, even when he is angry at Willie. What is more, if he does haul off and sock Willie, he can often invent some rationalization for doing so; e.g., Willie really wanted to be socked; or he hit Willie in order to stop him from abusing Annie; or he knows he was wrong in lambasting Willie, but he just couldn't help himself that day, and will absolutely, positively not repeat this kind of immorality again.

In regard to shame about his incompetence, Jimmie is likely to have a much harder time (a) preventing himself from being inadequate; and (b) making excuses when he is. For if he can't do his schoolwork well or play ball with the other kids in a competent manner, there may be little that Jimmie can do to improve his performance. All the practice in the world may not, if he is truly deficient, make up very much for his being ineffective in these respects. Moreover, if Jimmie is consistently poor at arithmetic or science, he is going to find it fairly difficult to find a good rationalization or other defense for his incompetence. He can always say that he doesn't like figures; that Babe Ruth was a poor mathematician; or that boys who do well in arithmetic are sissies. But this kind of "sour grapes" defense is not especially good or convincing; and underneath his rationalizations he may still sense that he is truly deficient in important areas and that it is highly inconvenient for him to have such deficiencies. Consequently, his feelings of shame may at best be temporarily shunted aside, but they may consciously or unconsciously remain to smite him.

This was true in the case of Sandra L., an eleven-year-old girl whose parents brought her for psychotherapy because she was not getting along with her classmates or with the other children in her neighborhood, although she was doing fine schoolwork. Sandra had as little guilt as any child I can remember seeing, not because she was psychopathic or overly defensive (as many children are) and therefore denied that any of her behavior was truly immoral. On the contrary, she was highly moralistic and freely admitted that she was unkind, dishonest, or thieving. In fact, whenever there was even the slightest possibility of her being immoral, she would lean over backward to accuse herself. On one occasion, when another girl copied some of her answers on a class test, Sandra vehemently accused herself of being evil because she did not go out of her way to prevent this girl from seeing some of the answers on Sandra's paper. On another occasion, when her mother had asked her what she spent some of her allowance on, and she had forgotten to include a bar of candy in her expenditures for the day, she insisted that she was an "awful liar" and contended that her lack of memory was entirely unforgivable.

Sandra, however, was so moralistic and so careful to refrain from sinning in the first place, and she was so ready to vociferously admit and atone for all her possible sins in the second place, that essentially she was a guiltless girl. She ceaselessly condemned others for their infractions of various social rules, but she hardly ever put herself in a position of doing something for which she really had to vigorously condemn herself. At the same time, with all her intelligence and physical competence, she could not prevent herself from performing less than perfectly in many ways. So she continually deprecated her activities and herself whenever she scored below 90 per cent on an examination, or noticed that her hair was too straight, or failed to understand a difficult passage in a book she was reading.

As a result of Sandra's inordinate demands on herself, she was overwhelmed with constant feelings of shame. She was terribly afraid to have anyone witness what she considered to be her inept performances and hence withdrew from many social engagements. This, added to the fact that she compensatorily became less sinning and more critical of others' presumed immoralities, made her decidedly unpopular with her peers. Then, when she saw that they tended to shun her, she vacillated between feeling that there was something radically wrong with her—and, of course, being horribly *ashamed* that there was—and feeling that she was "good" and "moral" while practically all the others were "bad" and "evil" for not living up to her wonderful standards of conduct.

If Sandra competed with other children in various performance realms, she could always be bested by them, even though she had a good deal of competence herself. But if she took a holier-than-thou moralistic position and rigidly stuck to being a goody-goody creature herself, the worst that could happen (and that was unlikely) would be that some of her peers could equal but never actually best her. So even when I convinced her that she did not have to perform ideally in various areas of academic and social achievement, she left herself the out of being able to behave impeccably in the moral area, and thereby outdistance her fellows. Queenness of the May was thus at least partly retained by Sandra, and her grandiosity remained unassailable. Only when I finally convinced her that underlying this kind of grandiloquence was a pronounced feeling of inferiority, and that this was most unlikely to be removed until she fully accepted herself whether or not she supremely surpassed others, was Sandra able to tackle her virulent moralism and to minimize her basic anxiety and ultracompetitiveness.

This is not to say, now, that morality or even moralizing is a bad thing. For a child to know what is right (that is, self-helping and other-accepting) behavior and what is wrong (that is, self-sabotaging and antisocial) action is fine; and to a considerable degree, his objective knowledge of right and wrong deeds (as psychologist Hobart Mowrer has shown) is one of the essentials for his being mentally healthy. But whereas morality consists of knowing and doing the self- and socially-approved thing, and whereas moralizing consists of teaching oneself and others what is right and wrong, moralism (or being moralistic) is the act of condemning human beings for being mistaken or immoral. This may seem to be a subtle difference, but it is a most important one. In fact, moralistic people become so preoccupied with how horribly wrong a given act is, and how punishable an offense it is, that they have great difficulty thinking at all about what can be done to ameliorate or change this supposedly horrendous deed in the future. Where, therefore, morality helps human beings to act properly and organizedly, moralism hinders them from behaving well and leads to emotional and other kinds of disturbance.

Resentment and Hostility

Statistically speaking, resentment and hostility are among the most "normal" emotions there are. Everyone resents injustice and hates being frustrated, and the world, of course, is full of injustice and frustration. However, that something is statistically "normal" hardly proves that it is desirable or healthy. The common cold, for example, is something that most of us have from time to time, but no one wants it.

Hostility, unfortunately, is a desirable and pleasant state in many instances. For by being righteously angry at others, one can easily demean them, then, by comparison make oneself feel enormously superior to them. In this sense, Hitler made himself feel infinitely superior to the Jews and the other "non-Aryans" whom he slaughtered; and virtually every bigot and tyrant likewise gains status in his own eyes over his victims.

Children especially "need" to feel resentful in many instances because they are so small and abusable and are so often taken advantage of by their elders. They nicely compensate for their inadequacy feelings and their relentless frustration by seeing others as miserable worms and themselves as would-be saviors. They gain false integrity or status in this manner—since they go up on the seesaw of life not because they have really accomplished anything in their own right, and not because they have truly accepted themselves in spite of their accomplishments or the lack of them, but because they have maneuvered someone else into taking the downward swing of the teeter-totter and therefore feel comparatively triumphant. As soon, therefore, as their opponent regains his equilibrium or (worse yet!) manages to wrench himself to the top of the swing again, they immediately lose their temporary advantage and usually become as miserable as they were previously happy.

Hostility, like all self-defeating emotions, has several component parts, some of them remarkably sane and some of them inordinately insane. The sane component of resentment is the displeasure that one normally feels when one is frustrated or unjustly treated by others. After all, if a child is prevented from doing what he wants to do or is punished by his parents for an offense he hasn't committed, one would hardly expect him to say to himself, "Oh, joy! What a great world this is!" and calmly go about his business. Instead, one would expect him to display a more appropriate annoyance, irritation, or displeasure—all of which would help him look for the origin of his frustration or unfair punishment, and try to take steps to minimize its future occurrence. Thus, he may be able to talk his parents into letting him do what he wants to do, or he may be able to show them that his punishment was not justified and that it would be better if they did not punish him again if the same circumstances should occur.

To the appropriate feeling of annoyance, irritation, or displeasure, the hostile child adds the unrealistic and unhealthy evaluation that the frustrating event or person should not be— has no right to exist. This is equivalent to his pigheadedly insisting, when he is displeased by any event, that the world must not be the way that it palpably is. He has every right to contend, of course, that if he is frustrated, there are many reasons why it would be better if these frustrations stopped. It would be. But it is a far cry from his telling himself, "It would be better if you stopped frustrating me and let me have my way," to "Therefore, you must not do so." For the first sentence merely states the truth, "I would like it if you stopped frustrating me"; the second states a falsehood, "Because I would like it, you must desist." Although there are many reasons why he would like your no longer being frustrating, there are no known reasons why this dislike should *necessarily* make you stop yourself from being the way he would prefer you to be. A child must learn to accept the fact that you may have very good reasons for frustrating him; and, even if you don't, you have a right, as a fallible human being, to be wrong or unfair, and need not be boiled in oil for so being.

Hostility, then, stems from a refusal to accept the facts of reality; from a grandiose notion that the world should be what a child wants it to be; from a (false) conviction that condemning human beings and severely punishing them for their annoying behavior will invariably help them to be less annoying in the future; and from the magical, absolutistic belief that the world underlyingly is an exceptionally well-ordered, just place, and that if things are temporarily out of kilter, they must soon be put to rights again. Since human beings seem to be born with a pronounced tendency to think crookedly and irrationally about themselves and the world, and to make their wish that everything be right father to the thought that it therefore must be, resentment of others for their undesired behavior is almost universal among our children (and our adults!) and is hardly a sign that they are exceptionally nutty. In fact, they are uniquely sane if they seldom are hostile; and to expect them to be this sane is in itself unrealistic.

Many children, however, are not only angry when they are seriously frustrated, but they are also resentful when they are only mildly thwarted; or they are resentful out of all proportion to the frequency or degree of their frustration; or they find severe frustrations when there actually are few or none. Whereas almost any kind of hostility is undesirable, the overly hostile reactions of these children are much more so, and they fall in the distinctly neurotic or psychotic range.

Jonathan C., by way of illustration, was a twelve-year-old boy whose mother was decidedly ingratiating and whose father, though a bit stricter, was rarely around the home, as he kept long business hours. Jonathan also went to a private school, where the classes were small and the atmosphere was most permissive. Finally, he was an only child, who did not have to compete with any siblings, and who had rather doting grandparents on both sides of the family. All in all, Jonathan was less restricted and frustrated than the great majority of children, and one would think that he had little about which to complain.

One would think, if Jonathan were to be believed, quite wrongly! For he was always complaining about everything imaginable, and not a few things almost unimaginable. If the weather was rainy, Jonathan bewailed the fact that he could not go out and play. If it was sunny, he insisted that it was too dazzling or too warm to go out. If other children were passive, Jonathan complained that they were too dull to play with. If they were active and alert, he insisted that they were smart-alecky. If he were advised to read, by his long-suffering mother, he would say that his eyes were too tired. If she asked him why he was not outside playing games with the other children, he would state that such games were too strenuous, and that he'd rather sit inside and read. No matter what happened in his life, or what it was suggested that he do, Jonathan always quibbled, quarreled, and behaved most irritably.

Why? It is hard to say with precision. Perhaps Jonathan was

merely a spoiled brat, whose low frustration tolerance stemmed from his being allowed to get away too easily with things by his parents and by others. Perhaps he had an inborn tendency to be anhedonic and to find little joy in many things that other children find thrilling and interesting. (Edmund Bergler eloquently terms this type of person an "injustice collector.") Whatever the original cause of his disturbance—and frequently such an original cause cannot be accurately ascertained, but can only be reconstructed, largely in relation to the biased theory of the psychotherapist who is trying to reconstruct it—it seemed clear that Jonathan had a negativistic, irritation-creating philosophy of life. And that philosophy was that everything should be made exceptionally easy for himself and that nothing in the way of frustration or pain should be permitted to enter his existence.

This kind of a philosophy, or some reasonable facsimile thereof, exists in the case of most inordinately resentful children who display low frustration tolerance. For, contrary to the views of John Dollard and Neal Miller, frustration does not *necessarily* lead to aggression in the human animal. As Nicholas Pastore, among others, has shown, it is possible for a child or an adult to be severely frustrated and for him not to become nasty and tend to strike out against others who are seemingly instrumental in frustrating him.

A realistic and unhostile view of the world accepts the notion that the child *can* stand what he doesn't like, that he is big enough and sufficiently independent to cope adequately with the hassles of life and to come up, if not exactly smiling, at least unperturbed. It accepts the fact that there are at least *two* ways of reacting to deprivation and restriction: (a) by idiotically foaming at the mouth and insisting that things are unutterably unfair and simply cannot exist (the child is more often than not telling himself something like this about an event and consequently making it worse); and (b) by wisely gritting one's teeth and acknowledging that if they are unfair, that's tough; they *do* exist and the world is not unspeakably atrocious just *because* they exist. This second attitude assumes that the harshness of reality *can* be coped with; the first view assumes that it can only be childishly and upsettedly reacted to, since it is essentially intolerable.

In the case of Jonathan C., he was loath to give up the cases that he kept amassing against his fellows. Admittedly, his rantings and ravings got him into difficulties with his friends, teachers, and adult nonrelatives. But he short-rangedly doted so much on feelings of excitement, superiority, and utopian demands that he found his life almost a vacuum when he tried to forego them. He made some small attempts in this direction but gradually sank back to his prior pathways of debasing others in order to illusorily raise himself.

Defensiveness

Children are more naïve than adults, and because they tend to be self-punitive and unforgiving about anything that ails them, quickly dart into defensive pathways when faced with the knowledge of their own inept or iniquitous behavior. What are some of the common psychological defenses that children employ?

a. Denial

Roland is actually a weak, puny boy who is unable to compete in rough-and-tumble sports with most of the other boys he knows. But he sees himself as a wiry, deft individual who just doesn't like football and soccer and who happens to enjoy handball. He believes that if he did like football, he would be a terrific quarterback, and sometimes has daydreams of acting in such a capacity and winning game after game. He completely ignores the fact that no coach would let him anywhere near a uniform in a football game, and keeps vigorously maintaining the fiction that playing the game is something he wouldn't want to do, anyway.

b. Repression

Joan is an exceptionally insecure girl who feels that she is good at practically nothing, and who mercilessly teases her peers to make them feel uncomfortable so that she can feel adequate in their presence. Whenever her parents or other adults ask her how she has been getting along with her friends, she pushes out of consciousness the actual facts of her teasing behavior with them and reports that she has been acting with great kindness, or perhaps that they have been teasing her but that she hasn't been reacting badly. She will not face the truth of her own behavior, for if she did she would consider herself cruel and evil; and she is already carrying a heavy burden of self-depreciation, and would then feel constrained to add to this. So she unconsciously forgets about this unpleasant aspect of her life and thereby consciously feels less ashamed than she otherwise would feel.

c. Rationalization

Dolores is not unusually bright for her nine years, but she has learned—or has taught herself—how to be a clever rationalizer. Whenever she does anything wrong—which she fairly frequently does, because she rarely learns from her past experiences—she immediately says that her younger brother pushed her into doing it, or that she really did it right and that he then refixed it so that it came out wrong, or that the standards by which her actions are being judged wrong are themselves mistaken. She always has some excuse for her own poor behavior—which means, of course, that she never really, in her own mind, does anything poorly, but is always a victim of unfortunate circumstances. Underneath, of course, Dolores would be so pained and self-hating by the admission that she had acted badly, that she could not bear to face this fact. Therefore, she rationalizes continually, that is, she comes up with a "reason" why her errors were not really erroneous and why everybody in the world, especially her younger brother (who is actually more competent than she, and of whom she is considerably jealous), is out of step but her.

d. Projection

Johnny is a conceited child who thinks that he knows the answer to practically everything, but who actually is full of false information, which he glibly rattles off whenever someone asks him a question. Because he is so glib, he actually fools people much of the time; and he almost always fools himself as well, as he sincerely believes that his false answer *is* a good one. At the same time, Johnny is adept at spotting conceit in others; in fact, he often finds it when it doesn't exist. For he is so nearly aware of his own conceitedness, and at the same time so determined to keep himself from facing it, that he projects this trait onto others, condemning them for being swell-headed, whether or not they are. He uses the classic defensive technique of projection, because thereby he is effectively able to deny that he himself has what he considers to be a blameworthy trait, such as conceit, and because he also is able to put down others and feel superior to them, for supposedly having this very trait.

e. Compensation

Georgene is a little saner than most children about her defensiveness. Other children commonly employ such mechanisms as denial, repression, rationalization, and projection, which themselves, when brought to the surface of consciousness and admitted by the perpetrator, are considered to be wrong—and even wicked—in our society, and which therefore have a good chance of boomeranging on the child who employs them. Georgene, however, rarely uses one of these poor or dangerous defenses; instead, she almost invariably resorts to the "good" defense of compensation. That is to say, when she finds that she is behaving poorly in one area of her life, she quickly searches for another area in which she can do well and mightily exerts herself to succeed in this compensatory area in order to impress others with her prowess. Thus, she did not do too well in her schoolwork and, after trying hard for a while in this area, has given up and now copies most of her homework from others. But she spends a great deal of time making herself up so that she will look beautiful; she goes shopping with her mother and looks for the prettiest clothes; and she arranges interesting parties for the other children she knows. As a result of this compensatory activity, Georgene is a popular child and is thought by many of her peers and their parents to be brighter and more competent than she is. She herself agrees with their assessments of her intelligence because she has managed by her compensatory behavior not only to win the acclaim of others (which in a sense is good and advantageous) but also to delude herself into believing that she does not have certain academic deficiencies and that she could do marvelously well at school if she kept trying. Instead, therefore, of merely wisely compensating for one defect by working hard at becoming proficient in another area, she defensively pretends that, whereas she is really able in *both* respects, she simply chooses to try in one area and not in the other.

f. One-upmanship

As Stephen Potter has shown with brilliant humor in recent years, and as Eric Berne has cleverly re-emphasized, human beings have a pronounced tendency to play games with themselves and others, and a great many of their ploys are designed to put down their associates in order to make themselves feel immeasurably one-up on these associates. William, for example, is a sharp fourteen-year-old who expends much more energy in demonstrating to others what miserable fools they are than he does in doing anything constructive for himself. He reads widely and has gathered a great fund of information, but he seems to be intent mainly on using this information to show his friends and relatives how supremely ignorant they are, and how they are not in his intellectual class. He deludes himself that he will someday put his knowledge to good effect by writing a great book. But he reads unsystematically and erratically, never truly masters any subject, and does not try to organize his information into any useful pattern. He is obsessed by a need to put others down while he himself presumably seesaws upward, far beyond their reach, but still within their awestruck vision. He is, therefore, largely motivated by power drives rather than by an intrinsic enjoyment of his knowledge-seeking activity.

g. Identification

Linda considers herself to be plain and dull, but she has magical notions of having her ugly-duckling qualities somehow transformed into their opposites. She has therefore made herself into an avid movie addict and continually views, at the movie houses or on TV, cinema productions that have, as their female protagonist, some beautiful and scintillating personality. She never tries to get the autographs of her favorite stars, as some of her friends do, or to start fan clubs for them, or to meet them in person. For she realizes somehow that coming into actual contact with these movie queens might disillusion her or might graphically bring to her attention the real differences between them and herself. But in a darkened movie house or in the dimly lit living room of her own home she can identify herself with the gorgeous images she sees on the screen, practically *become* the beautiful actress she is watching, and have the illusion that someday she, Linda, will be discovered and transformed into a film queen by a great producer (and become an *offstage* charmer who is incredibly attractive to all who meet her). She looks down on and is scornful of her brother, Tommy, who apes the stance, talk, and other mannerisms of his current baseball heroes, and who is sure that he is going to grow up to be just like them. She thinks Tommy is childish in this respect, but she completely fails to see her own puerility in compulsively continuing to identify with one movie queen after another.

h. Transference

Derek has the devil of a time relating to his father—who is not home a great deal of the time, and who is standoffish and unenthusiastic whenever he is around. Derek keeps trying to get closer to his dad but is almost always rebuffed. Rather than give up and face the fact that he is going to get nowhere with his attempts at rapprochement, Derek unrealistically rationalizes and insists to himself that his father does care for him appreciably but that he just does not have the time to show how much he cares. Meanwhile, Derek picks on any older man with whom he comes into contact—teachers, storekeepers, fathers of his friends—and does his best to get very close to them. Almost every man he sees is immediately viewed as a father image, and Derek takes toward him the sonlike attitude that he would like to take toward his own father if the latter were sufficiently around and interested. Naturally, the great majority of the men to whom Derek tries to relate rebuff his filial-like advances; but that does not stop him from transferring his feelings for his father to new men. Now that Derek has reached puberty and is beginning to have more specific sex drives, he is already becoming attracted to older males sexually, instead of to his female peers. If no fortunate circumstances intervene to help him become attracted to girls, there is a good chance that he will soon be picked up by older homosexuals and seduced into having sex relations with them. Because his needs for a kindly male parent are still so great, he could easily convince himself that he dearly loves an older man, and could wind up by becoming sexually attached to one.

i. Resistance

Carla strongly resists facing any unpleasant facts about herself, even when these are forcefully brought to her attention and the evidence for their existence is clearly shown to her. If her mother tells her that she is too loud-mouthed, she convinces herself that the mother is jealous of her easy volubility. If her teacher points out to her that she is doing her homework sloppily, she inwardly believes that the teacher is set against her or is simply unable to appreciate her special way of doing homework. If her friends suggest that she is too conceited, she calmly points out to them—and fully believes—that they are misperceiving her behavior. No matter what truths are shown to her, as long as they are uncomplimentary and indicative of her own fallibility, she resists accepting them and somehow manages to see things differently. Even when she goes for psychotherapy (to which she returns from time to time, only to insist, after a few weeks, that it isn't helping her and that she really doesn't need it) she resists the therapist's objective observations and evaluations and gives specious reasons why they are inapplicable. If Carla ever stopped being unduly resistant and accepted some of the unpleasant facts about herself, which others try to show her, she would savagely berate herself for being the way she is. Consequently, she finds it much "safer" to resist seeing these things and to remain continually defensive.

j. Reaction Formation

Ruth uses most of the common defensive maneuvers to avoid facing her own pathological behavior, which includes stealing, lying, and various other kinds of trouble-making. In one respect, however, she works hard—and that is in regard to maintaining seemingly good relations with her older sister, Mollie. Because Mollie is an earnest, responsible girl, who carries out all the promises she makes to others, and does her various school and home chores more than adequately, Ruth tends to be exceptionally jealous of Mollie—to the point of hating her. Instead of admitting this hostility to her sister, however, Ruth maintains the fiction that she adores Mollie and would do anything possible to help her. To bolster this fiction, Ruth often goes out of her way to lend Mollie her belongings and to buy gifts for her. In the process, she actually is something of a pest to Mollie, who could easily live without this kind of attention. But by resorting to the defense of reaction formation—that is, refusing to acknowledge her real hostility to Mollie but expressing, instead, kindness and goodwill—Ruth fools herself into believing that she is a "nice girl" who deeply cares for her sister.

From the foregoing examples, it can be seen that defensive children invariably fail to acknowledge some of their primary feelings, usually because they are consciously or unconsciously ashamed of having these feelings. Instead, they use various techniques of prevaricating and covering up these emotions, sometimes even going to the extreme of displaying opposite feelings. Defensiveness is almost always motivated by the philosophy that if the child has negative thoughts or behavior, he is a complete no-good for having them, and that therefore he'd better pretend to be a thoroughly different kind of individual. Although all kinds of neurotic behavior are, by definition, self-defeating, defensive acts are especially so, since the nondefensive neurotic at least has a chance of seeing what he is doing and then can consciously work at correcting his self-destructive thoughts and deeds. The defensive neurotic, on the other hand, has much less of a chance of *seeing* his true ideas and emotions and therefore almost certainly will not be able to work at changing them for the better. The time and energy he expends denying and camouflaging his true attitudes deflect him from working at changing them; and consequently he is caught in a perpetual vicious cycle from which it is most difficult to escape.

The truly grievous result of the various escapes from his fears .is that these defensive reactions almost invariably elicit withdrawing or rejecting reactions in others—often from those very people the child fears most. If they, in turn, punish him, they put into motion the same cycle of fear, defensive reactions, and punishment—"the vicious circle of maladjustment," which, according to Joel Davitz, places the child in a world of constant threat, unhappiness, and fear.

Compulsiveness

Although most neurotic children tend to be withdrawn, underachieving, and inert, a sizable minority of these youngsters are overexcitable and overactive. Most of the children in this class are compulsive, that is, they feel that they must act in certain specific ways. Rosalind, for example, was a typical compulsive worrier. Whenever she left the apartment in which she and her parents lived, she tried the door from three to ten times to make sure that it was locked. When she bought something in a store, she counted her change over and over to make sure that she had been given the correct amount. She made her bed every morning in a rigidly precise manner to make absolutely certain that the sheets and other covers were properly tucked in. Every day of every week she repeated many self-imposed rituals to insure that everything was right with the world and that she was assuming exactly the correct place in its scheme of things. If the slightest thing went awry in her ritualistic observances, she was terribly unhappy, could not concentrate on anything else (even when it was normally of an extremely pleasurable nature), and felt literally compelled to put the disordered thing or event right again. Rosalind was driven to avoid failure by slavishly complying to rigid behavior, leaving herself little room to become a normally assertive person and establish her own identity. Naturally, under these compulsive conditions, Rosalind did not function well, and everyone thought she was a bit nutty. Her cousin Oscar was equally compulsive but wisely chose more constructive goals for his compulsive efforts. He collected stamps, theater programs, and history books; and he necessitatively worked at filling in any item that was missing in all these collections. Eventually, he had remarkably fine accumulations in all these areas and won a great deal of approval from others for having them. People rarely thought of Oscar as being neurotic. Actually, however, he was so afraid of his inability to deal with uncertain and probabilistic areas of life—such as how to write a good essay or how to get along well with a friend—that he withdrew into more certain areas, such as collecting theater programs, which were finite in number, and which could be easily ascertained and hunted for. So Oscar, like Rosalind, was a worrisome person who continually sought for what Harry Stack Sullivan called "security operations" through which to make himself feel temporarily safe. He just happened to pick the kind of a security system which others honored him for finding—while poor Rosalind picked the kind of operations at which everybody laughed and for which they severely criticized her.

Summary

Childhood neurosis consists of stupid, ineffectual, self-defeating behavior by a youngster who is theoretically capable of saner and more intelligent responses to the world around him. Emotionally disturbed children invariably have irrational ideas which cause their immature and insecure feelings. These ideas include some form of absolutistic, perfectionistic shoulds, oughts, or musts. Thus, instead of telling themselves the sane idea that it would be nice if they performed well or if others treated them kindly, they actually believe the insane notion that they must perform perfectly and that others should always treat them fairly and sympathetically.

Once they take over from their parents, teachers, and other educational sources these unrealistic ideas, and once they keep indoctrinating themselves with these same falsehoods, children develop a wide range of neurotic or psychotic symptoms—including self-depreciation, grandiosity, shyness and inhibition, underachievement and ineptness, anxiety and tenseness, resentment and hostility, self-deceit and defensiveness, and compulsiveness. It is not, however, the particular forms their disturbances take which are important; rather, it is the concrete ideas and attitudes that lead to their symptoms. Unless these underlying crooked value systems are clearly seen (by the children themselves and by their parents) and are forthrightly attacked and uprooted, individual neurotic traits may come and go, but even when they do wane they will be replaced by other aspects of disturbance.

The symptoms that we have listed in this chapter, therefore, are valuable in that they indicate how a child may be neurotic and the ways in which his neurosis could manifest itself. With this list as a guide, it will often be possible for parents and other adults to discern that they are dealing with an emotionally aberrated child and that something should be done to help him or her with this aberration. But the symptom is not in itself the neurosis. Behind the symptom lies a cause, and before the former can be effectively treated the latter must be perceived and attacked. What follows will explain some of the detailed causes of various childhood neuroses and show how parents can understand them in order to help overcome them.

3

Helping Children Overcome Fears and Anxieties

"Anxiety can also be felt by animals, but it takes the voice of human conscience to transform the sense of physical failure into a feeling of guilt before existence. . . . The difference between his achievements and his duties is seen as an abyss . . . produce in him the mood of a permanent day of judgment."

—E. PODOLSKY

All children tend to have two major kinds of fears: (a) fears of external things and events, such as animals, noises, the dark, and moving objects; and (b) fears of their own basic inadequacies. The latter we often call anxieties, and these are the kinds of fears to which neurotic children, in particular, are prone. Whereas the so-called normal child almost always has some outside objects or happenings of which he is reasonably or unreasonably afraid, he may seldom be preoccupied with the idea that he himself is no good and that there is practically no difficult situation that he can handle successfully. Disturbed children frequently feel exactly this way.

At the same time, the neurotic child is not only likely to have more fears of outside situations than is the healthy child but often to have these fears in a more intense manner. He is not merely fearful of various things; he is excessively afraid. And he often reacts to the conditions of which he is afraid in states of utter panic, sometimes with a host of side effects such as various kinds of physical symptoms. Instead of consciously trying to avoid feared objects, he often refuses to admit that he is truly afraid and defensively avoids them, rationalizes his fears about them, or otherwise lies to himself and others in connection with them.

There is good reason to believe, moreover, that the highly disturbed child, and especially one who is psychotic, does not acquire all his fears simply from his early experiences and from the teachings of those around him. Certainly, these factors are important in his becoming terribly panicked—or at least in connection with the kinds of things of which he becomes unusually concerned about. He is not going to be scared of elephants if he has never heard of an elephant; and even if he has heard of or seen a representation of this animal, he is not likely to be abnormally afraid of it if he hears it mentioned only as a kindly, harmless animal.

Disturbed children, nonetheless, seem to have a strong inborn propensity to make certain things exceptionally fearful to themselves and can therefore use almost anything as grist to their fear-creating mill, whereas another child, without this strong tendency, might, with the same grist, shrug it off and carry blithely on. Even when they are told, for example, that elephants ordinarily do not harm people, or that they never roam around loose in civilized society, or that when tamed they are useful animals, they can easily upset themselves because of the size of the elephant, or his peculiar looks, or the fact that he somewhat resembles a fearsome hippopotamus, or about a score of other things that would hardly occur to or disturb a healthy child.

What can be done to help a disturbed youngster with this fearsomeness? There are several prophylactic and curative measures that can be taken in this respect:

(1) If it is known that a child has a strong tendency to be-

come frightened by dogs, the dark, loud noises or anything else, a special effort may be made to keep him out of the range of these things. He cannot, of course, be unduly restricted in this respect, or else he will tend to be deprived of large aspects of living. Moreover, if he is not allowed to experience and become used to a fairly wide variety of events, he may remain fearful forever, instead of gradually overcoming most of his childish panics. But, particularly when he is young, and when it is found that certain things will provoke immense fears if he is exposed to them, he should routinely be kept away from specific kinds of TV programs or stories or people (such as cripples) which are most likely to affect him adversely. As he grows older and can more adequately be shown that the things he fears are not truly harmful, he may gradually be subjected to an increasing number of potentially dangerous stimuli; but in his younger and less understanding years, it is probably wiser to keep him at least semi-protected in this respect.

(2) The easily upsettable child should preferably be kept away from excessively fearful adults and older children. If his grandparents happen to be unusually timid or panic-stricken individuals, he should not be allowed to see them except when other adults, such as his parents, are present, who can stop these fearful individuals from indoctrinating him with their own nonsense. Baby-sitters and other persons who are likely to have intimate contact with the child may sometimes have to be screened carefully, or else only allowed to be with him when there is some parental supervision.

(3) If you, as a parent, happen to be imbued with a great many intense fears, train yourself to suppress as thoroughly as possible these fears when you are with your child. At first blush, this might seem to be impossible, since fearful individuals can communicate their trepidation to a child by various nonverbal means (such as looking aghast, frenziedly biting their nails, etc.) even if they do not volubly *say* anything about their own disquietude. Or anxious mothers, fearful of their possible ineptness with their children, may overcompensate by fussing with them and unconsciously transmit their own anxiety. The fact re-

mains, however, that lots of children are brought up in homes where the parents fight with each other continually, frequently in a rather vicious manner. Yet, in some of these homes the parents are sensible enough rarely or never to do their backbiting in the presence of their children, who therefore grow up witnessing few outright squabbles, and sometimes are almost blessedly unaware that their parents are so combative. So even highly fearful parents can make a real effort to confine their emotional overconcerns to themselves and for the most part can refrain from inflicting them on their offspring.

(4) Children who are unusually fearful of external events can frequently be talked out of their fears if those who raise them will reason with them in a patient, kindly, and persistent manner. Allan Fromme notes that "a rational explanation of how little there is to be afraid of, or how unafraid we are, does next to nothing for a child." But there is evidence that this is by no means always true. Even though, when he is literally in a state of panic, a child may be unable to listen to any rational explanation of his fear—especially when he is determined to be fearful, partly in order to upset and dominate his parents—there is reason to believe that such an explanation may have a beneficial delayed reaction and be useful in inducing the child not to be equally fearful next time.

Repetition of rational explanations, moreover, may prove to be eventually helpful. In this connection, it should be remembered that one of the main reasons why a child is and remains neurotically fearful is not because a stimulus is truly fearsome in itself, but because he is vigorously and repetitiously indoctrinating himself with the ideas that he cannot stand the existence of this stimulus, and that he must be afraid when it is present. If his parents or teachers, therefore, will vigorously but calmly keep deindoctrinating him, and keep showing him that there is no reason he will suffer harm in the presence of this stimulus, he may eventually be convinced that what they are saying is true and may cease his self-propagandizations, which create and sustain his destructive fears.

(5) Blaming the child or making fun of him for his fearful-

ness usually won't help him at all but will tend to do him more harm than good. His propensity to be overfearful in the first place is partly derived from the fact that he has little confidence in his own ability to cope adequately with various aspects of his environment, and from his false belief that therefore he will be overwhelmed by certain things and events. If he is ridiculed for having such fears, he will usually feel even more inadequate and consequently will often become still more fearful. This does not mean that it is necessary for him to be shown that all his fears are perfectly sane and that there is no reason why he should give them up. On the contrary, he can definitely be taught that his exaggerated fears are not sensible and that there are several good reasons why he should forgo them. But objectively pointing out the nonsensicalness of his fears is a far cry from deridingly observing that he is an idiot for having them. The child, we must insist throughout this book, is not his performance; and no matter how idiotic the latter is, it presents no evidence that he is completely stupid, inept, or hopeless.

The child's specific fear, therefore, should often be concertedly attacked in an objective, unexcited manner. He should clearly be shown that this fear is groundless; that he need not retain it; that he will only harm himself if he does stick with it; that most other children do not have it; that there is practically no possibility of the feared object or event actually affecting him adversely; and so on. But concomitantly, he should be shown that he has a perfect right, as a human being, to be wrong; that he is not an inferior being because he is mistaken; that his being overly fearful in one area does not prove that he cannot handle any other area of life; and that he is not going to be singled out and punished, either by human beings or by any other powers that be, because he tends to stick for the present with his irrational fear. On the contrary, he should be taught that no matter how crazy his current fearsomeness is, it is *it* rather than *he* that is wrong, and there is good reason to believe that he can ultimately conquer it, and hence make himself unfearful again.

(6) Among the different kinds of methods that can be used to help a child overcome his extreme fearfulness, humor can be a

useful approach. After all, reducing an individual's belief in something to absurdity can sometimes aid appreciably in inducing him to surrender this belief. But here again, if humor is used, it should be good humor; it should be directed at the child's panic rather than at him. Thus, a child can be humorously shown that it is quite funny for him to be afraid of all dogs when some dogs are puppies, and even some grownup dogs are tiny, and when it is obvious that these kinds of dogs could not harm anyone, but are themselves terribly afraid of animals as big as he is. The child can be induced to laugh at some other child's fear of small dogs, and later be helped to laugh at his own fear. Or he can be shown humorous pictures or cartoons in which a large adult is terribly frightened of a small, fragile-looking dog, and be led to see how funny that fear is (and, simultaneously, how even adults can sometimes have fears). In various ways, his terror of external things and events can be attacked. But take care that you do not attempt to eliminate the child's self-acceptance along with his fears!

(7) It is frequently, though not always, possible to help the child become pleasantly familiar with a feared object. This was the famous deconditioning technique which was tried many years ago by Mary Cover Jones, a research psychologist who worked under the guiding principles of the noted behaviorist, John B. Watson. She placed a child who was afraid of rabbits, at one end of a long table while the rabbit was placed at the other end; she arranged things so that the child would be doing something pleasant, eating food, in this case, at his end of the table. Then, as the child continued his pleasant pursuit, she gradually brought the rabbit closer and closer to him. After a period of time, the child apparently began to think of the rabbit in relation to his pleasant eating experiences; and he lost his fear of it entirely.

This principle of deconditioning an individual's aversive response to a thing or a person by getting him to associate this thing or person with more pleasant situations can be used with adults as well as children—as Dr. Joseph Wolpe and his followers have shown in many experiments in behavior therapy. But it is particularly useful with children, who tend to be naïve, and who can often be deconditioned by their parents without their having any consciousness of how they are being affected. Roger J., for example, was a seven-year-old boy who was deathly afraid of the ocean, and who never went near the water when his parents took him to the beach every day during the summer. He would say that the water was too cold, or that he'd rather play in the sand, or would make up other excuses; but, when pressed he would admit that he just didn't like the ocean and was terribly afraid of going into it.

I dissuaded Roger's parents from trying to talk him into going into the water when it became clear that he was going to be quite recalcitrant in this respect. Instead, I had them, along with his two older brothers, induce Roger to play ball with them near the water's edge, and occasionally deliberately to throw the ball to him in such a manner that he would have to run into the water a little to catch it. They also encouraged him to return their pitches so that they would have to enter the water to retrieve the balls he threw at them. By making a sport of throwing the ball and catching it deeper and deeper in the water, and by thus luring Roger to concentrate on the ball rather than the water itself, they induced him to enter the ocean a good many times. He finally got so used to entering it that he thought nothing of doing so, and was thereafter able to begin wading and swimming and other water sports for their own sake. Within a month, he became a fairly good swimmer, and thereafter had no fear of the ocean or any other body of water.

(8) Calmness in dealing with a child's fears is one of the prime requisites for helping him overcome them. It is good for parent to recognize, in this respect, that all children's states of panic are hardly pernicious but that fear can be a constructive force, causing us to use caution and foresight. Thus, we certainly must teach our children the danger of running out in moving traffic on our streets. Consequently, it is well for the parent to know that a child's fear may be a sign of intelligence, common sense, and self-protectiveness and does not in itself mean that the child is severely disturbed.

Even if the child's fears are clearly excessive, there is no need for the parents themselves to become panicked. In fact, one of the main reasons why the child easily catastrophizes is because he sees the adults around him catastrophizing about various things that they do not like, and he begins to think that making mountains out of molehills is the appropriate way for a human being to react. Also, he may observe that life becomes somewhat exciting and interesting when his parents run around in a distraught manner; and he may decide to adopt a similar path of life to divert himself from some of the day's monotony.

If, therefore, your child becomes fearful or upset about something, for heaven's sake don't, yourself, become panicked about *your child*. Take his fears in stride, calmly showing him that you aren't scared stiff about his having them; indicate, by your manner as well as your words, that it is better if he conquers these fears, but that neither you nor he will die if he doesn't. Show him that it is indubitably preferable, but not an unquestioned necessity, that he be less fearful; that he will enjoy himself more if he is relatively fearless, but that he can still have a reasonably happy life if he retains several irrational dreads. As can you!

(9) Don't be deceived by your child's clever evasions of admitting his fears. Although the psychoanalytic school of thinking has its distinct limitations, and frequently finds motives for peoples' behavior that are farfetched and irrelevant, it has valuably pointed out that human beings set up all kinds of defenses against admitting how disturbed they are; some of these were listed in the previous chapter. As Fromme notes, "The most common piece of self-deception employed to minimize our fear is to convince ourselves that we do not like certain things rather than that we are afraid of them. We may, in fact, honestly dislike dogs, horses, swimming, and football, but the very reason we dislike them might be our fear of them. We satisfy ourselves, in short, with a half-truth and leave the underlying fear unchanged."

If, then, your child claims that he is not particularly afraid of other children, animals, or whatnot, but that he simply dislikes them and wants to stay away from them, take his "dislike" skeptically, and ask yourself whether he is using it as a cover-up for his fears. If you think that he is fearful rather than disliking, but still refuses to admit that he has any such fear, assume that he *is* fearful, and try to get him to overcome his fear, along the lines discussed above. It is preferable to help him to be conscious of anything he fears and to admit that he does fear it; but it is not always necessary for him to make this kind of an admission in order to help him overcome his dreads.

(10) If you, as the child's parent, have a fear of bugs, mice, airplanes, or anything else that he also fears, it is naturally advisable that you look into your own heart and get rid of your personal catastrophizing. Not that this is absolutely necessary, since you can pretend that you don't fear something or merely keep quiet about your own fears of it, and still be able to tackle your child's fear of this thing. But if you do actively display anxiety in relation to something (and its manifestations do manage to filter through), you will usually have a difficult time ridding your child of that same anxiety, for why should he not follow your own fear-ridden example?

How should you get rid of our own irrational fears? By vigorously questioning and challenging their validity. And by forcing yourself, by giving yourself definite homework assignments, to act against them. If, for example, you are afraid of insects, and keep showing your child how frightful they presumably are, you must ask yourself: "What is really so horrible about insects? What are they likely to do to me? Why do I think that I can't stand them? Who said that I must shudder every time that I see one?" If you keep asking such questions and keep checking your premise that you must quake at the sight of insects, you will soon begin to see that there really is no reason why you must. Only because you keep telling yourself that insects are horrible, ugly, awful, and remembering past instances of fright do you *make* them frighten you anew. To fully overcome your own fear of insects, you must stop running away from them every time one appears and must force yourself to look at them, to stay in their presence, and perhaps even to kill or handle them. Not that you have to become a roach fancier or collector or anything like that! But there is no reason why, if you really want to conquer your unreasonable fear of insects, you (or someone else) cannot catch a couple of roaches and have them race each other or put one in a jar and feed it for a few days. If you can get your insect-fearing child to join you in these pursuits, there is an excellent chance that he will overcome his horror of insects even more quickly than you overcome yours!

So much for fears of tangible objects and living things. Helping the child overcome his fear of failure and of what other people think of him is usually even more important, since this kind of fear—or what we usually call anxiety or feelings of inadequacy or worthlessness—is exceptionally common and leads to more pernicious results, in most cases, than does fear of animals or things. Why? Because a fear of something tangible usually involves the idea that one will be physically harmed by it; and that is more easily corrected in ordinary life-experience than is anxiety over being held in low esteem by oneself and others. (In the case of anxiety, one can always "manufacture" new evidence where none exists.)

Johnny J. was pathologically afraid of worms for the first eleven years of his life. Whenever he walked along city streets after a rainstorm and saw them on the street and sidewalk, he was revolted; he was particularly horrified at the possibility of his stepping on one of them and crushing it. When it did rain, he tried to get his parents to drive him to school, even though his school was only a few blocks away from his home, and normally he had no trouble walking there by himself. But going by car was a method of avoiding seeing any worms on the way.

Although Johnny thought that fishing might be a great sport, he shied away from it because all of his friends fished with worms. He did a little crab hunting (as no worms were involved in this activity) but found excuses not to go fishing. In his twelfth year, however, his best friend insisted that he come along on a fishing trip, and Johnny became so used to seeing him fish the worms out of the bait can and put them on the hook that he became inured to the sight of them. Before he knew it, he was fishing with worms himself—with his hooks at first baited by his friend, and then later by his own hands. After a few weeks of fishing, he was never bothered by the sight of worms again. His down-to-earth experience with them had obviously pushed out of his head the notion that he just couldn't even bear to look at them; and a year later he most unsqueamishly taught his younger brother, Joseph, how to dig for worms, collect them in a can, and use them to catch fish.

However, Johnny had much less luck with his fear of speaking up in public. Though bright in school, he avoided all classroom recitation, feeling that if he didn't know the right answer to the teacher's question, or if he knew it and didn't say it with distinction, he was a most inadequate person, and all the other students had a perfect right to laugh at him. So he made himself inconspicuous in class and managed rarely to be called on or to give any but the briefest answers when he was called on. Because he kept vehemently telling himself how awful it would be if he spoke poorly in class, and because he actually did speak badly most of the time, out of his very dread of doing so, Johnny never became used to recitations. Years of schooling, including several courses in public speaking, did not help him discard the idea that it would be terrible if he failed to be a great speaker; and every time he blundered in this respect, he felt so badly about his failure that his feeling of humiliation seemed to confirm his original belief. The usual self-fulfilling prophecy of doom thus kept recurring: Because Johnny believed it was awful to recite badly, he experienced terror when he did fail at reciting. Then this "terrible" experience made him believe that his original premise was correct. Actually, his feelings were creating further feelings, which in turn were creating still further feelings; and there were no facts to back his rotating premises, even though he strongly believed that there were.

When, therefore, a child feels that it is horrible if he appears poorly to others, it is very difficult to disabuse him of this feeling, since the feedback he received from it is largely created by his original feeling and not by the conditions existing outside himself. If he believes that a dog will bite him and it doesn't, he will ultimately be tempted to change his hypothesis about it and its dangerousness. But if he believes that people don't like him when they actually do, he may easily "see" them as hating him and will not give up his hypothesis about their attitudes toward him. Moreover, if a dog actually does bite him, he will probably discover that he is not severely hurt or maimed and may actually come to fear dogs less than he previously did. But if the people actively dislike him he will probably convince himself that he simply can't stand their dislike and will tend to feel even more fearful of their disapproval than he previously did. Or, without real evidence, he may imagine that people don't like him. While many of his fears of things will thus be self-corrective, his fears of people disapproving him will tend to be self-perpetuating.

"Failure," says Wendell Johnson, "is a matter of evaluation." If your goals are too high, or too unrealistic, "then you are likely to suffer from an inferiority complex, a low opinion of yourself . . . to be overwhelmed by the 'general impenetrability of things.' "

How can the child's fears and negative evaluations about himself be prevented or corrected? By slowly and persistently teaching him a philosophy of life that is radically different from that which almost all other children and adults in this society believe; namely, the philosophy that if there is such a thing as goodness or self-worth, he possesses it just because he exists, because he is alive, and not because he does certain things well or because other people approve of him.

Can this kind of a philosophy be taught to a child in the abstract? Not very easily, since a youngster is hardly an abstract philosopher, and is not likely to understand things unless they are stated with the most concrete kind of referents and applications. If you tell him, "Look, dear, you are a worth-while person just because you exist, and just because you are you," he will probably like the sound of what you are saying, and even repeat it. But just as soon as some other adult or child comes along and tells him, "I think that you're no darned good because you keep doing things badly, and anyone who does things so badly is just a bad person," he is more likely to start believing these others rather than you.

So try to be, on a thousand different occasions, more specific. When the child does something well, tell him so. But also let him know that even if he hadn't done so well he would still be a valuable individual, no matter what others might say. The trick here, of course, is not merely to say these kinds of things to the child when he behaves badly or unethically but to show him that you really mean what you say. If you tell him that you think he is a valuable individual while your eyes are flashing in anger and your teeth are wildly gnashing, he is most likely to conclude that you might like to believe in his goodness but that you really don't. When you are annoyed, irritated, or frustrated by your child's behavior, you are merely signaling him that you don't like what he is doing and would prefer very much that he act differently. But when you are exceptionally angry and upset about this same behavior, you are absolutistically telling him that he has no right to act that way and should therefore be punished and condemned. Annoyance at a child's deeds implies a kind of faith in him, for it is a means of showing him that you think he can change his annoying conduct and behave pleasingly in the future. Anger implies that you have no faith that he can change and believe that he is doomed forever.

Another major source of anxiety in children is the climate of fear and doom a parent can create as a result of trying to short-cut the learning of some rule. Thus, a mother tells Annie that if she gets her feet wet by going out without her rubbers she will catch pneumonia; another mother tells Ronnie that if he keeps shrieking his daddy will wallop him when he gets home. Such admonitions may (or may not) produce the desired short-range goal; but in the long run they may add up to generalized feelings of impending doom, guilt, and anxiety.

If you would raise a child to overcome his fears and anxieties and to find enjoyment in life, here are some ways in which you can help him construct and maintain feelings of self-worth and freedom from anxiety:

(1) Fully accept the fact that he is a child who has simply not had time to learn all the strange rules of the adult world; consequently, he is unusually fallible and must inevitably make innumerable mistakes that will be something of a bother to you. Realize, too, that going out and getting one's feet wet seldom

does produce pneumonia, and that children, as A. S. Neill of Summerhill never tires of pointing out, will outlive their childishness only if they are allowed to act it out, to be children, to learn the hard way by making mistakes rather than by merely being warned of the dire consequences of mistakes.

Try to view your child's behavior from his, rather than your, frame of reference. Naturally, you will tend not to dawdle over your food, or ask a stream of annoying questions, or go out to play ball when you have an important examination the next day. And naturally, from your way of looking at things, it is wrong for the child to act in these "silly" ways. But he has rather different goals from yours; and from the standpoint of these goals, his conduct is perhaps not quite as inappropriate as it first may seem. Thus, he may enjoy dawdling with his food or may like the effect that his dawdling has in throwing you off balance. He may feel that he can't keep quiet and that he must have immediate answers to all his questions. He may believe that being a good ballplayer is much more important than getting high marks on an examination. By holding these premises and acting upon them, he may indeed be childish; but he is a child, and that's the way most children are. Try to see his activities, therefore, from his own point of view and see if, from that standpoint, they are really as crazy or as vicious as they seem to be.

(2) Learn to tolerate normal inefficiencies, as they inexorably do exist, in the adult's as well as the child's world. The simple act of tying a shoelace becomes for a child not an exciting feat of independence but a bitter, frustrating defeat if an intolerant parent snaps at his fifth failure in an effort to get him off to school quickly. By displacing the onus of the shoe-tying failure onto the task (where it belongs) rather than the individual (Ginott suggests such comments as, "Shoes are difficult to tie, aren't they?"), a child learns to accept his deficiencies gracefully, is spared anxiety, and, his self-worth still intact, will cheerfully try again.

(3) Keep in mind that emotional disturbance has its own rationale and that neurotic and psychotic children do not employ the same motives, in many instances, as do less disturbed young-

sters. For one thing, once a child feels that others do not like him and that it is horrible that they don't, he frequently resorts to testing procedures, deliberately acting badly to see whether his peers and his elders will accept him. Or else, he may dislike himself so thoroughly that he thinks he deserves to be punished for his poor behavior, and he therefore acts in such a manner as to bring this punishment down on his head. Or he may be so afraid that he will fail his school examination, even if he prepares for it thoroughly, that he may intentionally engage in sports rather than studying, in order to give himself an alibi in case he does fail. For many reasons such as these, the behavior of disturbed children tends to be more idiotic and execrable than that of healthier youngsters, and you should keep this in mind when you are trying to appraise their conduct. Just as it would be foolish of you to expect a physically crippled person to run a race without faltering, you would be equally unrealistic to expect an emotionally aberrated child to engage in almost any kind of activity without making far more than the usual number of mistakes.

(4) Once you have ascertained that a child's behavior is poor, try to estimate what his chances are, with all the will in the world, of actually bettering his current performances. Children who are bright, who are not too young, who have not yet become habituated to a certain kind of behavior, and who live in reasonably good surroundings are more amenable to change than those who are less intelligent, very young, confirmed wrongdoers, who live in a slum neighborhood where most people ignore, or even set a premium on, antisocial actions. Don't make the mistake of believing that just because a child's deportment is unmistakably horrendous that he is entirely capable of seeing that it is and changing it if he wants to do so. Maybe he is, and maybe he isn't. Observe him carefully; find out what he *is* truly able to do and not to do; and then judge his deeds accordingly.

(5) If you honestly believe that your child's performances are correctable, and you are making a calm, concerted effort to help him improve them, keep in mind that haste makes waste in this regard and that it almost always takes a human being a considerable amount of time to modify his ways of doing things. For a

child to learn how to walk, to speak, to feed himself, and to play games well, a great deal of practice and effort must usually occur; and for him first to unlearn poor behavior and then to learn better replacements also normally takes time and practice, practice and more time. Be patient! Go over the same ground again and again—a hundred or several hundred times, if necessary. Don't get discouraged: Children aren't rebuilt in a day!

In regard to the last two points, it cannot be emphasized too strongly that the child is very much the result of heredity as well as environment and that, if he is born with a tendency to act in a certain manner, it is exceptionally difficult, and sometimes impossible, to induce him to behave in a manner that is radically different from this tendency. Even authorities who have been highly (and often too highly) influenced by psychoanalytic theories of the importance of early childhood training and conditioning have had to acknowledge the importance of organic predispositions toward certain kinds of conditioning taking place. Analytically oriented psychologist John Bowlby has guardedly stated, "It is useful to remember that recent work on the study of human beings and animals before birth has produced a steady accumulation of evidence that harmful changes in the environment before birth may cause faults of growth and development exactly like those which have in the past been thought to be due to heredity. This is a finding of great importance, which, as will be seen, is exactly parallelled in psychology. It is to be emphasized, however, that such findings in no way contradict theories of the bad influence of hereditary factors, except in so far as people hold that hereditary factors alone account for all differences in human behavior. Indeed, there is reason to believe that hereditary factors also play a part and that the greatest scientific progress will be made when the interaction of the two can be studied." And one of the leading authorities on child care, Anna W. M. Wolf, has noted that "there are differences in native constitution, as well as accidental experiences that cannot be predicted or controlled, that predispose one child more than another to find life hard."

Dr. Aaron Beck has made some exceptionally important discoveries in this regard about individuals who are subject to severe fits of depression. It has been noted for a good many years that such persons have a long history of traumatic events and that their childhoods seem to be much more difficult than those of nondepressed individuals. These data have been used to support the psychoanalytic hypothesis that if a child is dealt with harshly during his early years he will develop into a disturbed adult. Dr. Beck has found, however, that some children have what may well be an innate tendency to exaggerate the relatively minor slights and hard knocks that life passes on to them; that they are predisposed to what Bergler, as I mentioned, calls "injustice collecting" (or what I, more comprehensively, prefer to call *misery amassing*); and that *therefore* they turn up, when they are adults, with long histories of early "traumas." There is much reason to believe that practically all humans are dealt with fairly harshly during their early (and later!) days; that most of us soon come to accept the rank injustices and the inevitable annoyances of social living; and that when someone presents a picture of an unusually harsh early life, there is reason to suspect that part of this "harshness," and often a considerable part, is the view this individual takes toward his living, rather than the actual "awfulness" of the events of his existence, which a child less disposed to this kind of thinking passes over and forgets.

In view of these propensities of the child to be born—as well as to be raised—with a trouble-seeking mode of reacting to the noxious stimuli that are almost certain to assault him during his early (and later) existence, it is folly to believe that every youngster can be taught exactly what is the right thing for him to do and that he can be kept entirely out of harm's way, emotionally or physically. Certainly, his self-defeating and antisocial tendencies can be *minimized,* but there is no evidence that they can be entirely eliminated.

(6) Try to keep in mind that the main reason for anyone's anxiety is his dire need to be accepted, approved, or loved by all the significant people in his life—and sometimes by practically everyone in the world. Is there anything wrong with such a need? No, not statistically, since practically everyone in the world, and

certainly everyone in our society, seems to be sorely afflicted with it. In terms of mental health, however, it just won't work for the obvious reason—if you stop to think about it—that needing (rather than merely preferring) someone else's approbation means that unless you have this need fulfilled, you are a failure. Even when you are finding the acceptance you think you need, you have no guarantee that you will *continue* to win it, so you will continue to be anxious.

Stated a little differently: If you require the approval of others in order to like and respect yourself, you will never really have any stable self-esteem, for needing others essentially means not sufficiently liking yourself unqualifiedly and unequivocally, with or without their acclaim. And lack of self-esteem, low ego-strength, or insufficient self-confidence (which are all synonyms for the same state of personal insecurity) is, for the most part, a perpetual state of anxiety.

If, therefore, you would raise your child with minimal feelings of social panic and maximum feelings of self-worth, you should show him that you do not notably need others' love and that neither does he. Most graphically, in this respect, you can *let him see that you are not particularly hurt by his ungracious, inconsiderate, and sometimes hostile attitudes.* Naturally, you would like him to care for you and to be considerate of your feelings. But when (as is often likely to happen) his actions are not loving or kind, let him see that you can take his negativism well and that it doesn't send you off into paroxysms of self-pity, tears, and anger. As the noted child psychologist Bruno Bettelheim once pointed out to a panel of mothers discussing the problem of lying, parents far more frequently get upset when their children lie to them than they do when their children lie to their own friends. In other words, a false sense of their own inadequacy in bringing up a less-than-perfect child often results in a guilty lashing out at those children, who then generally misbehave further. There is, as several researchers have found, a significant and positive relationship between a parent's self-acceptance and that of his child.

Don't *demand* that he care for you, nor try to make him inordinately guilty when he apparently doesn't. Such demands show him (a) that you can't stand to live without his acceptance; and (b) that he, supposedly, can't stand to live without others' favors when they treat him much as he is now treating you. Both of these suppositions are false and pernicious. You *can* very definitely lead a happy life even if he hates you completely—if you *think* you can. So can he enjoy his existence, if not perhaps to the fullest at least to a vast degree, if you teach him to think that he can.

Which means exactly what it says! Teach him, as we have just noted, by example—especially by your own example. Point out to him that you, or someone else you know, or some famous person (Richard Wagner, for example) somehow managed to get by and be productive and creative even though others didn't uniformly like him, and many probably wished him dead. And teach him logically, philosophically, and empirically, that being loved is not necessary (though it is often greatly enjoyable), that it cannot be consistently achieved by virtually anyone, and that its lack still leaves a whale of a lot of sheer pleasure and vital absorbing interest in one's life. How do you teach him these things? The same way that you teach him not to run in front of cars, to do his homework properly, and to get along reasonably well with his peers, and by letting him, by a plenitude of trials and errors, see for himself that the things you are pointing out are true.

(7) Avoid the sorts of family tensions that are characterized by constant scraps between parents; such fighting denotes your own inability to handle the irritations and troubles that come your way. Prolonged exposure to a parent who dissolves into tears every time a roast fails or becomes nervous and irritable when confronted with too many things to do at once will undermine a child's confidence in his own ability to handle life's stresses when even his parent, a large and competent creature in his eyes, cannot. His ultimate reaction may be one of not wanting to enter the fearful adult world; he thus becomes fixated in infantile behavior to prevent it.

(8) Should you pamper a highly neurotic child who is ter-

ribly anxious about what other people think of him? Yes and no; unfortunately there is no unequivocal answer to this question.

First, let us consider the *yes* side. Disturbed children—we must again insist—are either biologically predisposed to be the way they are, or else they have been strongly conditioned to be that way by early influences. Or both. In any event, they are, by the time their anxieties, phobias, obsessions, and other symptoms are clearly visible, pretty well set in their ways, and if too much pressure is put upon them to change their disorganized ways, they may well balk, become hostile and aggressive, or sometimes give up entirely, view themselves as utterly hopeless, and withdraw into a world of their own.

Consequently, they must often be more or less pampered. Not that I would be defeatistic—but my theory of personality change strongly asserts that people don't alter very much, so far as their emotionally sick ways are concerned, unless they work, work, work; and I would consequently much rather see disturbed children work their little heads off to get better than to be passively conditioned from the outside by their parents and elders.

The fact is that highly neurotic youngsters must often be given in to *first* and be allowed to get away with all kinds of deviant behavior on many occasions before they can finally be helped to become less disturbed. They are so terribly fragile and/or hostile that they simply demand a considerable amount of mollycoddling; and it is sometimes wise to give some to them. Not only, as noted previously, should they not be roundly ridiculed and excoriated for their poor performances, but they should sometimes have these actions patiently ignored, or calmly acceded to, or occasionally even abetted. Thus, if a child has a terrible school phobia, it is sometimes the better part of valor for his parents to be understanding and keep him out of school for a while, rather than firmly insist that he go—even though he may not be particularly benefited, for time being, by this kind of pampering. At least, he may escape being further traumatized by it.

The point is, then: Be firm! Don't knock your children's heads in when they do something wrong and don't try to convince them that they are lice who should berate themselves for the rest of their lives for their contemporary wrongdoing. But do, quite definitely, show them that you and society consider certain acts muddleheaded, self-defeating, or immoral, and make clear that you intend to do your best, calmly and without mayhem, to persuade them to desist from such acts. If this kind of firmness, with appropriate penalties (but not malicious punishments), does not work, then you will know that you *really* have a disturbed child on your hands, and more serious measures, including psychotherapy for the child and/or you may have to be tried.

(9) Just as you should suspect any severe antisocial tendencies on the part of a child as being indicative of possible emotional disturbance, so should you be wary of the overly good behavior of any youngster. Children tend naturally to be little demons, especially when they are males. Therefore if they do not get into any mischief but act with complete benevolence, they may well be overinhibited and anxious, and their overpoliteness is not to be greeted with total enthusiasm. It is most convenient for you when a child is so afraid of losing yours and others' approval that he hardly ever expresses himself and is therefore the soul of "niceness." But such behavior may not in the least be convenient for the child himself—who may have all kinds of assertive feelings which he continually bottles up out of his dire love needs.

Even the child who is "naturally" nonassertive and has no trouble whatever in holding back his aggressive feelings, for the simple reason that he is rarely beset by such feelings, is not necessarily healthy. He may have exceptionally little native drive and may, unless something is done about his condition, be doomed to a passive, lusterless kind of future existence. Or he may have learned to squelch his obstreperous feelings at such an early age that it has become second nature for him to forgo them —just as it becomes second nature for a homosexual to feel sexless in the presence of a woman, although originally he may have had quite powerful heterosexual drives. It is almost incredible how "successfully" an individual can train himself, usually quite unconsciously, to go from one extreme of "feeling" to another—to make himself impotent, for example, because he originally was (to his own way of thinking) "too" highly sexed; or to become obsequious and passive because he first was "too" self-assertive and became guilty about being so.

If, therefore, your child is abnormally "good," is exceptionally loved by other children or adults, or supinely follows every rule that you and others give him, stop and consider whether he is already well on the way to selling his soul, and whether the advantages he may gain from this kind of ultraconforming behavior are really worth it. Try to discover if he is terribly anxious about losing yours and others' approbation; and, if so, get in a good, practical counterattack on his anxiety-creating attitudes. Show him that the purpose of living is just that—living, doing, acting, asserting, thinking, and expressing. Demonstrate to him the benefits of being himself, rather than of always being dependent on the notion of what others think he should be.

Studies have shown the dependent child to be far less inclined to engage in risk-taking activities, thus doing himself the additional disservice of depriving himself of new challenges and new contacts. With an overly inhibited child, persistent encouragement to activity is in order. Since he believes the results would be terrible if he spoke up in a crowd, or refused to do someone else's bidding, or got into a little mischief, and since he never or rarely actually risks doing any of these things, he has little or no feedback to convince him that his imagined terror has no reality, and that he might, in fact, enjoy doing many or most of the things of which he is so afraid.

Gently, firmly, if you can, push him. Get him among a group of his peers and encourage, almost force him, to speak up about something that you know perfectly well he is capable of discussing. If you find that he always does his best friend's bidding, see if you can persuade him, at least on a few occasions, to stand up for what he wants to do and not yield to what his friend wants. Of course, it would be unwise to become overenthusiastic in this regard. You don't try to teach anyone to have courage by having him jump over a cliff and hang by a limb. By the same token, don't try to teach an inhibited child to express himself more freely by fighting with the biggest bully in the neighborhood.

(10) Once a child becomes anxious about almost anything,

he generally has an inborn and socially acquired tendency to become upset and self-depreciating about being anxious. For anxiety is an unpleasant, inadequacy-creating feeling, and, like many other such feelings in our society, it tends to be socially disapproved. In fact, some of the worst worries of many of my patients is that they will feel and behave so insecurely that their friends and associates will see how upset they are.

Children may be more affected than adults by this tendency to worry about being worried. They are petrified lest someone *notice* that they blush, stammer, remain silent, or display other manifestations of terror; consequently, they become more terrorized. The usual vicious circle results: Anxiety leads to nervous symptoms, which encourage more anxiety, which in turn produces still worse symptoms.

What is to be done if a child is thus afflicted? First of all, he should be helped to see that his secondary problem—his worry about going to school because he will be asked to recite and will stammer when he recites—is a fairly common problem among other children, and even among adults. He should not be left to feel that he, and only he, has this difficulty, but should be shown that worrying about a nervous symptom is almost universal and that it is indeed a rare person who does not appreciably feel this kind of anxiety and react to it in some overexcited or withdrawing fashion.

Secondly, the panic-stricken child should be persistently shown that it is *not* so terrible if he does display to others his nervous mannerisms, thereby revealing how afraid he is. Certainly, some of his fellows may josh him or look down on him for this kind of display; but many others will easily understand how he feels, since they have had very similar experiences themselves. Moreover, those who do laugh at him or despise him for being insecure have a similar problem themselves but are displaying it in a different way; they, too, feel inadequate. But, instead of showing this directly, by worrying and appearing nervous, they are showing it indirectly, by feeling impelled to deride him, and thereby convince themselves that he is worse than they are, and that they are superior to him. Their "superiority," in other words, constitutes a cover-up for their own inferiority feelings. By realizing this, he can be made aware of their underlying weaknesses, which are hardly remarkably different from his.

Quite aside from this, of course, the child who is nervous about being nervous can be shown that he is a fallible being and that, as such, symptoms like nervousness must be part of his human lot. Yes, you can admit to him, it is not good to be afraid of speaking up in public or playing in a crucial ball game, in the first place; nor is it great to be afraid of being afraid. But that's the way boys (and men) are—anxious, fearful, scared stiff of some things. None of them is perfect, including him! And the sooner he faces the fact of his imperfections and graciously accepts them, the better it will be. It would be exceptionally nice if he could excel in everything, including fearlessness and lack of nervous symptoms; but, obviously, he's not going to make it, so he'd better live comfortably with his nonexcelling traits, too. If he can be induced to accept this lack of perfectionism—and, in particular, the absence of his being inordinately loved by every figure whom he chooses to make significant in his life—the basic problem of his feeling of worthlessness will be solved. Otherwise, only partial and palliative "solutions" are available, and he will be more or less ashamed and self-hating forever.

Anxiety, we have been contending in this chapter, consists almost entirely of the need to be approved and accepted by others (while fear may relate to actual physical injury or annihilation). One special form of anxiety, and perhaps the most prevalent form in a competitive society such as our own, is the dire need to achieve, which results in feelings of worthlessness about performance failure. The next chapter will deal with this aspect of the child's neurotic reactions.

4

Helping Children with
Problems of Achievement

---

*"I . . . became enormously aware of the tremendous amount
of ambition—self-defeating ambition—which I saw among
people. Everybody wanted to be the best, and that often
stopped them from doing anything. They're not content to be
good; everybody wants to be No. 1, and if they aren't they're
miserable. And many of them aren't No. 25 in the big league
of the world."*

—BRIAN MOORE

In the area of achievement drives, perhaps more than in any
other sphere, the parent must attack not only his child's irrational
thinking but that of a whole society. The undeniably large impact
of TV and movies on millions of people has resulted in the communication of a set of aspirations for the good life, not only in
materialistic but in personality terms as well. The "good" pros-
per, win wealth and fame, while the "bad" perish, are punished,
or suffer their own self-imposed feelings of guilt.

In a fast-paced society, untold numbers of children fall victim to their parents' needs for efficiency, to demands that they perform exactly as expected, and to condemnations when they fail. Too often the child's performances and achievements are viewed as indications of his parents' worth, and lack of achievement brings reprisals based on the parents' feeling of guilt that they are somehow to blame. This is most likely to occur when a parent's happiness comes to depend solely on his child's development, rather than on more solid footings. And love, as sociologist Theodore Newcomb has pointed out, becomes a premium, handed out on the basis of what a child can *do* rather than simply for *who he is*.

This emphasis on achievement rather than adjustment often takes a further toll in producing children who may excel in planning ability and actual performance, but who pay heavily for it in terms of tenseness, overaggressiveness, and domineeringness.

The bare fact is that the need to achieve is probably the best road to underachievement. Irony? Not at all: The need to have or do practically anything is usually your best insurance against having or getting this thing. For human need is never to be confused with urge, drive, or desire; indeed, it is almost their opposite.

Suppose, by way of illustration, that a child wants to do well in arithmetic and keeps working for what seems to be a very large portion of his waking hours at doing problems, studying mathematics books which are far ahead of those he is using at school, and even trying out original solutions to arithmetic puzzlers for which as yet there is no known solution. Is he a nut in this respect? Well, in one sense, yes, because we could say that he is somewhat obsessed with arithmetic. But is he an unhealthy nut? No, not necessarily.

There could be—don't forget—several good reasons why he is so intent on playing the arithmetic game (as against, say, the game of socializing more with his peers or engaging in athletics). First, he could really enjoy mathematics and have a natural bent for it. Second, he could be intrigued with the challenge of a rather difficult and mind-absorbing game while he gets bored rather easily with less difficult occupations, such as TV listening or reading history. Third, he may have decided that arithmetic has some real practical value, that he could use it to make money in the stock market, or to become a math professor, or as an integral part of the work he later expects to do in astrophysics. Fourth, he may want to impress others with his mathematical ability—may, for example, be interested in attracting a little girl in his class who herself is daffy about arithmetic and who is likely to be prejudiced in his favor if he also excels in that field.

For a variety of sound reasons, then, this child's powerful drive to get ahead in the field of mathematics may have rational components; and even though he spends a great deal of time and energy pursuing this drive, he cannot be said to be self-sabotaging or emotionally disturbed. Just as soon, however, as his bent for math turns into a need, a demand, or an unrealistic expectation, his behavior in pursuing arithmetic becomes truly neurotic.

Why? Because he then begins to risk too much—his entire self, in fact—and becomes driven by, instead of remaining in control of, his mathematical leanings. What is more, he may simultaneously tend to become a worse rather than a better arithmetician. For as long as this child strongly prefers to do well at mathematics, he consciously or unconsciously tells himself, "I want very much to succeed in this field, and if I do, great! But if I don't, that's too bad; and I still have various other alternatives for leading a happy life." But just as soon as he needs to succeed in this area, he surrenders most of these alternatives and leaves himself only with the possibility of success—or misery.

There is little wrong, then, if the child strives for achievement *in itself;* and in fact, this kind of striving is one of the main ways by which he will truly become a committed, active, creative human being. But it is unfortunately not in the nature of man to try to achieve in order to achieve or to reap the intrinsic benefits of achieving; it is more in his nature to strive to perform well in order to gain personal worth and self-confidence. Unfortunately, he tends to measure *himself* by his performance; and if the latter is inadequate, he usually considers his total being inadequate.

A child can ultimately become so fearful of failing that he

actually abandons all efforts, transferring most of his energies to alibiing. Ultimately, partly because he feels worthless unless his performance is shining, and partly because of his shirking, his performance actually *is* less than it might be, he concludes that things really are hopeless and that he will never be able to achieve anything. Or, even if he does perform exceedingly well, the next day he will simply have to prove himself anew.

Prescott Lecky has pointed out that if a child who fails a couple of arithmetic tests uses this past performance as unassailable evidence that he cannot do arithmetic, and then *defines* himself permanently as someone who will *never* be able to do arithmetic, he will abandon all efforts.

And even if the child does manage to perform well on a few tests, he often still feels the need to prove himself anew each day; the enormous strain engendered by such a need may result in the same abandoning of all effort.

Several things can be done, prophylactically and curatively, to help ameliorate your child's dire and self-defeating achievement needs. To wit:

(1) Try to raise your child so that he enjoys many achievements in themselves. Try to show him that the chess game is good because it is interesting; that getting a good mark on his arithmetic exam is intrinsically challenging; that being the best athlete in his class has distinct practical as well as competitive rewards (such as improved physical condition).

Show him, if you can, that various games and ventures in life are also good for the playing, whether or not he wins them. If he picks a good chess partner and continually loses to him, he can still enjoy having a good game; while if he picks a poor partner and continually beats him, the game may well be dull. Not that it is not good to win; for it often is. But it is certainly not necessary and can easily be dispensed with if the game itself is exhilarating.

(2) Teach your child that real achievement is rarely easy—and that there is nothing in the least disgraceful about its being a difficult and long process to attain. As Thomas Alva Edison remarked, "Genius is nine-tenths perspiration and one-tenth in-

spiration," and it is rare that it works out otherwise. There have undoubtedly been a few boy geniuses in all of human history who effortlessly, before their late twenties, turned out some remarkably good works of music, art, or literature. But few is hardly the word here: Such paragons of achievement have been almost nonexistent. Even the young Mozarts of the world have worked and worked and worked to produce their early inspired masterpieces; and the not-so-young Bachs and Beethovens have often worked harder. If your child, then, wants the real rewards of achieving, as well he may, let him know that they are virtually never to be had for the asking and that just about all human beings require practice, practice, and still more practice to achieve mastery in any field.

(3) Be aware of the value of positive reinforcement. Just as it becomes necessary to inform your child when he has crossed the limits of desirable behavior, so it is best, when he performs well, for you to give him a modicum of praise—lest all your comments on his behavior be negative. It is, however, just as harmful for you to couch this praise in terms of his being a better person as it is for you to criticize him in such terms. Thus, if Ronnie gets a 97 on his history exam, tell him, "You did very well on that test—isn't that fine?" You are thus skirting the issue of his being more worth-while because of his achieving, and at the same time you are showing him that praise as well as criticism of his performances can be forthcoming from your corner.

(4) Teach your child that perfectionism is great—as long as it relates to *performance* and not to *self*. Most fine artists are dissatisfied with their imperfect performances; so they keep changing, revising, reconsidering, and redoing, sometimes through many tedious versions of a work, until they put it aside as finished. Even then, they not infrequently return to it years later and make more changes. This is great; and relatively few masterpieces would exist without this kind of perfectionism.

Perfectionism as applied to the self, however, is radically different. For whereas the work-perfectionist tells himself, "This product or project will not be very good unless I do the best I can to keep improving it," the self-perfectionist notes, *"I will not* be very good unless my work is utterly faultless." This is exactly what you must teach your child not to do, since putting himself at stake when his work has flaws will not necessarily drive him to advance his work; on the contrary, it will usually or often make him so concerned lest he turn out a less-than-perfect product that he will be mainly focusing on "How dreadful if I don't! How awful if I can't!"—Instead of, "Now, let me see how well I can!"

Show your child, in other words, how to like and respect himself even when his best efforts to turn out a masterwork are failing; and, for that matter, even when he is not making his best efforts to turn it out. It is too bad when he fails to perfect what he is working at; and it is truly sad when he doesn't even try to perfect it. But "too bad" and "sad" are not equivalent to "horrible" and "unforgivable." And although the particular thing he is working at may be a real dud, *he* is only a dud by arbitrary definition, for he can work at innumerable other things, and he can (believe it or not!) enjoy himself immensely even though everything he ever works at turns out to be mediocre or poor.

Your child, then, should be taught never to confuse the *whole* of him—his self, his being, his total existence—with any particular *part* of him—such as his artistry, or his competence at sports, or his ability to make money. Perhaps his whole is actually the sum of his parts (and perhaps it is not, since all his performances in life may still not exactly equal *him*); but even if it is, it would be virtually impossible for anyone, including himself, to determine just what all his parts are, and how absolutely to measure or rate them. What is more, his self or his being is a process—something that continually changes, grows, develops, and is never static—while his achievements are largely products, things produced by this self-process. The self, therefore, cannot be rated in the same manner that its products or achievements can be assessed; and if it could be weighed and evaluated at all, we would have to use an exceptionally flexible scale with which to measure it, since the process that it is may produce "good" works today and "bad" ones tomorrow, may be highly applauded this week and heartily condemned the next. What, then, is this "good" self that was "bad" yesterday and will be "mediocre" (or heaven knows what) tomorrow? Is it really sensible to measure it at all? Most probably not, since the worst kinds of contradictions ensue in the attempt.

(5) Try to get your child to see that achievement and popularity are hardly the same; in some respects, indeed, they are almost opposites. What the public acclaims in the way of the performing or creative arts is often meretricious and superficial. Conversely, what the best authorities in a given field deem to be good is frequently highly unpopular with the masses. Your child, therefore, should preferably be reared to strive for what he considers to be a fine performance and not what others think is praiseworthy.

(6) Do your best to see that your child's preferences for great achievements are just that: *preferences* rather than *dire needs*. The fact that he wants, and even wants very much, to produce works of profound artistic, scientific, or even commercial merit is all to the good; but a strong desire is still not a need. When a child *needs* to succeed at something, he really means that if he doesn't attain his chosen goal he will view his failure as catastrophic—and that usually means that he will see himself as a Failure with a capital *F*. Theoretically, his enormous need to excel will drive him forward in such an energetic manner that he will be aided thereby. Actually, it will frequently impel him to become panicked at the mere thought that he may not perform outstandingly; and he will soon find himself dilly-dallying about working, giving himself excuses not to continue to work, and eventually (at least in some cases) spending most of his time worrying rather than working. Even when his needs do encourage him to work, they will tend to drive him to do so in such a frenetic, anxious way that his activity will be impaired and he will not by any means be truly focusing on doing the best job that he can do. Rather, he will insist that he must do the best job that *anyone* can do; and this distracting thought may thoroughly sabotage his best goal-seeking.

(7) Teach your child to take his mistakes with equanimity, and in some respects even to welcome them, instead of to excoriate himself for making them. Human beings, for the most part,

learn by trial and error; and unless they make plenty of errors, they are not likely to see clearly that they are wrong and why they are wrong. Children, in particular, are exceptionally fallible and often must make a mistake over and over again before they will profit from it. And why should they not? The idea that mistakes are awful and that you should not make them clearly flows from the ideas that you should be perfect, flawless, infallible. It would, perhaps, be nice if you were perfect since you would then tend to be superior to all other people and would reap certain advantages thereby. But it would also be something of a bore, for the good reason that much, perhaps most, of the interest and excitement in life consists of its nonpredictability—of seeing whether you will live up to certain challenges and discovering whether you will succeed at something or fall flat on your face. No matter: Even if it were thoroughly desirable that you be infallible, you simply are not going to be. Only angels are flawless— and there are no angels.

Your child, then, should not be protected from mistake-making; but, better, inured to this inevitably human process. This means, of course, that you, his parent, should show him that you can gracefully accept your own errors—that you see quite clearly that you are prone to doing things badly on many occasions and that you are not in the least ashamed of so doing. Not that you necessarily like bumbling; but you fully accept yourself when you do bumble. If you give your child the impression that you do plenty of things badly, that you expect to keep erring forever, and that you can calmly tolerate your mistakes and (by looking them squarely and undefensively in the eye) learn a great deal by them, he will tend to follow your sensible lead and learn to view his own errors with a good degree of equanimity.

(8) Teach your child to laugh at himself. Human beings really are a funny race. They are incredibly inconsistent; they almost routinely practice almost the exact opposite of what they preach; they behave with enormous stupidity even when they are unusually bright; they make the most ludicrous boners from birth to death, from morning to night, from country to country. Since your child is more than likely to contribute his share, and per-

haps a few extra dividends, to the fount of human inanity, why not let him know that it often is funny when he puts his foot in his mouth and unsteadily hops around on his other leg until he bumps his nose into something.

This does not mean, of course, that you should laugh at your child's silly antics and ridicule him for being a human boob. It means, rather, that you should laugh good-naturedly at yourself, at man in general, and at—or with—your youngster, too; for he, like the rest of us, is not to be taken too seriously, and is certainly not expected to be a saint.

Eugene L. was as close to being obsessed with proving his own superiority as a boy of fourteen can be. He dressed in the plainest possible manner, so that no one would think him vain. His time after school was spent almost entirely in doing his homework, praying to God to make him a good boy, and collecting religious objects. He refused to participate in any "worldly" events, such as sports and parties; and he even looked down on those who were occupied in reading good fiction or scientific works since he deemed such material too "secular." He was determined, although he was not a Catholic, to become a great religious leader, such as a Pope. Only then, he said, would he be convinced that he had led a truly worth-while life.

Eugene, as one might easily suspect, had practically no sense of humor. He was quite bright and could easily see the point of any joke or witticism; but he scorned resorting to this kind of "frivolous" behavior. He particularly believed that television and other shows that featured comedians were a complete waste of time because they "got absolutely nowhere" and "made no contribution to human knowledge"; and if any of his acquaintances at school started to discuss a comedy show they had seen or commented on the latest issue of *MAD* magazine, he became tense and fidgety and either stopped the conversation with a cutting remark or managed to break away from it as soon as possible.

When I saw this overserious boy for psychotherapy, I tried to get him to admit that there were other things in life than the narrow scope that he insisted on confining himself to and that no form of human happiness, as long as it did not impose upon others or needlessly harm them, was illegitimate. I tried to show him that even his religious views were basically designed to help people be healthier and happier and that, at bottom, they were just as hedonistically oriented as were the views of most secularists. I also tried to get him to see that he wasn't by any means as purely altruistic or selfless as he liked to think that he was: because, fairly obviously, he was playing his own kind of one-upmanship game with the rest of the world and was striving with might and main to be holier-than-thou in order, really, to prove himself to be better-than-thou.

As might be expected, I at first got nowhere with Eugene. He was very willing to discuss with me the possible validity of my interpretations of his behavior, but he always had a brilliant reply to counter my view. If I said that happiness was something that all human beings, including himself, strove for, and that even masochists, in their own peculiar way, were trying to be happy, or at least less guilty and unhappy than they at the moment felt themselves to be, he would answer: "Yes, I have to agree with what you say, since it does seem to be true; but don't forget that there are various kinds of happiness, and that the high-minded, contemplative form that I am espousing is much better than the kind of happiness usually 'enjoyed' by the masses. And just as there are good games to play, such as chess or fighting to conquer cancer, so are there poor games to play, such as checkers or collecting autographs from celebrities. So why should I try to be 'happy' in the way that you or my parents seem to want me to be?"

I tried to explain to Eugene that I didn't care what way he chose to enjoy himself—as long as (a) it was really his own choice and his own way; and (b) he stopped despising others for picking whatever ways of life were most satisfying to them. I merely doubted that he was truly selecting his own mode of living, but felt that, instead, he was compulsively driving himself to the "highest" form of achievement that he could imagine and that he was doing so because he really could not accept himself as he was—with his human limitations and ungodlinesses. The "proof" of my hypotheses was in part that he utterly refused to accept others the way they were and insisted on condemning them for being "inferior" to him. Essentially, I said, he was an intellectual fascist—one who holds the arbitrary belief that individuals possessing certain traits (such as those who are intelligent, cultured, artistic, creative, or achieving) are intrinsically superior to individuals who do not possess these traits, and that the members of the former group deserve to live while those in the latter group really deserve to be annihilated.

Eugene admitted he was fascistic, in this sense of the word, but claimed that being so was much better than accepting the "sloppy" and "decadent" views of the majority and going along with the "weakness" of democracy. I tried to show him that democracy certainly had its deficiencies and that there was no reason why he had to ardently advocate it; but that there were good reasons why he should allow others to be as democratic (and, if necessary, as "weak") as they wanted to be, and that unless he gave them this right, they had an equal right to put him into jail or eradicate him for his ideas. Without trying to win Eugene over to the majority view, I tried to get him to see the value of living and letting live and of accepting a world in which there were many individual differences instead of one "superior" sameness.

He still proved to be a rough customer, and for many weeks I accomplished nothing with him. I noticed, however, that whenever I dropped some of my own serious arguing demeanor and resorted to wry comments on some of the foibles of humanity, including some of Eugene's own extremist views, he would laugh heartily, like the child he really was, and even cackle in a manner normally indigenous to children much younger than he, or to the members of his peer group who were bent on the "frivolous" activities which he so violently deplored. So, to a considerable degree, I turned our sessions into amusing sallies and encouraged him, too, to quip to the best of his ability about many of the topics we kept discussing.

What a change soon transpired in Eugene! Whereas he previously would begin almost every psychotherapy session by soberly reading to me excerpts from some religious-minded thinker who was thundering a jeremiad against the follies of mankind, and would smugly wait for me to agree that this negatively-filled statement was indubitably accurate (which I rarely did), he now started off by reading me some of his own essays on man—and they were usually brilliant, biting satires which were howlingly funny, and which kept both of us in stitches from five to fifteen minutes. I laughed heartily with him and encouraged him to write other material in the same vein; and before Eugene quite realized what was happening, I was showing him that he had a fine humorous talent, and that he might even seriously consider becoming a comedy writer or a humorous novelist.

Then, a little to my own surprise, I discovered that Eugene was not only reading these sardonic missives to me but was also declaiming them to various of his peers, to see how much they enjoyed and appreciated his wit. Within a few weeks, he even went to the trouble of organizing a literary club at school, where the members brought in their own writings to be read for criticism by the other members of the club, and where just about every session featured a reading of some of his own recent humorous declamations on the foibles of man.

The next thing I knew, Eugene was one of the most popular boys in his school and was also being asked to outside parties to give his acerbic recitations. He not only grew in his ability to write humorous sketches, but he soon found that commenting in a semi-religious manner on the idiotic nature of man was limited and eventually boring, so that he included a wider and wider range of topics, some of which had nothing to do with his original views. One of his most amusing talks, for example, was on the difference between classical music and rock and roll; and in this instance he satirized the devotees of the classics as well as of the more popular forms of music, and it would have been difficult to discern any amount of snobbery in his humor. He also began to give more thought and effort to his manner of presentation, rather than just to his subject matter, and he became so good at developing special tricks of the comic trade that he began to consider seriously whether he should not become a public performer on a more professional basis. He even enrolled in an acting class and from time to time wondered whether playing Falstaff, or some other famous comic character, might not be his particular cup of tea. So matters kept developing, until Eugene was rolling merrily —and I mean merrily!—onward, and no further guidance from me was needed. Within eight months after I first started to see him, he had gained considerable insight into his previous behavior, and was more than willing to admit that he had become scrupulously religious mainly because of his dire need to outdo his fellows, and because he could not think of any other area in which he might better outperform them. He also realized that his motivation had been essentially *un*religious or *anti*religious, in that instead of being devoted to any deity or higher cause, he had actually been obsessively-compulsively devoted to proving what a great person he, himself, was. He finally saw that what is usually called religiosity, in our society, is little more than a subtle game of one-upmanship, stemming from the "religious" individual's serious feelings of inadequacy and his driving need to show himself and others that he is not really a sinner now that he has somehow managed to put himself on the right hand of God. Seeing this, Eugene gave up all his scrupulosity, joined the Ethical Culture Society, and stopped condemning others for their less-than-godly behavior. His humorous propensities won out over his overly serious views of himself and the world, and he became a much more relaxed and tolerant individual.

This does not mean, of course, that every youngster who is approached in a humorous manner in order to ameliorate his depression, guilt, or overachievement drives will wind up as a comedy writer. Eugene had specific talents in this respect, and if he had not had them there is no telling how the method of playing on his sense of humor would have worked. The fact remains, however, that almost all emotional disturbance is a taking of yourself and the world too seriously, with a consequent acquiring of an exaggerated belief in the horror of what is transpiring in your life. Neurosis does not consist of giving a significance or a meaning to the things that happen to you—for that kind of thing is good and makes your existence infinitely more interesting and absorbing. It consists, rather, of your giving an *exaggerated* significance to events, and particularly to negative events, that may or do occur. The more, therefore, you are able to laugh at yourself and others, in a kindly way that is fairly devoid of status-seeking, the more you are likely (as eventually occurred in Eugene's case) to tone down your rueful, pessimistic view of yourself and the life you lead.

A final word on helping children with their problems of achievement. I in no way want to depreciate the values of human mastery and excellence which Robert White, John Gardner, and some other contemporary writers have recently touted. By and large, the closer that a child can get to the best level of performance of which *he,* personally, is capable, the better off he is. For doing well at various tasks provides an intrinsic enjoyment that is not often surpassed; and in the highly competitive, practical world in which we live today, it has distinct advantages. The child's problems in connection with achievement do not arise when he tries to do well, but when he insists that he must do perfectly well—that he must do *the* best instead of *his* best, and that he must only accept and value himself, as a person, if and when he does remarkably well in his performances. For when he acquires such an exaggerated need (instead of a healthy, strong desire) for achievement, the child tends either to overproduce in a self-destructive manner or (probably in most cases) to withdraw from the field of competition and to become a serious underproducer. As is usual in most affairs, the individual's goals in achievement should be for some sort of Aristotelian mean between the two extremes: sober-minded rather than somber-minded striving, or the ability to laugh at himself in a lighthearted way without being too frivolous and irresponsible.

Is it easy to raise your youngster to strive for excellence without his winding up on the rocks of overachievement or in the straits of underachievement? It certainly isn't! You have about as good a chance of helping him keep safely in midstream in this regard as you have of getting him always to drive his bicycle at exactly the right speeds in precisely the safest places. Children are simply not born for full moderation; and there is no reason to believe that your child will be a notable exception to the rule. So do your best—and don't, unrealistically, expect too much. Otherwise, you yourself will tend to be a would-be overachiever who may well, for that very reason, fall on your face.

5

Helping Children
Overcome Hostility

Displays of temper tantrums and hostility are the normal lot of children—so much so, in fact, that some authorities consider them "physiological functions," along with many other childhood emotions. Is this an accurate view? Not entirely. Emotions become physiological once they are created—but the actual creating of them is largely a cognitive (thinking) process.

"But how can that be?" you may ask. "Isn't it true," as the well-known psychologist John B. Watson showed early in this century, "that if you hold or restrain a very young child who still is unable to talk, that he will frequently become enraged? Isn't anger, therefore, virtually an automatic process, that is quite independent of thought?"

No, not exactly. It is true, of course, that in infants as well as in lower animals, who apparently have little or no ability to converse with themselves, manifestations of anger will "automatically" flow from frustration or physical pain. Obviously, however, even infants or children must view frustration or pain as noxious. For if it were seen as pleasant (as is occasionally true, for example, when a young child is snugly held or put in swaddling clothes, and apparently likes this kind of restraint even though it is also frustrating), probably no anger would result.

Frustration, in other words, must be interpreted as bad before it is reacted to negatively. Thus, if the child is confined to his room and he does not mind being cooped up (because, say, he is tired or because he wants to avoid playing with other children), he will not see his confinement as being frustrating and painful and will take it quite cheerfully. But if he is confined when he very much wants to go out to play in the street, then (even if it is storming and playing in the street is precluded) he frequently *feels* (meaning, *thinks*) that being made to stay in his room is intolerable, and he erupts in temper-tantrum modes of behavior.

The reason why the child so frequently becomes angry at others or at his environment is not because he must, on a purely physiological basis, react in that manner, but because he is not mentally equipped to react more appropriately. No matter how bright he may be, he still tends to think disjointedly about himself and the world simply because he is a child; and it is his disjointed thinking, rather than his physiology itself, which makes him angry.

Gerald A. was a well-built nine-year-old of average intelligence who persistently threw temper tantrums whenever he was tired or deprived, and who got into more fights with other children than any other youngster in the neighborhood. A slight look of disdain, or the refusal to give him an ice-cream cone—almost anything could, and did, set Gerald off; and once he was started, he railed and ranted, and ripped up everything in sight, for what seemed to be an endless period of time. His outbursts, moreover, would cool him off only temporarily; and within ten minutes of the termination of one wild scene, Gerald could easily be embroiled in another one—and be just as enraged all over again. His face would become so purplish, his eyes so popping, and his fists so tightly clenched whenever he did become angry, that it looked as though he were about to have an epileptic fit; and sometimes it almost seemed as if he did have one. This, combined with his tendency to flare up so quickly, convinced his parents, his teachers, and his physician that there was something radically wrong with Gerald's physiological responsiveness, and the solution finally decided upon was to keep him under fairly heavy dosages of Dilantin and other sedatives most of the time. But even medication did not seem to help very much.

I was skeptical of the hypothesis that Gerald's main difficulties were caused by his physical supersensitivity, largely because he seemed to take unusually well to the classroom situation and virtually never got upset about anything during regular school hours. At lunchtime, when he interacted with the boys and girls in his class, he often got overexcited and hostile; and immediately after school, when he played with the other boys in the schoolyard, and then walked home with a few of them, he began to show signs of temper outbursts. But no matter what his class was expected to do—including staying after school on detention because several of the members had acted up during the day— Gerald was able to accept these restrictions quite easily and even to be helpful and philosophic about them when talking to the other members of his class.

The answer to this seeming paradox was easy: I found that Gerald was madly in love with his teacher, a charming woman who had three children of her own and who apparently knew how to get on the best side of most of her pupils. For her, he would do almost anything; and if she deprived him of something or pointed out his failings, he took her actions with the best of grace; while if anyone else, including his long-suffering parents, balked him in almost any way, he became enormously resentful and rebellious.

This dramatic splitting of his behavior made me highly suspicious that Gerald was hardly reacting to inner physiological impulses when he became temper ridden. A little further probing showed me what was actually going on with this youngster. He believed that practically everyone in the world existed solely for the purpose of doing his bidding and making things easy for him and that when anyone acted otherwise, this person deserved instantly to be put in his place and made to feel miserable. After discovering, experimentally, that the easiest and best way to make most people, especially his parents, feel weak and upset was to throw a fit of temper, and absolutely refuse to be appeased until they had given him his way, Gerald began practicing his epileptic-like fits, and sometimes quite consciously (and at other times unconsciously and semiautomatically) threw himself into them, in order to control the behavior of those around him and to make sure that they did not balk him.

Actually, at the time I saw him, he was getting rather sick of his tantrums himself and was a little ashamed of being forced to resort to them at his age—since he thought that they were only appropriate for children two or three years younger than he. But he had not as yet figured out any satisfactory substitutive behavior and, therefore, was still resorting to them. When I showed him that he could usually get what he wanted in life by taking a calmer and firmer stand, and that he could thereby eliminate the disadvantages of his terribly angry actions, Gerald was more than willing to try other methods of coping with the world around him. In a few months he was able to become as disciplined outside of class as he had previously trained himself to be (because of his feelings for his teacher) during the classroom activities.

My experience with Gerald taught me to be duly skeptical of the spontaneous "physiological" reactions of other hostile children. Not that anger reactions, themselves, aren't part of human physiology, for they certainly are. Once the child (or adult) upsets himself about virtually anything, his nervous system tends to take over, and from there on in he may resort to kicking, biting, rolling on the floor, and other kinds of physical acts over which he has practically no control, and which literally "run away" with him. What is more, neurological circuits are often set up in this process which are self-perpetuating: so that anger leads to physical lashing out, which in its turn incites the child to greater feelings of anger, which in their turn result in more lashing out, and so on and so forth, in an almost endless chain, until the point of physical exhaustion is finally reached, and the vicious circle finally halts.

Although, then, disordered emotion is a physical response, it is mediated through psychological (or philosophical) attitudes. The child believes that something (such as being restrained or losing contact with his mother) is terrible; therefore, he becomes panicked or enraged or otherwise upset. His belief, when he is below the age of one, is not very clearly articulated, and it would be difficult for him or anyone else to define it clearly. He is fairly easily diverted from it just because it is so diffuse, and he may be grim one moment and smiling the next. He does not have the sustained kind of philosophy, and hence the sustained kind of emotions, that he will more easily have a little later in life. Although he can easily get upset, he is probably not neurotic or psychotic in the way an older child or adult is—just as a rat or a guinea pig who is made "neurotic" in the laboratory is probably not disturbed in the same manner as a human being is. For the very core of emotional disturbance, as we usually see it in later life, is a fixed or rigid set of ideas which do not conform to reality; and the child, before he is able to talk, probably has few if any true fixations or bigotries—even though he may cry and scream.

Just as soon, however, as the child is able to use language, his reactions to things become almost entirely translated into words and sentences. When he emotes after the first few years of life, he does so almost exclusively because he has first told himself some definite sentence or meanings such as, "I very much like this" or, "I hate that!" and his "emotions" almost entirely consist of the sensory and other physical "feelings" that result from his telling himself these ideas.

There is a great deal of clinical, experimental, and observational evidence which shows that children do not become angry because of a *direct* biological predisposition, but because they are born with a tendency to communicate irrational ideas to themselves, which then set off physiological responses we call "emotional." They inherit nervous systems which are acutely sensitive to stressful stimuli. Their almost immediate response to potentially irritating events is, then, some kind of physical response (such as a knotted stomach, nervousness, sweating); and when they feel these physical responses they know they have become angry or hostile.

Unfortunately, the anger itself, once it arises, is so powerful, and tends to feed on itself in such a self-governing manner, that everyone—especially the individual feeling it—forgets about its philosophical antecedents, and tries to do something about it. This is a fatal mistake, since there is no good way of dealing with extreme hostility once it rears its ugly head. There are many ways in which the child can try to stop it—such as squelching it, telling himself that he shouldn't be angry, trying to prove that he really isn't angry, or other suppressive techniques—but they rarely work and at best are temporarily palliative.

There are also several ways in which the child (or anyone else) can try to evaporate his anger by expressing it fully, e.g., blowing off steam, telling off the persons at whom he is angry, socking a pillow and pretending that it is someone he despises, having a temper tantrum, etc. Though these expressive methods often work better than the suppressive ones, they are still palliative rather than curative, and do little or nothing to prevent the individual from quickly becoming angry again. In fact, some of the expressive methods, such as having a fit of temper, make the experiencing of anger so gratifying and such a good means of controlling the behavior of others that the child becomes addicted to them, and hence becomes more rather than less angry.

What, then, can you do for a child who frequently has outbursts of hostility and rage, not only to help him with his current eruption but to show him how to decrease his general level of anxiety and to live more comfortably with himself and others in this often frustrating world? Several things, including the following:

(1) First and foremost, be calm yourself. If you allow yourself to become exceptionally peevish and critical because your child is having a temper tantrum or is unduly aggressive against other children, you will be directly and indirectly teaching him that it is proper to get upset when others do not act exactly the way you want them to act, and will thereby be encouraging his own overly peevish and critical reactions. For if *you* can't stand people being the way they are, why should *he* learn to stand their poor behavior? So the best kind of a model you can be for him is a calm,

nonangry model, stating your complaints but without attacking, using hate words or insults. No matter how much you preach the advisability of this kind of behavior, you will not be very convincing if you are practicing the opposite kind yourself.

Your own anger can create the danger of what Thorne calls an "epidemic of negative reactions." Angry responses by the parent or child can infect everyone in the area, setting up a vicious circle of reinfection and creating a disease far more severe than the often petty action setting it off. Thus, a child's simple act of breaking a cup sets Mother to shrieking at what a malicious child he is, which in turn impels him to further temper tantrums or misdeeds. Driven to a real fury, Mother spanks him in a white-hot rage. The whole situation might have ended quietly had Mother simply told Adam that cups should not be played with, as they break easily.

(2) Remove, if you can, unnecessary frustrations from the child. Although, as we noted above, anger is not a direct reaction to frustration, but a reaction to what the individual tells himself about being frustrated, the fact remains that children almost invariably do tell themselves nonsense about the irritations and annoyances to which they are subjected: Consequently they do anger themselves continually by this nonsense. What is more, they have great difficulty, in most instances, learning how not to feed themselves negative conclusions when they are frustrated. It often takes them a number of years even partly to learn this. If your child, therefore, responds in an angry manner to deprivations, it may be well for you to see that these are reduced to a minimum.

This does not mean that you have to be ultrapermissive and let your child get away with practically everything. This kind of spoiling is bad in that it often increases the child's inability to tolerate frustration, for the more he sees that he can cajole or bully you into not sending him to bed on time, or letting him have a piece of candy when he is not supposed to have it, the more he will tend to believe that it is terrible when he finally is sent to bed or deprived of the piece of candy. And, indeed, it is fairly arbitrary if he has not been previously told that there was a time when he must be in bed.

At the same time, there are many frustrations in life which are truly unnecessary, and there is no reason why you should not remove these, as well as you can, from the child's existence. There is no law, for example, that he has to get up early on Sunday morning to go to Sunday school; and there is no reason why, if he strenuously objects to doing this, you should make him get up just because you believe (probably without any confirmatory evidence) that such attendance is a good thing. On the other hand, he does have to be at grade school on time each morning; and it is better if you insist that he tolerate that kind of frustration.

So it is quite realistic to reduce a child's frustrations to a minimum—since, just because he is small and weak, he has to suffer many annoyances that adults can easily avoid. There is no point, however, in "protecting" him from many of the harsh realities of life that have to be faced. Moreover, even though it is wise to reduce his frustrations when he is quite young, it is often equally wise to *increase* them gradually as he grows older. For, as he approaches late childhood and the teens, he does have to learn to assume various responsibilities—such as taking care of his own clothes, making his bed, cooking simple meals, and so on. If you never require him to do any of these things, he will usually be overly dependent on you and others. He will be ill equipped to go away to college, enter the armed forces, get a job, and do the innumerable other complicated and often unpleasant things that a normal young adult has to do. So try, with your child, to achieve some kind of Aristotelian mean between the two extremes of being unduly demanding and overdisciplining, on the one hand, or exceptionally lax and overpermissive on the other hand. If he is to become a mature, self-sufficient individual, he must learn to tolerate a considerable degree of frustration and annoyance; but he can be taught to do this gradually, without being unrealistically expected to do so at too early an age.

(3) Young children easily become irritable and angry and sometimes have wild outbursts of temper when they are over-

tired, just as many adults are prone to similar fits of anger when they are fatigued. This may well be because they cannot think clearly or effectively when they are tired. Consequently, it is well to see that children are not kept up too late even when they seem to be doing well. Encourage them to get sufficient sleep each night (or take additional naps during the day) so that they will not be vulnerable to fatigue-induced anger. When children are tired, they may become suddenly irritable and nasty, and suitable steps should be taken to see that they are rested. It should not be cavalierly assumed, however, that most temper outbursts stem from fatigue, a cold, or from some other physical origin; some children, as their normal condition, possess the same kind of overreactivity that others feel only when run down.

(4) Do not condemn or punish a child for his hostility when he is unusually hostile. Show him, as a means of teaching him what is and what is not socially acceptable behavior, that he has behaved poorly. But do not, out of sheer intolerance, fall prey to the deadly mistake of deprecating him as a person even for what may appear to you to be malicious and spiteful behavior. For there is no evidence that he is totally worthless just because one *aspect* of his behavior is; nor that he will keep repeating this behavior; nor that even if he does continue to get violently angry at others, he deserves to be outlawed. It is highly likely that a child who throws repeated tantrums is biologically predisposed to do so; and certainly if he is too unintelligent or too neurotic to stop himself, he should be sympathized with and helped, rather than punished, for this kind of affliction.

A dramatic contrast in the outcomes of two ways of treating the chronically negative child was shown in a developmental study by Chess, Thomas, and Birch. Two children, Jane and Tommy, showed signs of being difficult children from the time they were only a few weeks old, constantly crying and making violent demands. Jane was quietly removed from the social scene every time she sat on the floor and threw a tantrum, and in time her negative and hostile behavior diminished. Tommy, on the other hand, had a mother who felt harassed by a child so far from her expectations. She so often gave in to her frustration by shouting at Tommy that nothing she did seemed to satisfy him, that she ultimately had on her hands a child who *was* satisfied by nothing. Tommy simply stepped into her definition of him and made it his own definition of himself.

Is punishment, then, never justified in correcting the child and helping him be less hostile than he now shows himself to be? No, it is not, if by punishment we mean deliberately depriving or hurting him with a deprecatory attitude. Penalizing (or what may be called objective punishment, without the concomitant attitude of personal depreciation) may be used, at times, as a deterrent, and as a means of discouraging future misbehavior. If your child is continually hostile and keeps savagely picking on other children (and especially younger children), you may justifiably penalize him each time he does so by taking away some privilege, by putting him in an "isolation" room, or even (occasionally) by hitting him just about as hard as he has hit the other children.

But you should not, as you penalize him, give him the sense that "I think you are a wicked *child;* and the reason I am taking you to task is because I think you deserve to suffer for being wicked!" (A. S. Neill recounts how a father, as he slugged, declaimed, "I'll teach you to swear, you little bastard!") Rather, your attitude should be, "I think you are a basically good child, who has committed this poor behavior, and who is perfectly capable of doing better next time. Since there seems to be no other way of teaching you how to correct your ways, I am unfortunately having to resort to depriving or hurting you to help teach you this lesson. But I still don't think that you are worthless, and can still accept you and love you while I am helping you act better."

In other words, a child's hostility should calmly and firmly be brought to his attention, and, if necessary, corrective measures should be taken to help him stop it. But the correction should be accompanied with respect for his being and with unqualified acceptance of him as a person, even though it does not include respect or love for this particular hostile behavior. His hostile acts, and not his total self, should be censured.

(5) Try to keep in mind that the child's hostility is an ex-

pression or symptom of his underlying attitudes and beliefs and that expressions or symptoms of human behavior are themselves normal and even healthy. If anything, it is the value systems behind these expressions that bear investigation and possible correction. Thus, if a child firmly believes that other children should do his bidding and that it is thoroughly awful if they don't, he will be compulsively and almost inevitably hostile to other children on numerous occasions. If he held this basic value system and were not often angry, that would indeed be miraculous—and we would then have to suspect that he actually was, underneath, very angry, but that he was somehow squelching or repressing his anger, and unhealthfully refusing to display it. Sooner or later, however, his anger might arise in the form of ulcers, hives, or some other unpleasant result of sitting on his own hostility and not allowing himself ever to let off steam when other children refused to do his bidding.

The point here is that you should not try to discourage your child from displaying his feelings of anger (or of guilt, love, or virtually any other strong emotion) once it seems highly probable that he actually has such feelings. For, the consequences of encouraging him to stifle his emotional responses are often more dangerous than the consequences of his expressing them, even though he thereby gets into some difficulties. Either conscious suppression or unconscious repression of deeply simmering feelings may have grave consequences, such as the storing up of *all* aggressive feelings, creating difficulties socially, and often producing, as Robert Sears has shown, strong *self*-aggression.

It must not be inferred from this that you should encourage your child to express his emotions fully whenever he happens to experience them. If, for instance, he becomes angry at several of the boys in his class, and froths and fumes at them, perhaps even uses brute force against them, it will only be a matter of time until they feel forced to retaliate. Moreover, if he lets go full-steam ahead when he feels angry, he will frequently set in motion a feud which manufactures its own fuel, keeping himself (and his opponent) constantly re-angered. Actually, just as love tends to beget love, hate also tends to beget hate, and in the very act of telling others off, he can give himself further reasons why he loathes them, and may aggravate rather than temper his own rage.

As an alternative, you might get him to verbalize his anger against a schoolmate's bullying and, by rephrasing it in such terms as "Bruce must feel terribly inadequate if he has to try to prove his strength by beating everybody up," get him to understand the reasons for someone else's annoying conduct. In addition, you might calmly explain the possible consequences of attempted retaliation, and how its alternative—calmly accepting Bruce's bullying as the undesirable consequence of one person's disturbance —is really the most advantageous and least upsetting. As is often the case, the mere ventilation of anger leads quickly to its dissolution. Listen with sensitivity, sympathizing where appropriate, but without agreeing that his angry reaction is a very effective one.

The important point is, in other words, to show the child that it is not really Bruce who is making him angry, but that he himself is producing his anger by what he is telling himself about Bruce (i.e., that he shouldn't be the way he is and that he can't stand it). Implant in him the philosophy that it would be nice if we had all the toys we wanted or if people never acted poorly toward us, but things are never exactly the way we would like them to be in this far-less-than-perfect world. And things are far worse if we double our anger and discomfort by fuming about them.

Can a child really be shown that he is creating his own hostility and that he can do something effective about changing it? Not very easily! For he likes to believe that other people and things are causing him to act in certain ways—and that, therefore, he is not responsible for his bad deeds. "The book fell on the baby," he says—forgetting to note that he let the book fall. Or, "Johnny hit me!" he screams—neglecting to add that he first hit Johnny. He may take, of course, full responsibility for the good things in life, and he may even believe that he makes the sun rise every morning by asking it to rise. But if something nasty happens, then he frequently wants no part whatever in its causation—because he realizes that he is going to be blamed, or even condemn himself, if he is held thus responsible.

Once the child is shown that he is not an ogre for creating and displaying his hostility, he can often (though not always) be shown how to diminish and eradicate it. Thus, you can demonstrate to him—a thousand times, if necessary—that his anger arises from the sane belief, "I don't like this thing that is happening to me," and the mistaken belief, "and therefore, I can't stand it, and demand that it shouldn't happen!" And you can persistently, firmly encourage him to contradict and challenge this wrong belief.

Twelve-year-old Hilda C. kept insisting to me that she had a perfect right to be angry with her mother because the mother was unfair in her treatment of Hilda. "She keeps after me all the time," Hilda exclaimed. "If she asks me once to wash my hands before eating, she must ask me at least ten times each meal. And I mean ten! Isn't *that* enough to get angry about?"

"No," I calmly said. "It isn't. Not that she's not a terrible pain in the neck to you; for let us assume that your story is right, and she is."

"Oh, she is, all right! And that's putting it very mildly. She's also a pain in the you-know-what, too!"

"O.K. So she's a pain in the you-know-what, too. But you are just as much of a pain yourself."

"To her, you mean? I am not!"

"No, not to her, perhaps; but to someone even more important to you than her—to yourself."

"How am I a great pain to me?"

"By angering yourself unnecessarily about her. That way, you cause yourself much more pain than *she* gives you."

"Says you! Why, you should just see her! Ten times each meal —not a single one less! You'd think I *never* washed my hands, the way she goes on, and on, and on."

"That's beside the point," I persisted. "That's what *she* does to you. But how about what *you* do to you—that's much worse."

"Me?" Hilda fairly screamed. "I don't do a darned thing to myself. *She* does!"

"That's the way you see it, I'm sure; but it just isn't so. *You* do."

"NO!!! *She* does!"

"No, *you* do."

"How? How do I do anything to me?"

"Simply by taking her seriously. If she actually does tell you, at least ten times every meal, that you should wash your hands, then I'll admit that she's highly annoying—a real pain in the neck. But by taking her annoyingness, and frantically insisting to yourself that she *shouldn't* be annoying, you are multiplying her original pain-in-the-neckism by about ten times. Which, come to think of it, is ironic! She's telling you ten times too often to wash your hands, and you're telling you ten times too much that she shouldn't be a pain in the neck—which means that you are making yourself suffer about ten times as much as you have to."

"But you do admit that she's annoying, don't you?"

"Oh, yes. I'm accepting your story that you don't like her telling you to wash your hands so often, and that it's unnecessary for her to do this, and that therefore she's needlessly annoying to you. I don't expect you to say to yourself, 'Good-goody! Mother's telling me to wash my hands all the time. Isn't that great!' "

"Well, I'm certainly glad that you don't expect me to think *that!*"

"No, I don't. But I also don't expect you to keep whining, like a two-year-old, 'How *can* she keep telling me to wash my hands, when I wish she'd shut her big mouth? She *shouldn't* be acting the way she does act, that meany!' "

"But she *is* a meany! *Should* she be acting that way, if she weren't?"

"Why *shouldn't* she be?"

"Well—uh—because it's not *right.*"

"But why *should* she be always right? It would be nice if she were right; in fact, it would be lovely. But she isn't, according to you. She's terribly wrong, Now, why *shouldn't* she be?"

"Well, *should* she be?"

"Why not? Why shouldn't she be exactly the way—according to you again—she actually is? Who said she shouldn't be?"

"Why, *everyone* would say so. Everyone who really knew the way she was, at least."

"Oh, no. You mean everyone might agree with you that she was wrong to tell you ten times each meal to wash your hands. But not everyone would agree that she *shouldn't* be wrong. I wouldn't, for one."

"Oh, *you!* You probably wouldn't say that anyone shouldn't be wrong."

"Yes, that's exactly what I *would* say. It's *sad* that people are wrong; it's a pain in the neck if they are. But that's the way it is: sad and a pain in the neck. And that's the way the whole world is: full of people who make mistakes. I still see no reason why they *shouldn't* be, when in fact they most certainly are."

"Well, I *do!*"

"Yes, you do, because you're obviously saying, 'Because I don't *want* them to be the way they are, they *shouldn't* be.' "

"What's wrong with that?"

"What's right with it? Who are you to rule the earth and tell others exactly the way they *should* behave?"

"Don't I have a right to tell them I think they're behaving wrong?"

"Yes, you certainly do. You have a perfect right to say to them, 'I don't *like* you to act the way you're acting; I think it's wrong; and I would *like* you to stop and to act differently."

"Well, isn't that what I'm saying about my mother?"

"No, far from it. You're saying that, but you're also saying a lot more. You're adding, 'Because *I* don't like you to act the way you're acting, you should absolutely and positively stop acting that way, whether you want to or not.' "

"What's wrong with that?"

"First of all, you're not *requesting* that your mother change—you're *demanding* it. Secondly, you're really giving her no good reason for changing other than the fact that you want her to—and you're forgetting that she has just as much a right *not* to want to as you have to want her to. Thirdly, you're really saying that everyone, the whole universe, agrees with you, sees that she is wrong, and demands utterly and absolutely that she stop being wrong."

"But *shouldn't* everyone agree with me?"

"Why should they? It would be nice, again, if they did; but that hardly means that they *will*. And even if you and everyone else in the world agreed that your mother was wrong and that she *should* stop asking you to wash your hands so many times before each meal, will all your agreements make her stop?"

"No, not necessarily, I guess."

"But that's just the point. You're demanding that you and the universe should necessarily stop your mother; and you have no way of enforcing that demand."

"Am I demanding that she necessarily stop?"

"Aren't you? When you say, 'She shouldn't keep asking me to wash my hands,' don't you really mean that she absolutely, positively, necessarily shouldn't?"

"Hmm. I never thought of it that way. Maybe you're right. Maybe I am demanding that."

"Think about it, and you'll see that I am right and that you are demanding that just because you want something to be, it should exist—which is just like saying that because you want school to close for a week, it should."

"No, not exactly. No matter how much I want school to close for a week, I know that it won't. But my mother could stop acting the way she does, and there's a much better chance that she will than school'll close for a week."

"Is there really that much of a greater chance? Of course, she could. But what are the chances that she will? Besides, your statement to yourself obviously says, 'Because she *could*, she *should*.' But does that make sense?"

"No, not always, I guess."

"Not by a long shot! I *could* give you all the money I have; but that hardly means that I *should*. And even if you were starving and needed all my money to eat with, it then *would be better* if I gave you all my money (for you, at least, though not necessarily for me); but that's still hardly a reason why I absolutely, without any argument, *should*."

"So I'm really like a dictator when I demand that mother should stop asking me to wash my hands, when I mean that I want her to and it would be nice if she did, but let's face it, she probably won't."

"Right. You're saying that you need her to behave the way you desire but could well live without; and that if she *doesn't* behave the way you need, you can't stand it—which, of course, you can. And your belief that you can't stand her not giving you what you desire (and what you erroneously think you need) causes your anger. Not *her* poor behavior, mind you, but *your* belief about it."

"Hmmm."

I didn't exactly convince Hilda during that session of psychotherapy; but at least I gave her something to think about. And after several more weeks of pounding away at the same ideas, I finally started to convince her that she was causing her own anger and that she didn't have to do so. Hilda, as you can see from this conversation, was an unusually bright eleven-year-old, and with other youngsters of lesser intelligence a simpler approach to this problem would have to be taken. But in one way or another, children of average or even somewhat below average I. Q. can often be shown that their hostility to others is self-caused and that injustice or annoyance alone is not sufficient to upset them.

(6) At times, it is wise to let a child get his anger out of his system. This particularly goes for very young children, or for those who are not too bright, or for those who are exceptionally seriously disturbed. None of these would agree that they are causing their own angry reactions and that, therefore, they could do something effective to minimize and eradicate these reactions. Even older and wiser children, already too far gone in their rage, are for the moment beyond salvaging and cannot simply be talked out of their tantrums. At these times and in these cases, as Helen Thomson has indicated, "It's pretty futile trying to convince him that he's getting himself all worked up over nothing. Don't waste time arguing with him. Once a storm has struck, you can't talk him out of it."

If the child's hostility is verbal, you should have no trouble in letting him express it, since you will not, of course, be hurt by his words, gestures, and attitudes—unless you yourself sharpen these up and stick them into your own heart. You may well be disappointed or saddened by the fact that he is hurling invectives at you, but you cannot possibly be *hurt* by his mere words. The only way in which you can ever become mentally or emotionally hurt is by giving the same kind of importance to these words as your child is giving to them. Thus, if he says that he hates you for depriving him of something he wants, and you feel hurt or depressed or angry at his saying so, you are really agreeing with him that you are somewhat worthless, and that his opinion is accurate. If you did not agree with him, but convinced yourself that in spite of his disapproval, you are a perfectly valuable human being in your own right, you would not feel hurt, depreciated, or threatened by his verbal barbs.

So, no matter how roughly your child speaks about you or others, let him sound off when he is highly enraged and when he seems beyond control. Just let him rant and rave, and either say nothing in response, or even say, "Yes, you may be right, dear. I did treat you badly; and you do have a right to be angry at me for doing so. But even parents make mistakes, sometimes!"

If your child wants to take out his hostility in blows or other physical manifestations, that's quite another thing, and in most cases you must forcibly restrain him. Even relatively light blows may do you or others serious injury at times; and throwing things around can be dangerous. You may, as psychologist Dorothy Baruch suggests, give him substitute objects instead of the real thing on which to vent his physical spleen—a pillow, for example, instead of your own stomach; or a doll to pinch, instead of his baby sister. But if he actively resorts to violence, you will usually have to restrain him—while pointing out that he is really a good boy, but what he is *doing* is not tolerated in civilized society.

As usual, one of your best methods here is your own good example. If you throw things around when you are angry, and physically lash out at others or threaten to knock their blocks off, there is an excellent chance that your child will erroneously construe this to be a good kind of solution to anger, and tend to use it himself. If you act nonphysically, or use a punching bag to get some of your feelings of hostility out of your system, there is a greater likelihood that he will begin to resort to this kind of solution. Children *are* imitative.

(7) How can you get this somewhat subtle idea—that he is not a bad child but his notions are—across to a child? First, by explicitly stating it over and over, telling him quite definitely: "Look, dear. I cannot tolerate your hitting me or others, because you may injure us, and it is my responsibility to protect myself and these others from being injured (just as it is your responsibility to protect yourself from being harmed). So if you actually go around taking out your anger on me, your little brother, or any other child, I will have to stop you—by force, if necessary. This does not mean that I will then think you are really a bad boy and that I don't love you at all. Your getting angry like this is not at all lovable, but the rest of your behavior is all right. Besides, though you may show this kind of unpleasant anger today, I know that you do not always get angry, and that you may be very pleasant tomorrow. So I am not condemning you as a whole, and I do not think that you have to condemn yourself for doing this wrong thing. But you can—and I shall have to insist that you must—learn to do fewer wrong things like this, and to become less physically angry. Otherwise, you will have to be penalized for hitting others, just as your blows penalize them. So watch your step—and take it out on a pillow or something else instead!"

Secondly, by your actions, you can literally show the child that you are calmly penalizing him when he strikes out at others and that you are not as angry and hating as he himself is. Immediately after penalizing him for his reprehensible physical acts, you can show him approval, acceptance, and even reward for other kinds of behavior and thereby convince him that you do not consider him unworthy as a human being. Moreover, you can help him be kind to himself after you have restricted him from harming others—thus showing him that you think him a person who is worthy of gaining pleasure and happiness, and not a devil who should be condemned to live miserably in hell.

(8) When there is not time to get to the very bottom of your child's anger, or when it is too late to start interpreting and arguing him out of it, you can frequently use some kind of diversion as an effective means of calming him down. If you induce him to be quite active—to run an errand or play ball—he may not have the available energies to devote to hostility. If you get him absorbed in a game, in eating, in watching a TV show, or in some other activity, he may become so diverted that he will forget what he is angry about. If you somehow get him out of the anger-inciting situation—take him away from the boy with whom he is fighting, for example—he will often act on the principle that out of sight is out of mind, and will simply fail to respond in an angry way any longer. None of these diversionary methods is more than palliative, since they will not encourage your child to refrain from being angry the next time a poor situation occurs—but they can be very helpful when nothing else seems to work. Moreover, once your child gets diverted from his immediate anger, he can frequently be shown later how he incited himself to hostility and how he can do something to avoid doing this again in the future.

(9) Try to be as fair as you can in your dealings with your children. Life, after all, is decidedly unfair to almost all youngsters, since it makes many demands on them which are onerous and which they cannot easily avoid or meet. Since this is so, the least you can do is to be as just as you can yourself, and to lean over backwards to understand children's viewpoints and to make allowances for them. One of the main ways you can set an example of fairness is by persistently curbing your own tendencies to arbitrarily lash out and condemn your children's behavior; by resisting the temptation to whack them simply because they choose to ply you with questions when you are in an extremely irritable mood.

Yet, since a certain amount of unfairness is inevitable in life, you should therefore teach your children that this is so, and you should not be too surprised when they are specifically treated unfairly—even by you. Moreover, they do have the possibility of first trying to eliminate some of the unfairness that does exist (by, for example, being fair to others themselves, or by choosing to avoid consistently unjust people) and of then gracefully lumping that injustice which they cannot eliminate. It is likely that, by becoming involved in the workings of human failings, they will tend to better understand them, focus less on "flagrant" injustices—become, in short, less frustrated and more tolerant.

(10) One of the main causes of children's anger is jealousy or envy of others. They see some other child with more toys, more money, or more abilities than they themselves possess. They become terribly frustrated because he has more and then make themselves angry about their frustration. You may, of course, try to keep your child away from other children who have certain advantages over him—but this is rather impractical. Or you may try to compensate him for his relative deprivation by trying to give him more toys, more candy, or what you will, in order to put him on a par with certain other children. But this, too, unless you are very wealthy, is unrealistic; and besides, it will hardly reduce his low frustration tolerance.

The point is that the child's anger does not spring from his deprivations or disadvantages in themselves, but from his belief that he should not—positively ought not—be deprived or disadvantaged. And this belief may often be effectively tackled: by pointing out to him that, alas, all men are not created equal, that many social and economic inequities do exist, and that he nonetheless can live happily in a competitive world where he will often be a loser—as everyone is many times in his life.

Besides, you can often teach him that Jack's having a bicycle or getting good marks in school hardly makes him a better boy —it only makes him a boy who has certain advantages in one small area of life. Moreover, Jack's bicycle or good marks really say nothing at all about your child and his characteristics, for it is unlikely that Jack's advantages will prevent your child from someday acquiring similar advantages, too. Even if Jack's attributes make him the captain of the ball team, and your child is thereby deprived of being captain himself, this hardly means that (a) your child is a poor ballplayer; nor that (b) other children will hate him if he is a poor player; nor that (c) other people's looking upon him as a poor player will thereby make him an inferior person. Jack is Jack and he is he; and there is no reason why he should have all the advantages that Jack has, nor why he is no good if he misses out on some of these.

Jealousy and envy generally are rooted in the fact that the jealous individual believes that he doesn't amount to anything because the persons of whom he is jealous have benefits that he misses, or that the world is horribly unjust for depriving him of their advantages. Both these propositions are false; and you can consistently show your child, if he is afflicted with these negative feelings, that they are falsely based, and can keep demonstrating that he is worthy of existing and worthy of enjoying himself even if others have certain superior attributes and even if he is relatively deprived.

Summing up: Many children have little toleration for frustration. They demand to be king of the roost and they demand that everything in their life run smoothly. When actual frustration occurs, they view it as dreadful, believe that they cannot put up with it for a single minute, and make themselves resentful toward the world and hostile toward other people. Their anger seems to stem from their frustration, but it actually rises from their unrealistic demand that they should not be balked or mistreated. When these children are quite young, not too bright, or seriously disturbed, and especially when their temper tantrums are well under way, often the only thing that can be done to help them is some kind of diversion: Prompt them to express their anger harmlessly in some physical or verbal manner; help them become absorbed in some other kind of activity; try to remove the source of the frustration; treat them with unusual fairness yourself; accept them fully even when they are behaving badly. For more permanent and curative results, these palliative measures will not work. Instead, you should try to show the hostile children what is the basic cause of their anxiety: the overdemanding, unrealistic sentences, or implied philosophies of life, that they are telling themselves; and try to get them to challenge and contradict these negative, self-agitating viewpoints. Mainly, you should emphasize over and over and over that the world is *not* the perfect place they would like it to be, and that, to lead more comfortable and happy existences, they had best learn to tolerate their real (and imagined) deprivations, injustices, and other grievances. If you yourself serve as a good model in this respect, if you calmly learn to uproot the main sources of your own resentment and unblamefully persist in showing easily angered children what they are doing to create needless anger in themselves, you can slowly but surely help many of them to become much less hostile, even when they are faced with unjust and difficult life situations.

CHAPTER

6

Helping Children Become Self-Disciplined

"Unless we give children time to organize their sensations and impressions—in short, time to react to their environment— we shall continue to see a profusion of moralists and rebels . . . rather than someone who has had time to organize his responses."

—A. GREGG

The main thing a child is not is self-disciplined. He is a born dawdler, goofer, and short-range hedonist. This does not go, of course, for all children, any more than anything is true of all of them. There are some youngsters who naturally seem to like following sensible routines, keeping themselves and their premises in order, and putting off present pleasures for future gains. But how rare they are! The vast majority of children are hardly in this category—any more than the vast majority of adults are. Would that they were; but they definitely aren't!

Not that discipline is necessarily a virtue in itself. In some ways, it is even a handicap. A small number of children, for example, are compulsively well ordered. They rarely enjoy themselves in the here and now because they are anxiously focused on what will happen to them in the future. They keep their possessions scrupulously neat, save practically all their spending money, walk along a street making sure that they do (or do not) touch lines on the sidewalk, and otherwise compulsively adhere to senseless, self-imposed rules that needlessly restrict them and render them entirely unspontaneous. Children like these are overly fearful and demand absolute certainty. They have become socialized, but at the price of overdependence, lack of initiative, and submissiveness. Concerned with preserving their security and love, they avoid the sorts of risk-taking which would lead them down fascinating new avenues of life. Theirs is an obvious attempt at overdiscipline—and an effort has to be made by their elders to help them be less compulsive and more alive.

In the case of the more usual child—he is the one who has a much harder time keeping himself in line, and who frequently resists attempts by his parents and other adults to induce him to follow an ordered kind of existence—this child dillydallies continually; he says he will do something in a minute, then lets the deadline go by unchallenged. He does many pleasant things to extremes; he overeats, overbicycles, and overtalks. He balks at doing numerous unpleasant or difficult tasks such as his homework or the household chores. He frequently won't sit still in school and makes up his own rules when engaging in games; he is very inconsiderate of other children and adults when he wants to do something—such as run, yell, or beat up the furniture.

Most of this type of behavior is childish and should be accepted as such, coming as it does from a child. Only when his behavior becomes dysfunctional to himself or others should he be disciplined; curbing a child every time he acts like one can prevent him from developing the self-reliance and self-confidence that eventually leads to self-discipline.

By all means, then, be permissive and allow the child to explore the many fascinating aspects of his existence—romping in the woods on a picnic, exploring the treasures of the local drug store after school, the tinkling sounds of a spoon on a glass. Let him do as many things as are feasible—but not as many things as are possible. Rules for his behavior should definitely be set, but these should be minimal and critical. Such rules as not crossing the street in traffic will protect the child and his friends from harm. And if he does not obey these rules, there should be precise and invariant penalties.

The critical issue in discipline, then, is first one of deciding where the limits of desirable behavior should be drawn, then, secondly, of deciding how to deal with transgressions. As Mary Fisher Langmuir has pointed out, when parents ask "How can I discipline my child?" they generally mean, "How can I make him stop?" or "How can I get him to do what I want him to do—or what he ought to do?" Too often, discipline becomes erratic because it is geared to a parent's mood rather than to his child's age, temperament, abilities, or the harmfulness of his misbehavior. Lamentably, there can be no easy set of guidelines by which the parent can automatically decide when discipline is in order. He must only remember to make his rules clear and consistent. In general, children should not be allowed to be tyrants to themselves or to blackmail others into acceding to their whims. They should have definite bedtime hours; be required to eat on a certain schedule, if that is most convenient to their parents; go regularly and on time to school; obey a minimal set of rules about keeping the house in order and the furniture in one piece; and otherwise conform to the normal set modes of behavior that are necessary for cooperative family and social living. If they are firmly and calmly told "this is it, that's the way things are," and there is no nonsense or caviling about it, they will usually develop patterns of reasonably well-disciplined living and become socialized animals.

Remember, however, that there are vast differences in temperament among children, which are frequently evident even in their cradles. A child who is clearly supersensitive must often be indulged in the same kind of behavior which in a more relaxed, easygoing child would definitely not be tolerated. A case in point is one easily riled patient of eleven whose mother must remain outside the family apartment from 3:30 to 4:30 every afternoon so that this supersensitive child can do her homework in peace: Nothing but this kind of pampering works with this particular girl. Try to assess your child's unique temperament by observing his patterns of reaction; then discipline him accordingly. Even a mild rebuke to a shy child unaware that he has not properly thanked his hostess at a birthday party may bring on waves of guilt, shame, and further shyness; whereas a high-spirited youngster would be completely impervious. The exuberant child who is constantly getting into scrapes and being punished for them, on the other hand, could turn into a negative, sulky child, who resultantly gives up having his exploring instincts.

To insure that your child is benefited and taught by your discipline, first make clear what he may not be allowed to do; and secondly, clarify why such behavior is undesirable. Study after study of anxious children has shown that these children had parents who threatened, who punished inconsistently, or who failed to impose any carefully delineated, definite controls on their behavior. When a rule is set—as the requirement that children be fairly silent when their parents are sleeping—children should frankly be told that it may disturb them, but that it is necessary for the comfort of others and that therefore they will simply have to obey. And—consistently—when they fail to do so, they must be chastised. At the same time they can be informed that others also have to obey many onerous modes of living for their benefit and that good social living demands a mutual kind of give-and-take.

Children are much more likely to develop sensitivity to others' needs if they are treated as reasonable, basically good creatures who want to do the right things, rather than be forced to act in certain ways simply because their parents commanded them. Even very young children can be given a good deal of free or democratic choice in their own upbringing. Thus, they can often be allowed to choose the clothes they wear, decide whether or not they will eat carrots at a given meal, and be given a voice in family conclaves. The more free choices they are given, the more they may be able to tolerate the forced choices which they are also required to make. In any event, it should be made perfectly clear to them that sometimes, where feasible, they can be allowed to do what they want—because at those times their voices are harmless to others and are important to themselves. But at other times it should be made clear that they cannot be given too much leeway and simply must obey certain principles of behavior—or suffer clearly defined consequences.

Permissiveness and punishment—it cannot be too strongly emphasized—must never be indiscriminate or absolute. A mother may lash out and slap her whining child in the toy department of the five-and-ten one day simply because she is in a bad mood; while another time she may largely ignore the whining or, to stop it, buy the child a toy. As a consequence, the child will fail to learn that he is not to wail when toys are not in the day's budget. Rather, he may reap from such experiences one or more of the following undesirable conclusions: (1) Whining pays. (2) The world is a very confused place, whose rules he cannot understand, and that therefore he must always be anxious lest he unwittingly do the wrong thing. (3) His mother is a beast who condemns one minute and rewards the next. (4) Lashing out at the world when one is frustrated (as Mother has just done) is an acceptable way of handling occurrences not exactly to one's liking.

When a child clearly does not wish to do something that he considers bothersome (such as going to bed) that you, as his parent, feel is necessary for him to do, it is most important to stand firm. Children are wheedlers, blackmailers, and bullies. On many occasions they will do almost anything to get their way; and you as a parent must consistently and unwaveringly show them that enough is enough, that screaming, writhing, crying, getting sick, or complaining will not work.

May it not be harmful if the child whimpers half the night before he consents to go to sleep in a room by himself, or if he has a violent fit of temper because he has to walk home from school instead of having you drive him home? Yes, it may be, particularly if he is a neurotically stubborn child and insists on suffering rather than conforming to what he considers to be difficult rules. The fact remains, however, that pampering this kind of a child in most instances will do him still more harm; it will encourage him to be whiny and blackmailing on into adulthood, when he will have an infinitely more difficult time getting his way. Therefore, the better part of valor, in the great majority of cases, is to let him pull everything in the book and even make himself miserable for days, while still calmly insisting that, like it or not, he is going to have to sleep by himself or walk home from school. If days and days of continued discipline of this sort simply do not work at all, and the child continually becomes terribly upset when you stick by your disciplinary guns, then he may be an autistic or otherwise seriously disturbed individual who simply *cannot* follow the usual rules, in which case you may have to treat him differently. But don't give in too quickly or too easily on this score: At least nine out of ten "difficult" children are partly the product of spoiling and too easily intimidated parents; and consequently you'd better look into your own heart before you assume that your child needs unusual pampering.

This is as good a point as any in this chapter to repeat, once again, the point that we have to keep making throughout this book, namely, that raising a sane and well-balanced child is largely a matter of raising a sane and well-balanced self. For you must usually be the main model for your child—and this goes in the realm of discipline as in practically all other fields of behavior.

Let's look for a moment at you, then. Are you something like Mrs. V., an exceptionally well-meaning mother who just couldn't bear to see her son, Michael, screaming until he got hoarse every night when she tried to get him to bed before 11:00 P.M., and who therefore let him stay up as long as he liked? Most of Mrs. V.'s friends and neighbors thought that she was a remarkably kindly, loving mother, for she seemed to have few thoughts other than those regarding seven-year-old Michael, and the two of them appeared to have a truly warm, mutually interdependent relationship.

Actually, Mrs. V. was thoroughly scared of everyone. She hated sex, but she had intercourse with her husband almost every night because she was afraid he would criticize her if she didn't.

She dreaded her mother's pointing out her mistakes to her, and she dressed, shopped, and cooked mainly to conform to her mother's views. She had only one woman friend, to whom she kowtowed in the most nauseating manner, and to whom she never fully expressed her own views. And she was enormously afraid that her own son, Michael, would not love her, and gave in to his every whim, to make certain that he, at least, remained on her side.

Mrs. V., in other words, was completely overdetermined in her behavior because she feared the slightest disapproval of others; she had no true *self*-discipline or willingness to accept the consequences of her own beliefs and desires. Michael, seeing this, knew that his mother was foolish and did his best to bully her into acquiescing with all his wants. Moreover, seeing that she was disordered in her own doings, he could find no good reason for disciplining himself. She was a short-range hedonist who could not face the possibility of a temporary loss of approval as a consequence of fulfilling one of her longer-range goals.

So it goes in most cases where a child refuses to accept any discipline. It is his parents, rather, who won't accept any wrestling with him and who weakly refuse to take the consequences of forcing him to discipline himself. This is often an outcome of their own feelings of inadequacy, their fears of guilt at acting "hostilely" toward a child and—as the mistaken Freudian viewpoint contends—injuring him for life by withdrawing affection and approval. Their weakness becomes, in a sense, his weakness —even though the outward manifestations of their disorders may appear to be radically different.

Will your serving as a good model of strength and self-discipline in itself induce your child to order his life in a reasonably sane manner? Not necessarily. On the contrary, there are many instances of children of outstandingly well-disciplined and productive parents who became so discouraged about their being able to live up to the fine models being set for them that they ran in the opposite direction and made themselves into alcoholics, drug addicts, beatniks, or other kinds of sorry individuals. For if a child feels that he must measure up to, or compete with, his parents' superlative behavior, he may come to believe that he has little or no chance of ever doing so successfully, give up in disgust, and consciously or unconsciously drive himself to an opposite kind of conduct.

Self-discipline or long-range hedonism, therefore, must be taught to the child as something that he should achieve for himself, for his own good, and not as a means to impress or to surpass others. This is difficult to do, since it is a child's nature to go for immediate gains and short-range hedonism, he must learn to strive for what Sigmund Freud called the "reality principle"— he must learn to give up present pleasures in order to acquire future gains. Nonetheless, the child can persistently be (and unangrily) taught that if he eats too much today, he will have a stomachache tonight; if he plays hooky from school today, the truant officer will be after him tomorrow; if he refuses to go to bed on time tonight, he will be sleeping in class tomorrow. Or, to put it the other way around, you can steadily point out to him that the stomachache he feels right now, and the trouble he is in with his teachers and principal, and the tiredness he experiences in class each has a prior cause, and that if he is to avoid feeling these unfortunate effects again, he'd better look at these prior causes and make sure that they rarely happen again.

The child is nothing if not hedonistic and pleasure-bound. And that is good, not bad—as long as we use his hedonistic tendencies to show him that he must, for his own sake, exert a good measure of self-discipline. For he wants to be free from physical ills, wants to get along well with others, wants to avoid trouble in school. And he can only accomplish these goals if he eats well, considers the feelings of others, and obeys certain educational rules. We, naturally, would like him to follow these rules, too, since it is to our advantage that he do so; and, besides, we like him and want his good. But whether we are pleased with his conduct or not, he still has to get along in the world; and there simply is no other way for him to do so very satisfactorily if he fails to discipline himself.

This is the point I have to keep teaching and reteaching my psychotherapy patients, and which you will have to keep teaching your child if you want to avoid his becoming a psychotherapist's patient a little later on—that there is no other way—there is no magic, no pathway to happiness and success other than constant self-discipline. Practically every child, naturally, thinks that there should be: that is, that there should be magical fairy godmothers, and easy ways out. That is why fairy tales are so popular; they provide the demanded magic. So do myths, fantasies, dreams, Hollywood films, novels, and plays. But only in fiction—never in real life. The grim fact is that there are no fairies, genies, or angels; and we, all of us, eventually have to provide the good things in life for ourselves. Bringing up a child in an ultrapermissive manner may appear to be stimulating to his own creativity, but he will one day grow up and be shocked at what the world is really like.

So bring up your child realistically. Inform him, at an early age, that there is no Santa Claus, that the gifts and candies he receives are not conjured up by magic, but are produced by hard, hard work, and by due sacrifices of time and energy. Let him do some of this hard, hard work himself; let him earn some of his spending money by running errands and merit having a room of his own by helping to keep it clean. Don't inform him, pessimistically, that the whole world is bad, and that he'll never get any great good out of it: for that would tend to take away his motivation and make him cynical and inert. But inform him, realistically, that the world has many good and many bad aspects and that if he would gain more of the former and less of the latter, he must normally participate in some kind of action.

Let him know, moreover, that self-discipline is not a high-sounding, ethereal term with vague referents: It specifically means, for the most part, some form of deprivation. To become a fine athlete, you deprive yourself of excess food, slothfulness, and other unathletic pleasures. To become a notable scholar, you give up a good deal of lolling around, reading superficial magazines, watching endless TV shows. Many of the formal religious groups of the world realize that discipline and deprivation go together and therefore encourage their adherents to fast, sacrifice, or go through various other kinds of self-depriving rituals and ceremonies. But they sometimes go to extremes and accept discipline, or its ritualistic symbols, as ends in themselves, to be practiced because they make the individual intrinsically "good" or beloved of God. This belief, to say the least, is highly dubious, for an individual can be essentially good and be loved by any god in which he believes, without wearing hair shirts or living on bread and water for a month.

"Good," however, does not mean happy or accomplished. You are good, in the existential sense of this term, merely because you exist, because you are alive. You are good whether or not you are happy and whether or not you do anything well. You are good just because you are you—and it is good to be yourself, and not anything other than yourself. But being good, you still would be better being happy, fulfilled, and enjoying. And to be happy you would often first be achieving or masterful in some pursuit of your own choosing. These goals—happiness and accomplishment—are not arrived at merely by existing. To achieve them, you normally have to do much more than merely be; and one of the things you usually have to do is to discipline yourself in various sensible ways.

Teach your child, then, that he is not a worthless human being, not a rotter if he is undisciplined. He has the choice, as a human being, of being as unfocused and unjelled as he wants to be; but he must also pay certain penalties if he chooses to be so. If he does have organized goals and ambitions (and having these will itself usually tend to make him a more vitally absorbed, hence happier human being), he'd better get off his behind and do something about them. This means, obviously, not doing something about other things which are counter to his goals. This means working and practicing to make himself more competent to achieve his ends. This means discipline—and discipline imposed by himself, not by you or any other outside forces. Guard against expectations that your child must acquire self-discipline as early as possible; rather, help him gradually adjust rules to his growing capacity for independence and self-direction.

Realism, then, is still the core of a good philosophy of discipline. "To make a child's whole pattern of life the expectation of getting what he wants when he wants it" (and never mind about anyone else), English and Foster note, "is dangerous preparation for being an adult." Worse, it is even dangerous preparation for being a child. For children, too, have to pay the piper; and if they do not accept the consequences of their doings, they will soon get into trouble. That is what the disciplined attitude is: Knowing that what you do today leads to almost inevitable results tomorrow; and knowing that to get the good things of life on the morrow, you have to give up something or exert some special effort today. By your own persistent words and deeds you can teach this to your child—once you fairly rigorously teach it to yourself!

How about making the punishment fit the crime, and using the firmness of your hand as well as the firmness of your mind to convince your child that he simply must be disciplined? When we ask this question, we immediately run into the controversy that still exists among experts about spanking. On one side, we have authorities who insist that under no circumstances should you use the rod, even at the expense of slightly spoiling the child, because children invariably interpret spanking or other forms of corporal punishment as meaning that their parents are angry at them and hate them; and if so, the corrective value of spanking brings with it too many enormous disadvantages, and is just not worth it. On the other side, we have equally respected authorities insisting that spanking is harmless, that children are often relieved by being physically mauled for their misdeeds, and that as a deterrent to future wrongdoings and lack of discipline spanking is quite efficacious. Which of these views is correct?

Neither is entirely true for all children at all times. My own belief is that spanking and other forms of physical punishment are normally to be avoided for several reasons: (1) It is a rare parent who can spank a child without getting terribly angry in the process; and although the spanking itself may do the child more good than harm, the anger that goes with it can be very harmful. (2) The facts show that spanking is often quite ineffective as a method of penalization: Some children hardly mind it; others almost enjoy it; and still others find it so harsh that they feel themselves unjustly done in by it, and rebelliously vow to be even worse behaved in the future. (3) Even when physical punishment does work, it may easily drive the child's desire to misbehave underground, so that he still very much wants to do so, but merely covers up this preference and pretends that he is a little angel. His overt behavior may then be "satisfactory," but his underlying thoughts and feelings may be positively murderous, and there is no telling where or when these may ultimately display themselves. (4) Spanking is too easy a method of penalization, and most parents who employ it frequently do so because it is easy. It allows them to avoid the more difficult but much better educational corrective methods of talking to the child, showing him why he is wrong, and indicating that he should try to do better for his own sake. The main message that spanking usually conveys is that "We, your parents, demand that you change your ways; and by heaven, you're going to, if we have to whale the living daylights out of you to make you do so." It does not convey the more educational message, "We feel that you are harming yourself by behaving in this manner, and we hope that you will change your ways for your own good, as well as to make things easier for us."

On the other hand, it cannot be denied that physical punishment of a child has certain advantages: (1) Some children seem to learn to correct their behavior only by this kind of disciplining, since they close their ears to verbal persuasion. (2) Some parents are not very adept at talking their children into better behavior and can say more with a single blow than they can with a thousand words. (3) Spanking is a dramatic form of penalizing that sometimes is more emphatically remembered than other forms of penalty. If you deprive a child of his allowance or of seeing television when he behaves poorly, he may soon forget the onerousness of this kind of deprivation or may become inured to it. If you penalize him by physical blows, he may remember the real penalties involved in his misbehavior. (4) As noted above, spanking sometimes relieves a child's guilt. He feels that, now that he has been concretely punished for his acts, he is not as bad as he thought he was when he performed them. If he is not punished, he may continue to berate and penalize himself even more drastically than you, his parents, might do. (5) Physical chastisement is sometimes quicker and more effective with younger children than any other form of disciplining. If you argue with your three-year-old about the disadvantages of his running across the street by himself, he may enjoy the argument and not let himself become too affected by it. But if you slap him roundly every time he runs in the street, he may quickly learn not to do so, and you may save him from actual injury thereby.

What shall you do, then, about physical punishment, in view of these pros and cons? I would advise not that you discard it completely from your disciplinary apparatus, but that you use it quite selectively and discriminatingly where the child just will not be deterred by other approaches, when you can apply it un-angrily, the same way you might deprive the child of something that he wanted; that you do not get too much satisfaction from it yourself; and that you accompany it by other forms of explanation and persuasion, even though these are given some period after you have done the hitting or spanking.

Use physical chastisement, in other words, as a temporary and palliative expedient. Do not delude yourself that it will work permanently or that it will do the child maximum good. But if you have exhausted other disciplinary means and it appears that anything but spanking or its equivalent is going to be too time-consuming and difficult to make practical, then you may use this kind of a penalty. Remember, however, to distinguish between penalty and punishment: The former is a mode of frustration that is objectively applied to an individual (or a lower animal) to help in his training when his behavior has gone beyond the allowable limits of deviation; the latter is applied with hatred and devaluation of the person's being. To penalize a child is often necessary; but to punish him is almost always to help him depreciate himself. As Dr. George Sheviakov has stated, penalization *"is* necessary; a part of real life, a powerful deterrent and discourager, but *it should represent the logic of life rather than the impulse to retaliate"* (italics in the original).

An excellent way of ensuring that discipline will not appear retaliatory is to follow Selma Freiberg's technique—making discipline a logical consequence of the misbehavior. Thus, if a child is persistently unruly while his parents are doing their bookkeeping, they might tell him to leave the room and come back when he thinks he can be quiet. To withhold a cherished privilege, such as going to the zoo on Sunday, becomes not a logical penalty for making noise, but a retaliatory measure whose effect will be to deprive a child of an important privilege, thus stirring up resentment, feelings of injustice, and probably further misbehavior.

A final word: No matter how effective your technique of teaching discipline may be, it still is essentially imposed from without, and your child must make an almost magical jump so that he teaches himself *self*-discipline, or control from within. This is why you should not give him rote rules to follow, threaten him with censure by others, or use external pressure and penalization to any considerable degree. The object is not merely to socialize him, so that he will not bother you and others, but to *train him to train himself,* so that he will not unhappily bother himself for the rest of his days. Naturally, you want to see him as a happy and not too conflicted child. But you also hope that he will be a reasonably well-controlled adult and will be able to carry on successfully and enjoyably in his life after you have long since failed to exert any real power over him. So your job, if you are a truly responsible parent, is to try to help him become an *independently thinking* instead of a *dependently suggestible* self-controller. By using some of the more democratic and interpretive means outlined in this chapter, you are most likely to achieve that child-rearing goal.

7

Helping Children with

Sex Problems

Sigmund Freud and his followers have emphasized an important truth about child sexuality; namely, that children often do have sex urges and problems and that the improper handling of these urges and problems frequently helps them to become neurotic adults. Along with this truth, unfortunately, the Freudians have also intertwined a significant lie or gross exaggeration, to wit, that *all* children have enormously significant sex lives and that *all* their early sexual experiences greatly influence the rest of their lives.

That children do have sex feelings has been attested by many independent observers who have not been particularly swayed by Freudian theories. Albert Moll, Alfred C. Kinsey and his associates, and Glenn V. Ramsey have all presented data showing that youngsters of one year or less may become thoroughly aroused and may even have orgasms, and that older children engage in all kinds of sex activities. Indeed, in recent years considerable doubt had been thrown upon the old belief that sex offenders who molest children are terribly nasty individuals, since studies by Paul Gebhard and his associates have shown that in many cases the child himself is something of an aggressor, and that even when he (or she) is seduced, he frequently engages quite enjoyably in sex activities with the adult and is not at all averse to continuing them. Therefore, the Freudian thesis that children do have sex lives long before they reach the age of puberty has been fairly well validated.

At the same time, there are several notable loopholes in the Freudian version of child sexuality. For one thing, there is no evidence whatever that *all* children have an important sex life. On the contrary, it would appear that many normal youngsters are not sexually awakened before puberty; and some of them in fact, seem to be unaroused and unappeased sexually until their late teens or early twenties.

Secondly, there is no reason to believe that all, or even that most, children go through the well-organized stages of pregenital and genital development which Freud attributed to them. According to his theories, all boys go through a pregenital phase, in the course of which they are first oriented toward oral pleasures (sucking, biting, kissing) and then toward anal pleasures (defecating, inserting their fingers or other objects into their rectums). Following this pregenital phase, males are supposed to attain a genital stage of development, in which they directly become interested in their penises, and want to have gratification through using them. In the course of this genital phase (which may be arrived at any time from their second year onward), they reach several substages, including (a) the masturbatory phase, when they want to give themselves satisfaction; (b) the latency period, between the ages of around six and twelve, when they presumably become guilty about masturbation and therefore repress most of their sex urges and actions; (c) the homosexual phase, when they fall in love with and want to have sex relations with other males; and (d) the heterosexual phase, starting up sometime after puberty, when they ardently desire and want to copulate with girls.

As for the Freudian-hypothesized pregenital phase, there is much doubt that this exists at all. Certainly, youngsters take pleasure in using their mouths and sometimes (though hardly always) in employing their anal region for stimulation. But there is no evidence that this *sensual* satisfaction is truly *sexual*, and much reason to believe that it is not. It is true that teen-agers and adults become specifically sexually or genitally aroused when they kiss; but it would not appear that many children of a younger age do likewise. It is probably only *after* the genitals are rendered supersensitive by the influx of androgens that occurs in human beings around the age of puberty that all kinds of previously nonsexual sensations—such as strokings of the skin—become sexualized and lead to erection and sometimes orgasm. Freud seemed to take this postpubescent phenomenon and to *assume* that it was true of prepubescent years as well; but he appears to have been wrong in this assumption.

The Freudian notions of oral sexuality are again mistaken, since they equate the sensual orality of the child—that is, his sucking, biting, and kissing—with his later tendencies to use his mouth, tongue, and teeth in specific sex acts. Actually, I have seen and known about a number of children who were continually sucking lollipops, kissing others, chewing gum, and engaging in other kind of oral activities when young; and yet, when they finally engaged in adolescent and adult sex relationships, they were almost completely genitally inclined and took little pleasure from oral sexuality. Where oral fixation should "logically" have occurred, it definitely did not. Moreover, many other individuals, in all parts of the globe, who are raised in various oral and non-oral ways, manage to acquire a common sexual proclivity such as an addiction to oral-genital relations.

Once the genital phase of sexuality, which the Freudians posit, has been reached, children still do not follow the subphases of development that they are supposed to follow in accordance with psychoanalytic views. The so-called latency period frequently does not exist at all, since many children remain sexualized from their third or fourth years to their teens, and during this time continue to practice one form or another of masturbation or even begin to have relations with other children or adults. When the latency period does come about, it seems to arise not because children become guilty about their sexuality and therefore repress it, but because they are able, at the age of six or so, to become much more active and independent than they ever were before, and hence become absorbed in many nonsexual activities which were previously not available to them. Sex, in comparison, takes a back place in their lives—at least until the onset of puberty.

When puberty is reached, many or most males, once again, do not seem to follow classical Freudian-hypothesized patterns. Instead of most of them entering a pronounced homosexual phase, only a sizable minority of them do. Even those that do engage in homosexual activity—such as mutual masturbation with other boys—frequently do so not because they are particularly attracted to members of their own sex (indeed, they may be avidly dreaming of girls at this time) but because this type of activity happens to be more easily available than heterosexual relations. And many boys—perhaps, in fact, the distinct majority—go through no real homosexual phase whatever, but remain consistently attracted to girls, both amatively and sexually, from their early childhood to the end of their lives.

The Freudian notions of the great importance of the Oedipus complex in childhood sexuality are too lengthy to be discussed in detail here. Suffice it to say that they, too, have been anthropologically and clinically questioned in recent years, so that it would appear, at most, that only relatively few children in today's world are seriously afflicted with Oedipal conflicts and that when they are, it is their general feelings about wrongdoing and the dire need for their parents' approval that truly bothers them, rather than their specific lusts after their mothers and their fears that they will be castrated for being so lustful.

Granted that the orthodox Freudian theory of childhood sexuality leaves much to be desired, the fact remains that children often have clear-cut sex problems. If their parents do not help them concretely with their conflicts in this area, both early and later misery will likely ensue. Let us now consider some of the main difficulties in this regard and how they can be handled.

Masturbation Problems

Sex surveys consistently tend to show that a good many boys masturbate before the age of puberty and that the vast majority begin to do so before they are out of their teens. Considerably fewer female children masturbate; but here, too, it can safely be said that at least a large minority of girls engage in some kind of self-stimulation by the time they reach their late adolescence. In the case of many children, masturbation is concentrated in two different periods: first, when they are between three and six years of age; second, when they have attained puberty. In early childhood, the practice is usually quite normal; even infants one week old have been observed to rub their genital areas. In adolescence, it is not only frequent (Lester Kirkendall estimates that most teen-age boys masturbate about three times a week), but it is also beneficial, in that it serves as a harmless form of sexual release when other outlets are not easily available.

During the so-called latency years, between six and twelve, masturbation often wanes in the wake of satisfied curiosities and the discovery of a world full of other fascinating things—trees, frogs, dolls, and school. Periodically, though, it may rise to a prominent place again when a frightened youngster, recently scolded, instinctively begins to touch his genitals for comfort—often without being aware that he is doing so.

Whereas it was once believed, wrongly, that masturbation led to various ailments, and notably to mental illness, it now seems much more likely that severe emotional disturbance sometimes leads to an overconcentration on autoerotic activities. Thus, when a child is terribly anxious over almost anything, or when he feels that he is rejected by others, or when he thinks that there is little or no possibility of his getting along successfully in the world, he *then* will sometimes resort to steady or even constant masturbatory activities—*even* when he does not particularly feel a sex urge.

It should be noted in this respect that all kinds of nonsexual excitement can induce the individual, quite automatically and spontaneously, to become sexually aroused. When a boy, for example, is in the midst of a difficult test at school, and he is afraid that he is not going to answer the questions properly, he may suddenly notice that he is sexually excited. Then, just because he notices this excitement and becomes concerned about it, he may become sexually aroused again when he is in a similar situation—not by the examination itself, this time, but by his fear or expectation of having an erection in the course of it. In consequence, he may be led to masturbating during exam situations, or when he is studying for an exam, or whenever he becomes fearful about sexual arousal, or when he becomes generally fearful.

By the same token, as Hadfield has indicated, a child may begin to masturbate, guiltily and resentfully, just because his parents have previously caught him in this act and have made a great to-do about the practice. This same sex guilt may later be extended, so that this child grows up to be impotent, perverted, or otherwise neurotic. And then, in a circular fashion, the individual's impotence, perversion, or neurosis may lead to further compulsive masturbation.

Masturbation, in other words, tends to become a problem when it is done for nonsexual reasons, and particularly when there are guilt, anxiety, depression, or other negative emotions connected with it. If it is engaged in because the individual is trying to withdraw generally from life and its supposed dangers or to avoid other forms of sex (such as heterosexual petting or intercourse) because they appear to be too difficult to learn, then it becomes a problem. Even then, it constitutes in most instances a general neurotic problem rather than a sex problem; and it is harmful not because it is a sex act but because it is an act that is done for disturbed reasons.

One of the main bugaboos concerning masturbation is that it will be done too frequently or "excessively." In a physical sense, this is almost impossible, since the sexual mechanism, in the case of both boys and girls, is such that if the individual really masturbates more than he is healthfully able to do, he (or she) loses desire and therefore is persuaded to discontinue. However, children who masturbate for nonsexual reasons may spend inordinate amounts of time doing so, to the neglect of other valuable pursuits. Hadfield notes that "physiologically the child who constantly masturbates becomes nervous from the persistent over-excitation of its nervous system." This may or may not be true, since the child who does constantly stimulate himself sexually may do so just because he has an overexcitable nervous system to begin with or because he is psychologically upset.

Charlene J., a ten-year-old girl I saw not so long ago, is a case in point here. She was brought to me because she was stimulating herself constantly in class and often in other public situations. Both her parents and the child's physician felt that she might well do herself some neurophysiological damage by this persistent masturbation; and although I doubted this, I did think her compulsive sex acts warranted investigation. While talking with Charlene I soon discovered that she was very jealous of her fifteen-year-old sister, who engaged in a goodly amount of petting with boys, and who apparently went out of her way to tell Charlene how delightful it was to have them pet her. Charlene, who considered herself much less good-looking than her sister, and who also thought that it was terribly unfair that she was too young to be able to get boy friends as yet, felt exceptionally inadequate and desperately searched for a way of compensating for her "terrible" handicaps. She therefore devised what she called a "self-petting" routine and tried to outdo her sister by giving herself the kind of stimulation the older girl achieved with boys. Moreover, since much of her sister's petting took place at parties, on park benches, in parked cars, and other semipublic places, Charlene thought it quite appropriate for her "self-petting" to be done in equivalent public view.

Charlene's parents and physicians were notably wrong about her doing neurophysiological harm to herself, since she wasn't achieving any orgasms, but was simulating them, and at times fooling herself into believing that she had them in order to vie successfully with her older sister (who, being better physically developed, actually was achieving almost seizure-like climaxes in many of her petting affairs). I worked with Charlene in regard to her jealousy and was able to show her that her worth as a person did not depend on competing successfully with her sister, nor on being more grownup than she actually was, and she was able to accept herself without these qualifications and to stop her public masturbation entirely. She resorted to only occasional private autoeroticism, until she had reached her own puberty three years later, and therefore no longer had sex problems.

Although occasional or even frequent masturbation by a child is generally harmless and should be ignored, compulsive or public self-stimulation is a sign of disturbance, and the reasons for it should be investigated. Perhaps the child requires more attention and approval; or is too bored with his existence; or is being overly pressured about his school or other achievement; or is unable to relate to other children. These possible causes of his upsetness should be probed and appropriate measures should be taken to rectify them.

The Problem of Sexual Preoccupation

Some children appear to be quite preoccupied with sex words or acts. In many instances they tend to use these words or display these acts in a highly provocative and adult-taunting manner. Four-year-old Nonie, for example, may be happily engaged, day after day, in a game of "doctor and nurse" with her three-and-a-half-year-old cousin Ricky and may think nothing of undressing Ricky completely and doing all sorts of "sex" things with him. Or five-year-old Tommie may take delight in experimentally pouring milk down his younger sister Annie's "gina" and may perversely seem to increase this kind of activity when horrified adults are around.

Such activities are usually normal, just as are such evidences of children's natural curiosity as throwing stones in the water to watch the rings, or pulling a flower apart to see how it is made. Doctor-nurse games are often beginning efforts at sex-role identification, children's attempts to imitate familiar adults' behavior: thus, Ricky's playing doctor is often replaced on the next visit by his being the father in a game of "house." Allowed to explore, the child's curiosity becomes fairly speedily satisfied.

Children of all age levels frequently undergo a phase in which they become obsessed with "dirty words"—toilet and sex talk. Often such phases are triggered by contact with age-peers who, often because of the clandestine way in which sex, toilet training, and the like were handled by their own parents, have become obsessed with the topics these parents' attitudes have suggested were taboo. The result is huddles behind the garage where sex "knowledge"—most of it fantasized and erroneous—is passed down from the little "expert" to his awed playmate; or mischievously and often maddeningly relayed to parents in the form of incessant repetition of newly learned "dirty" words. Again, this obsession is not in the majority of cases to be considered a sign of moral depravity, but rather an indication (a) that the child is simply living out a normal developmental stage, or (b) that there has been some mishandling of the sex question, either on the part of peers and their parents, or on the part of the child's parents in their failure to teach him some of the facts of life. In the latter case, some gentle intervention and open discussion would most likely move the area of sex alongside the other affairs of life the child is gradually learning to regulate—and in so doing prevent its potentially dangerous compartmentalization, its relegation to an alien, hush-hush area of life.

The task of combating shame and guilt concerning sex and the body is often difficult. Even in homes where the issue of sex is handled with gentle, unemotional firmness, the moralists and sex-haters, and the rules of society (such as the fact that a child must close the door when he urinates and button his pants when he's through) militate against his having complete sex trust. The child must frequently be given a double-barreled kind of teaching— that is to say, taught on the one hand that sex is perfectly proper, but on the other hand that many people in our society do not deem it to be proper and that therefore he must watch his step when in the presence of these people. This, of course, is an attitude similar to that which we teach children about religion; namely, that our own religion (or lack thereof) is fine, but then one does not necessarily go around converting others to it, and instead is discreet about various aspects of it because of the obvious religious prejudices that exist in almost all communities.

So with sex. You may teach your child, if you wish, that there is nothing dirty about sex, and that it is all right for him to keep the door open when he goes to the bathroom to urinate. But at the very same time you must let him know that many or most other people have quite different ideas on the subject and would be horrified if he urinated in *their* homes in the same manner that he does in his own. These others, you can explain to him, are quite probably wrong about their puritanical sex views; but they have a right to their own wrong opinions; and if he is to get along satisfactorily in the world, he has to honor their right to have these opinions.

An interesting case in point, in this connection, is that of Joe and Hal, two cousins in their ninth year. Both seemed to have unusually liberal parents, since they talked freely about sexual matters and seemed to have more information than any of their peers in regard to sex affairs. Joe, however, took care to keep the usual rules of his community in regard to dress and toilet arrangements, while Hal seemed to go consistently out of his way to leave his fly unbuttoned or to urinate in a friend's house with the door wide open. Investigation showed that Joe's parents were truly enlightened sexually and had done their best to give him the facts of life, but at the same time realistically to show him that he'd better behave circumspectly in regard to these facts when he was with other children or adults. Hal's parents had told him practically nothing about sex and had only shamefacedly answered the questions he put to them. He had picked up most of his information on the subject from Joe and other boys. But he was never satisfied with what he knew, was always trying to get "deeper" information, volubly flaunted the information that he did have, and exhibitionistically showed himself to others in order to "prove" that he was as enlightened as Joe.

Hal, obviously, was unhealthfully preoccupied with sex and was compulsively resorting to shocking behavior. Although he had eventually acquired all the facts known to Joe, and perhaps even more, his attitudes about sex were remarkably similar to those of his parents, so that he did not effectively utilize these facts. His preoccupation with sex continued until he was thera-peutically shown that sex in itself is not bad or shocking (even though many adults consider it so) and that he could soberly use sex information without having to display it ostentatiously.

To insure that your own child does not become highly obsessed with sex, on the one hand, or woefully underinformed about it, on the other hand, you might well remember (and teach him) that private and public behavior are often much different: as when we eat with our fingers at home, but not necessarily the same way in a public restaurant. From an ideal standpoint, this may not be too good, since honesty is a fine trait, and perhaps it would be better if all of us honestly acted the same way in public as we do in a more private setting. But the fact remains that society as yet does not tolerate this kind of a single standard of etiquette; and it is therefore necessary for us to raise our children to be somewhat hypocritical and two-faced in regard to public displays of eating, sexuality, and many other behaviors.

Preventing the Development of Fixed Homosexuality

Although it is often contended that confirmed homosexuality is inborn and that nothing can be done to prevent it in some individuals, there is considerable evidence (which I have reviewed in *Homosexuality: Its Causes and Cure*) that this is not true. The fact is that our lack of proper sex education, our distorted emphasis on the attainment of perfect "male" and "female" roles, and our encouraging much of our populace to grow up with overweening feelings of social-sexual inadequacy often make it easier for many of our youngsters to become predominantly homosexual instead of heterosexual adults. This kind of miseducation is largely responsible for the fact that one out of ten of our males is basically homosexual for a number of years of his life and an astonishingly high proportion of our females is more or less frigid.

In treating many fixed homosexuals, I have noticed time and again that they were raised with exceptionally puritanical views about heterosexual relations—but that they received little information on homosexual activities. The latter were considered to be so heinous by their parents that they were not even mentioned. Thus, male homosexuals had often been told when they were children that it was wrong to "sully" or "dishonor" girls and that they'd better stay away from all intimate male-female contacts. This, under pain of such teachings, they frequently try to do. But if they are sexually normal, they have powerful unsatisfied urges and often will experiment with homosexual participations. Since they have only been taught not to engage in sex with *girls,* they frequently enter into homosexual affairs with relative open-mindedness, find that interhuman sexuality is more satisfactory than self-stimulation, and become addicted to homosexuality.

This is particularly true when, in addition to having a lack of sex knowledge, a boy is raised with the idea that he has to compete mightily for the prettiest and most personable girl available. As he grows into adolescence, a boy so indoctrinated often becomes terribly afraid of failing in the heterosexual rat-race and finds excuses to withdraw from the possibility of being rejected by girls. If he then finds that certain other boys, some of them older than he, are spontaneously attracted to him and willing to go out of their way to woo him, he may find this kind of game much less difficult than heterosexual courtship and may be eased into a pattern of exclusive homosexuality. By this time, moreover, he feels so far behind the other boys who have been dating and petting with girls for several years that he despairs of ever being able to catch up with them; and he feels more motivated than ever *not* to take heterosexual risks.

If, then, you would prevent your child from developing into a fixed or exclusive homosexual (which is not the worst thing in the world, but which will prevent him from achieving a wider range of sexual enjoyments and from subsequently achieving a good marital and family relationship), you would be wise to encourage him, as he approaches puberty, to participate in social-sexual relations with members of the other sex and to teach him to some degree *how* to do so. Show him, when the time comes, that his worth as a human individual is not dependent on his dating and mating prowess: that it is *desirable* but hardly *absolutely necessary* that he win an attractive heterosexual partner. Teach him how to compete adequately for a satisfactory mate—but how to refrain from berating himself or considering himself worthless if, somehow, he does not completely succeed in this respect.

Sexual Ignorance and Guilt

Most of the major sex problems that afflict children and that lay the groundwork for their developing into sexually neurotic adults are not specific symptoms or deviations, such as compulsive masturbation or fixed homosexuality. Rather, they stem from a general dearth of adequate sex information and a plethora of negative, puritanical ideas about virtually all aspects of sexuality. Exceptionally few children, for example, are plagued with problems of impotence or frigidity. In fact, the more sexually anesthetic a child is, in our society, the better he or she is likely to get along—especially from an adult viewpoint! But sexual inadequacy among our adults is a most common problem; and some of its important roots are definitely in childhood. It consequently behooves us to give our children the kind of sexual information and attitudes that will protect them from acquiring later-life problems rather than the kind that will only prevent them from developing dramatic symptoms during their early years.

Most books on child-rearing recommend that you give a youngster relevant sex information, starting at an early age, but that you take care not to give him too much or too detailed knowledge, since this may only serve to confuse him. My own view is that it is better for you to err on the overdone than the underdone side in this respect. If you give meager facts, it is almost certain that he will pick up additional ones, usually in a distorted manner, from his peers, from TV shows, from books, and from other sources. Moreover, he may add his own imaginative ruminations to the knowledge you give him, and may come up with some startlingly wrong answers.

Thus, if you tell your child that a husband "plants" a seed in his wife's stomach, he may literally envision his father's digging into his mother's belly with a trowel—and he may be startled when he later discovers the true story of how impregnation takes place. Or if you give him the idea that sex is only for making babies, he may later associate it with hurt rather than with pleasure.

It is interesting that Dr. Mary Calderone, Executive Director of the Sex Information and Education Council of the United States (SIECUS), emphasizes that parents should not give a child the impression that married couples engage in sex only to have babies. States Dr. Calderone: "You should make it clear that sex is something in which parents can express their love for each other from the time of marriage until they die. It is something mothers and fathers have between them that underlies the continuing marriage relationship." I quite agree. But what Dr. Calderone rather inhibitedly fails to add is that young people, in this day and age, should also be taught that *un*married couples also delightfully engage in sex, that they need not beget children in so doing, and that knowing the facts of life includes a realistic acceptance of the incidence and the potential goodness (as well as the actual dangers) of premarital sex relations. To teach a child, that sex is or should be limited only to marital relations is as puritanical as teaching him, as in the old days, that it is solely for purposes of procreation.

Actually, unemotionally presented sex education is still rare. It is practically nonexistent in our public schools, and it is in the formative stages in some of our best private schools. It is so seldom given in the home that a five-year study carried out by William Blaisdell with 25,000 teen-agers revealed that only one out of fourteen received sex information from their parents before acquiring it from other children, and only one out of twenty-two obtained any parentally-instilled information about venereal disease. These facts have led the Rev. George Hagmaier, professor of religious education at Catholic University, to conclude that "Sex education in the United States is in the Neanderthal stage. It is ironic that in our so-called sexually liberated society, sex is still a dirty word."

In view of this deplorable state of American sex education, it is usually best to give your child the full facts about intercourse, pregnancy, birth, and other aspects of sex and reproduction when he is quite young, and even before he starts to ask questions. In the school, says Dr. Calderone, sex knowledge should be taught at the kindergarten level; and in the home, I would add, even before. The truth about sex should be given in the simplest language at first—though not, as Bob Lardine points out, by using "nonsensical, baby-like words to describe parts of the human anatomy." Although the salient facts need not be overly detailed, there is no reason why they should be highly poetized or distorted and thereby rendered "nonsexual" and "innocuous."

It is important, morever, that sex information be given objectively and unemotionally, just as other information is normally given. If you, as the child's parent, have unusual difficulties in giving him the facts of life in a dispassionate, informative manner, you should think seriously of having some friend, teacher, physician, psychologist, or other trained person educate him in this respect. If you decide to give the information yourself—which is probably the best procedure in most cases—you should be well read and otherwise informed in this area.

Regarding your own sex education, you can gain from perusing a number of books such as Hugo Beigel's *Sex from A to Z*, the Kinsey group's *Sexual Behavior in the Human Female*, Warren Johnson's *Human Sex and Sex Education*, William H. Masters and Virginia Johnson's *Human Sexual Response*, my own *Art and Science of Love*, and *The Encyclopedia of Sexual Behavior* which I edited with Albert Abarbanel. Walter Stokes points out that "it is of the greatest importance that both parents should share all of the reading and should be ready to discuss it with the child if he has questions. In such discussion, parents should not pose as all-wise oracles. They should acknowledge ignorance or uncertainty when such is the case and should prepare the child to cope with the great diversity of views about sex that he will encounter as he grows up."

Do your best to provide a climate in which the child can feel free to pose his questions on sex. This means that you'd better curb your inclination to grab him and drag him into the house in horror when you catch him playing with his female cousin's genitals in the garage or to wash his mouth with soap when he is enjoying the sound of a newly acquired but socially unacceptable addition to his vocabulary. As Bettelheim suggests, "As a grown-up, you know that sex is something we don't enjoy in public . . . but *first* you have to learn if it's enjoyable or not."

You must, naturally, decide where limits are to be drawn—for I am not advocating unbridled sexual expression for the child, such as swimming in the nude in public pools. But draw the line uncondemningly! Make it crystal-clear to your youngster that even his sexual exhibitionism or homosexual behavior does not mean that *he* is a bad person. Preventing a child's (and later, his adult) compulsive sexuality will be most effectively ensured by your policy of being nonjudgmental—by your calmly explaining to him why playing with Sherry's genitals is not the best way to learn about sex and by your providing a suitable alternative for satisfying his curiosity. (Haim Ginott suggests, "Ask us about Susie; but no undressing!") Down-to-earth explanations of procreation, menstruation, and other sex issues are a far better insurance of later sex (and general emotional) health than making a highly charged deal out of a child's activities. Such to-dos have often backfired by causing guilt and shame or an obsessive preoccupation with the very facts of life that parents were trying to suppress.

If a child is establishing a pattern of fixed behavior—as may happen in the area of masturbation—search hard for the cause. A retreat into compulsive self-stimulation can be born of a dire need to be loved, which the world at large can seldom satisfy; hence the child renders to himself this love-substitute. (Sometimes the problem is in part augmented by a reality situation, such as a new baby taking all the attention away from him; or a period of tense nagging by his mother.) Do your best to instill the rational principle that he is a significant human being whether or not he is loved by all his friends. When he refuses to be deprived of constant gratification, gently but firmly explain his low frustration to him. And rid him of the complications of such irrational philosophies.

The child who is perpetually anxious about whether or not others like him, or who must constantly have every whim gratified, will invariably have a dire fear of being caught (at masturbating, for example) and further rejected. And thus he performs his undesirable behavior all the more frantically. Or he feels he is so vile and inept that he cannot stop masturbating, and that thought gives birth to further repetitions of the deed.

The really dangerous way of handling sex is imperiously and emotionally insisting that your child not perform certain practices. There is, as Fritz Redlich warns, the danger that the child will develop terrible self-loathing and lack of confidence when he finds he cannot (especially when half-asleep) keep himself from doing what he has been so forcefully told is unnatural and vile. Even the healthiest child, who has no masturbatory problem, can be spurred on to compulsive autoeroticism when faced with a moral prohibition.

Don't, James Hymes warns, look at your child's habits at six or seven as if he were a teen-ager. If he likes to run around nude, is preoccupied with his genitals, he is hardly a sex maniac or an exhibitionist. Or, if he seems fearful of having anyone see him undressed, he is not marked for impotency or frigidity. To the fearful and the precocious child, explain that the body is neither dirty nor to be feared and let your explanations keep pace with his expressed or implicit need for answers. A child who has some difficulty in separating his body from his own personal worth may acquire the idea that it, as well as himself, is dirty and bad. And such an attitude is likely to grow up with him. "If sex is dirty in the nursery," says A. S. Neill, "it cannot be very clean in the wedding bed."

Keep pace with your child, but keep a little ahead as he approaches puberty. He should be prepared for bodily changes; else his first wet dream or her first menstruation may become a hideously fearsome event rather than adolescent baptism.

Allow some leeway in masculine and feminine behavior (in the very young), since boys will play with dolls and girls will act like tomboys. Let your youngster have playmates of both sexes. Remain calm when he plays "doctor," and the chances are that he will develop a healthy attitude toward sex, satisfy his curiosity for a while, and begin to develop normal sex-role identification.

One of the most gruesome cases of sex miseducation that I have encountered occurred in the cases of Cecelia and Monique Z. Cecelia, the older sister, was largely raised by her mother, and was taught that sex was only for procreation, that even the most minor forms of petting might well lead to pregnancy, and that practically all sex terms were dirty. Although quite an attractive girl, she shied away from dating boys and could not even stand most other girls because they were always talking about dating, love, and marriage. When she was fourteen she met a seventeen-year-old girl, Dora, who seemed to share many of her own puritanical views; and before long, they were intimately and almost exclusively sharing their various pursuits. By the time Cecelia was sixteen, she had unwittingly fallen into a full-blown lesbian affair with Dora and she had no interests in virtually anything but being with her inamorata.

When Cecelia's lesbianism was discovered and she was sent to a psychologist for treatment, her parents were shown that their puritanical rearing had much to do with her disordered sexuality. Since the mother still had her own sex problems, it was agreed that the father would be more responsible for the sex education of Monique, who was six years younger. Whereupon the father then went to almost opposite extremes, indiscriminately presented Monique with all the sex facts he could find, forcefully pushed her (from the age of eleven onward) into heterosexual affairs, was frankly seductive with her himself, and taught her to defy and flaunt practically all of society's sex mores. The result was that Monique had an illegitimate child when she was fifteen, found little enjoyment with her husband, whom she married at seventeen, and (much to her parents' horror) left her husband and entered into a lesbian affair when she was eighteen.

Although it was clear to me (when I saw Monique for intensive psychotherapy) that neither her nor her sister's sexual aberrations stemmed wholly from their extreme forms of sex education, since there were several other nonsexual causes involved in their severe emotional difficulties, I was also reasonably sure that parental extremism helped to contribute considerably to their disordered lives. This is usually true: Any extreme way of sexually informing or censoring a child is likely to lead to poor behavioral results; and in this, as in so many other aspects of human living, it is well for the parents to seek the Aristotelian mean between either of two extremes.

A final word: Proper sex education is synonymous with proper emotional education, or education for living. The object of teaching your child the facts of human sexuality is not merely to make him sexually guiltless and proficient, but to help him be generally self-accepting and competent to face life. If he truly likes himself and is able to direct his own existence, the chances are that he will discover what is sexually good for him, even if you do not specifically demonstrate very much in this respect; while if he feels that he is worthless and undeserving of happiness, all the sex information in the world will probably be used miserably by him. Likewise, if he is able to master his general anxieties, he will probably be able to master fears surrounding sex.

This is not to say that you should not give your child adequate sex data, since good intentions plus ignorance can still pave his road to hell. But the facts are not enough; his *attitudes* toward himself and others are even more important and must serve as a foundation in which the proper facts can be successfully embedded.

No matter how well you raise your child, he or she is bound to make sexual mistakes—such as overfocusing on sex, to the harm of studies or of the rest of his or her development. Or he or she may go to the other extreme and squelch sex desires so thoroughly in an effort to concentrate on academic achievement or some other aspect of life as to anesthetize the sex drive and thus be unable to enjoy the full and proper satisfaction of married life. Your job is to accept these "mistakes" with understanding, try to inform your child fully and objectively on sex matters, and never be remiss in giving him or her a direct answer to sexual questions. Will you thereby be a perfect sex educator? By no manner or means! But at least you'll be doing your best to approximate sanity in an area that is presently remarkably lacking in common sense.

8

Helping Children with
Conduct Problems

Most of the neurotic symptoms that we have been discussing in this book are defeating to the child himself but not necessarily to those with whom he associates. Thus, if the child is anxious, has severe problems of achievement, is undisciplined, and is sexually aberrated, he is likely to suffer severely; but it is quite possible that those around him will not suffer equally and may not even be aware of his disturbances. There are, however, a number of problems which the child inflicts not merely on himself, but on others, and these are notably dysfunctional in many instances.

If, for example, a child is emotionally disturbed and resorts to stealing because of his disturbance, he immediately impinges on the rights of others—and these others almost invariably take an exceptionally dim view of his problem. Instead of seeing him as an emotionally upset child, they concentrate mainly on his symptom; and since this symptom is unpleasant and antisocial, they tend to condemn him roundly for displaying it.

In truth, what parents automatically construe to be maliciously antisocial behavior more often than not is the child's natural tendency to selfishness—and, resultantly, to thoughtlessness. Nowhere is this more the case than in the area of destructiveness. When two boys tear up a sheet, their sole thought often is that it would make a super sail for their toy boat. Not taking the time to put herself into her children's frame of reference, a mother sees only wanton destruction of property and vents her anger in genuinely hostile shouts and blows. And a bewildered child concludes that it is wrong to play, create, and be inventive.

In either case, whether poor conduct is volitional or unwitting, parents rarely take the time to understand why the child acts as he does because of their indignation over the fact that he does. Driven by the censure of those around him to condemn himself enormously for behaving poorly (especially if his original impetus for being antisocial was some degree of self-depreciation), he will become increasingly self-blaming, and hence emotionally aberrated.

Let us examine some of the specific problems that these children often display, to see how you can understand and counter them if they should ever arise in connection with your own child.

Lying

Practically all children (as well as all adults) lie at one time or another, and most of them engage in a good deal of prevarication. Why? For several fairly obvious reasons: They are frequently punished if they tell the truth; they can get away with things they don't want to do by lying; they can make themselves "superior" to others by boasting of deeds that they have not performed; they wish so heartily that certain things would occur that they actually see them, in their mind's eye, as occurring; they are afraid to admit their mistakes, for fear that they would be despicable if they did; etc. None of these reasons for lying are exceptionally good, in that there invariably are, at least in theory, better ways of dealing with the situations about which the lies are manufactured. But the fact remains that children are not too capable of finding the best solutions to various difficulties, and the lies which they tell are one form or another of second-best solutions in many instances.

There are, moreover, occasions in which it is actually wise and sane for a child to lie. If he would be unduly and unjustly penalized for truth-telling—for example, thoroughly thrashed because he has unwittingly spilled a jar of jam—it is highly rational of him to pretend that he has not spilled it, and even to manufacture conditions which tend to show that someone else is responsible for his misdeed. Or if he knows that his parents or some other child would be completely shocked and hurt by his telling them his true feelings about them, it would be perfectly proper for him to tell a white lie, and to keep some of his feelings to himself.

Many times, too, a child appearing to relate a most farfetched tale, may actually be telling the pure truth, only to be punished for it by an overly suspicious parent who is underconfident in her child. Thus, when Danny brings home a miniature puzzle and boasts he has won it in a gym contest, Mother, going by his poor past athletic performances, accuses him of having taken it from a friend. Be sure of your own facts before accusing your offspring of lying.

Nonetheless, there are many occasions when children self-defeatingly or pathologically lie. If Jimmy, for example, tells how well he did in an essay contest at school, when there actually was no such contest, or when he submitted one of the worst papers in the contest, he is palpably avoiding facing reality, and is showing that he has a dire need to impress people with his nonexistent prowess. If Sandi tells her parents that she is doing her homework regularly, when actually she practically never does it, and is falling further and further behind in class, she is not merely cleverly avoiding some onerous work, but is probably seriously avoiding activity that simply has to be done, and that she will soon be severely penalized for not doing.

Lies such as these, which are falsely ego-boosting on the one hand, or which are techniques for getting away with murder on the other hand, are pathological not merely because they are untruths, but because they are prevarications which simply do not work. For Jimmy, in all probability, will be found out in his lies about the essay contest or about similar things which he boasts about having done when he clearly has not done them; and then he will actually sink *lower* in other people's eyes, when his whole intent, through lying, is to have them think *better* of him. And Sandi will probably not be able to get away with her maneuvering, and will either have to catch up on her homework all at once, or be forced to take the subjects she is avoiding all over again and then have to do more work than she would have to do if she had stopped her nonsense and buckled down to the work.

The first thing to note, therefore, if your child is engaged in pathological lying, is that his behavior is aberrant just because it is self-defeating and not because it is simply dishonest. Since this form of lying is already handicapping your child, it is foolish for you to take a moralistic attitude toward it and attempt to penalize the child even more. It is far wiser, in most instances, if you try to understand the source of the lying—the philosophic assumptions which the child holds that drive him to lie. And again—search yourself and determine to what extent you may have been responsible for implicitly planting those philosophies.

These sources, as usual, are the same as those behind other kinds of emotional disturbances, namely, the two basic irrational ideas: (1) that the child must do things perfectly well and be acclaimed for his performances; and (2) that he simply cannot tolerate frustrating situations or difficult tasks, and should not have to put up with them. If, instead of attacking the child and his lying, you forthrightly but kindly attempt to tackle the irrational ideas that impel him to lie, you will have a good chance of helping him.

Thus, you can show Jimmy that even though you know that there was no essay contest in school, or that he did poorly in the one that was held, you still like him as a person, and would like to help him do better when the next contest is held, you will be on the road to convincing him that he does not have to be the best essayist alive in order to win yours and others' approval. And if you show him that you can respect and help him even though you know that he is lying, you may particularly persuade him that he does not have to be perfect to get along in the world, and that imperfect creatures such as he are still lovable. On the other hand, if you show Jimmy that you know darned well that there was no essay contest and that he's a little rotter for pretending that there was and that he won it, his basic insecurity will probably be even more enhanced, and he will quite possibly have a greater need to make up exaggerated stories about himself the next time.

In Sandi's case, if you kindly but firmly show her that it is quite understandable why she should lie about doing her homework, and why she should not do it in the first place, but that nonetheless this kind of irresponsible behavior will get her nowhere in life, and will inevitably bring her more disbenefits than gains, she will see that you are really on her side, rather than against her; that she certainly is not getting away with anything; and that the chances are that you are right, and that she'd better do her homework in the future when it is due, not because *you* think she should but because *she* will be severely penalized if she doesn't. On the other hand, if you point the finger of guilt at Sandi and condemn her thoroughly for lying about the homework, she may become angry, rebellious, and highly defensive, never admit to herself that she is goofing, and use her resentment against you as a beautiful alibi to keep goofing.

Calmly accept, then, your child's lying. Determine whether it is done for sane or crazy reasons. If the former is true, ignore it. If the latter is true, you may still be wise to ignore the lies themselves, but to get, instead, at the irrational philosophies that underlie and cause them. Or you can bring the lies to the attention of the child, but show him that you are only doing so in a helpful, corrective manner, and not because you think that he is a hopeless child who has to lie, and who should be punished severely for doing so. In any event, remember that the lie is not the issue; it is the *reason* for it that must be sought out by you and intelligently handled and uprooted.

A highly effective breeding ground for lies is a climate of hypocrisy. Much of society is concerned with irrational rules of etiquette whereby men doff their hats to women they don't respect (or even know) and tell relatives how nice it is to see them when their visit is really a bore. There is no need to go to another extreme and encourage your child to tell his hostess, "I think your party was stinky"; on the other hand, he should not be forced into paying completely unfelt obeisances. Rare is the child, as any parent knows, who does not with fair regularity blurt out, with complete ingenuousness, some rather blunt remark. Yet what is more natural than a curious child, spying a lady getting onto his bus, asking loudly, "Why is her stomach so fat?" What chance has a child, dragged off the bus by a red-faced mother, or slapped for similar questions, of becoming anything but a liar himself? "The best way to make a child a liar for life," says A. S. Neill, "is to insist that he speak the truth and nothing but the truth."

Tattling

Like lying, tattling may sometimes be fairly healthy. A child who has a great deal of confidence in his mother and believes that she is on his side, no matter what he does, may routinely confide in her all sorts of things about his peers that they would just as soon not have her know; but he may not in the least be malicious in this kind of tattling. Or a child who is exceptionally talkative may unwittingly, in the course of many things that he expresses, give out information that would better be left concealed; and, again, he may have no hostility when he does so and may be considered to be reasonably normal in this respect.

Much tattling, however, is of a negative nature. Mary tattles on Susie and Janie because she moralistically feels that they have done the wrong thing, that she would never do anything similar, that they therefore deserve to be punished, and that she should be seen as the fair-haired girl of the neighborhood for not doing what they did. This kind of tattling, although Mary may not in the least realize it, is part of the power struggle that she much of the time engages in; and, as the authors of a noted United States Department of Health, Education, and Welfare booklet on "Behavior Problems and Fears" indicate, "it suggests that the tattler is weak, and has to come to an adult for support."

If your child tattles and does so in a manner that shows his jealousy of and hostility to others, do not chide him for being a tattler, for that (as usual) will tend to make him still less secure, and hence potentially more hostile. Try the following approach:

(1) Let him see that you are not shocked by his description of the nasty behavior of the people on whom he is tattling but that you rather expect them to be the way they are. Not that you necessarily condone their behavior; but that you are not horrified by it either, and that you certainly are not going to condemn them for it. Tell him something along these lines: "Yes, dear, I see that Lionel lied when he told his mother that he was going to be with you and actually he went to the movies. And it would have been better if he had told the truth. But children like Lionel do lie every once in a while, and we cannot expect them to be little angels and never lie. Now, are you really so surprised that Lionel acted that way? And can't you see that his behavior is rather common? This doesn't mean that you should lie the way that Lionel did. But if you did lie to me, the way he did to his mother, I'm sure I'd understand it and think little of it. We often do undesirable things like lying; but that's the way we are— humans who easily make mistakes."

(2) If your child persists at tattling, gently but firmly show him that his is not the best kind of behavior and that it has distinct disadvantages. For example: "Well, I can see that Bob was wrong in bullying that other child; and I'm glad that you see that he was wrong and that you are determined not to do that kind of thing yourself. However, dear, if Bob finds out that you told me about this, when he specifically asked you not to say anything to anyone about it, he's going to be very displeased—and you may be the one whom he starts bullying next. For you wouldn't want anyone to tattle on you like this, would you, even when you had definitely done something wrong? No, I'm sure you wouldn't. So don't you think it would be better if you merely tried to persuade Bob not to do any more bullying, rather than go off and tell everyone, the way you're telling me now, what a big bully he is?"

(3) See if you can't do something to tackle your child's basic insecurity, so that he will not feel impelled to tattle on others in the future. Show him, if you can, that he is not a better individual if he makes himself superior to others by proving that they have done worse things than he has done; but that, instead, he is a valuable person to himself, and even to others, if he accepts the fact that he is not flawless and other children are not ogres and if he makes few comparisons between himself and these others. If he wants to do fine deeds—not in order to prove how worth-while he is, but because of other satisfactions that often go with doing them—that is fine. But if he has to knock others down, that is not fine, and does not increase his stature one bit. If he really wants to be a strong individual, he will gracefully accept the good deeds of others—and for the most part forget about their weaknesses.

(4) Be a good model to your child by looking into your own heart and stopping some of your own backbiting of others before it even gets started. If your child continually hears you putting other people down, thereby showing how "great" you are, he will tend to imitate your behavior; and much of his tattling may stem from this kind of imitativeness.

Stealing

As we noted in the illustration that was used at the beginning of this chapter, stealing is sometimes done as a method of false ego-boosting by children. They feel great, as they "get away with" the stolen goods, thus proving how clever they are; or they impress their friends with their prowess at thievery; or they buy the love of their peers with stolen goods, thus proving how "nice" they are; or, rather than depreciate themselves for their various lacks and misdeeds, they preoccupy themselves with the diverting action of stealing, which distracts them from some of the other serious problems they have to face.

This does not mean, again, that all stealing by children is necessarily pathological. A child may truly be deprived, even hungry, and may steal to make up for this deprivation. Or he may hobnob with a neighborhood gang for whom stealing is the norm and where he would be left out if he did not engage in theft. Or he may have a mother who is incredibly careless about leaving money around the house, and who continually tempts him to take some of it because he knows perfectly well that she would never notice that any part of it was missing.

A young child, especially, is quite apt to see a shiny red truck at a playmate's house or in a store and quite cheerfully (to a mother's later horror) take it home with him. The child's thought is solely that the object is pretty and should be fun to play with; the fact that it belongs to someone else never entered his mind. "They are not immoral," says Bettelheim, "since they have yet to learn what morals are. They proceed from the simple premise that what they want is justified by the fact that they want it, and the only problem is that adults so often have different ideas."

As usual, however, when a child's stealing is fairly persistent, and when it covers up some other negative feeling about himself, it is truly pathological, and should be duly brought to his attention and checked. And the first step in this regard, as we noted previously, is to point out to the child that his behavior is wrong —meaning that it needlessly harms other human beings and helps create the kind of a disordered world in which he would not particularly like to live himself—but that he is not to be condemned for performing this wrong behavior. He is a person who has the power to change his behavior and to desist from stealing in the future.

Try to determine whether your child has a terrible feeling of injustice, and whether that is encouraging him to steal. Even if he is treated well by you and his associates, he may have an idea that he should be treated still better, and that consequently the world is unjust. If so, try to show him that it would be very lovely if things were made easier for him, and that perhaps you even will try to arrange this to some extent, but the fact still remains that he can put up with deprivation and even injustice, and (since the world is the way it is) he will just have to do so if he is to live happily. Teach him, in other words, not to overfocus on the horror of being frustrated or deprived; that in an imperfect world we cannot, by simply willing it, have everything we desire; that in the very act of doing one thing we like (such as going to the circus), we must give up another (such as watching a TV program scheduled for that time). Reassure him that he is not the only person in the world who must see his wants unfulfilled; we all are deprived daily.

If your child's stealing symbolizes his wanting something other than the actual objects he is taking—denotes, for example, that he really wants more attention than he is getting or that he wants to excel at something—try to get at the basic source of his thievery rather than at the act itself. For if you manage to stop him from stealing—by, for example, taking him away from tempting situations or penalizing him so severely that he sees that the game is not worth the candle—and you still have not done anything about his underlying reason for stealing, it is most probable that he will use some other form of negative behavior as a compensatory device. Thus, instead of stealing to gain attention, he might bully other children, make a spectacle of himself in class, resort to other unsavory devices. So, the symptom of stealing may sometimes be eradicated fairly easily; but the cause may perniciously go marching on unless you make an honest attempt to understand and do something about it.

Bullying

When a child engages in a certain amount of intimidation of others, this is not to be thought of as necessarily being disturbed behavior, since most of us are born as well as raised with a strong tendency to want to be king of the hill, and it is very difficult to be king unless we somehow convince others that they should kowtow to us. A healthy, leading type of child, therefore, does practice some amount of browbeating when he is with other children (or even adults), and it would probably be a shame if you tried to beat all of this trait out of him.

Constant and vicious bullying by your child of his playmates and schoolmates is another thing entirely. As with many other seemingly "strong" and "assertive" acts, this kind of bullying is actually a form of weakness; it signifies that the child apparently cannot stand to be with equals but insists on forcing others to act more weakly than he and often resorts to brute force or dire threats to get them to act this way. Such bullying may stem from the fact that the child is bullied, in his turn, by others; from his way of seeing life only or mainly as a dog-eat-dog kind of existence; from his being overly deprived in various ways; from his grandiosely thinking that he has to run everything his way; and from other pressures caused by his external and internal environment.

The correct counter-bullying procedure? Not, certainly, greater bullying itself. For if you threaten your child with physical punishment and otherwise coercively harass him because he is intimidating other children, the chances are that he will become even more malcontent and intolerant. He may actually stop his bullying; but he will take out his disturbance in some other manner. Moreover, he may only become a more subtle kind of bully, one who makes sure that other children do not report his activities to their own parents or to you.

As ever, you should try to find out exactly why the child resorts to threatening tactics. If he threatens others out of his own underlying feelings of weakness and anxiety, then you should attempt to show him that he does not have to have these feelings. Teach him to discriminate, if you can, between physical and mental strength so that he will realize that a truly strong child does not have to be the mightiest one on the block, and that real emotional strength often consists of living comfortably with one's physical weakness, instead of impressing others with how muscular one is. Show him how some of the biggest and brawniest individuals have turned out to be mentally weak-kneed, in that they were ultrasensitive to what others thought of them, while some of the puniest individuals have proven themselves to be unusually tough, in that they bucked the world with their views and were not intimidated by others. Teach him that it is no disgrace—although it may well be disadvantageous—to be physically weak or even to be cowardly, in the sense of avoiding fist-fights with bellicose members of his peer group. Teach him that it is even more disadvantageous—though, again, not disgraceful —for him to be intellectuallly namby-pamby and not to have a pronounced mind of his own.

Although it is well, in our society, to teach your child, if he is a male, that boys are different from girls, and that in some respects masculinity is a trait to be desired, make sure that you do not overemphasize this trait and make him feel that it is the most desirable of all characteristics to have. For masculinity usually connotes physical prowess and (oddly enough) supersensitivity to insult—both of which often make an individual mentally vulnerable and hence far from strong. Females, moreover, can well be powerful individuals, in the sense that they know what they want in life and have no intention of being diverted by the negative opinions of others; and it is silly to call all such females "masculine," since they may be highly "feminine" in various other ways.

For both sexes, the ideal that should be taught is not one of outward "masculine" or "feminine" characteristics, but of inner or characterological strength. A girl may be large-breasted and highly emotional, but she can still be shown how stand on her own feet and to say "yes" when she means yes and "no" when she means no. A boy may be small and frail and still learn how to think for himself even when most of his peers are conforming in unthinking ways. Where one's physical characteristics are largely inborn and difficult to change, one's attitudes and ideas are much less subject to heredity and can be significantly modified over the years. It is therefore pernicious—as I show in *The American Sexual Tragedy*—to overemphasize physique and other external manifestations of "manliness" or "womanliness"; and if we must designate certain human traits as desirable, then it would be far wiser if we selected those that can be worked upon and changed, such as standing one's own ground in spite of what other people think, than if we choose anatomical attributes which are largely beyond our own control.

If your child is bullying others mainly because he has low frustration tolerance and cannot stand—or thinks he cannot stand—not to have things his own way, then this is the idea that you should counterattack. Try to show him that it would be nice for him to have others continually do his bidding, but that this is hardly necessary; and that if other children do not kowtow to him, he can easily stand their doing what they want rather than what he wants. Teach him, again, that being overly annoyed at being frustrated is not being strong—as the movies, unfortunately, would often have us believe, as they show gangsters punching others in the jaw when they are thwarted—but that it is actually weak. A truly strong individual is tough-*minded* rather than just tough-knuckled. He does not like the rebuffs and unniceties of the world; but, at the same time, he does not whine about them and think that they must immediately be righted by his making things rough for others.

Your main technique, then, in trying to overcome your child's bullying should be corrective rather than punitive, educational rather than restrictive. You have to try to teach him (or her) the proper kinds of attitudes, ones that will tend to prevent him from having bullying tendencies in the first place, rather than ones that will induce him to stop himself after he has already started to intimidate others. This takes some time to do in most cases, since children can mainly first correct themselves after the fact—after they have already made mistakes. It is only after they have uncondemningly corrected themselves for a fairly long period of time that they then start, as it were, correcting themselves prophylactically, beforehand. And although—as in learning to tie their own shoelaces—this process at first has to be well thought out and carefully worked upon, it later becomes semiautomatic and requires little effort. At first, therefore if you use the right teachings with him, you may expect your bullying child to become more adept at squelching his threatening tendencies. But ultimately he may lose the tendencies almost completely, and just not think of intimidating others to get his own way.

Destructiveness

If your child is destructive, and particularly if he resorts to vandalism and other kinds of public sabotage, you may well have a real problem to handle. Not that a certain amount of this kind of behavior is not healthy, for it is. Most children at times chalk up sidewalks or fences, take light bulbs out of public buildings, damage other children's possessions, and engage in many other kinds of minor vandalism. Largely, they do it to show off or to save face with their peers; but sometimes they do it quite on their own because they are in a bad mood or because they want to see how much they can get away with.

Some types of seemingly destructive behavior on the part of children, as Shirley Camper points out, are even constructive. Thus, a child may take apart a watch because he is curious to see what makes it tick; and he may thereby destroy it without having any intention of so doing. Or a child may enjoy working with a hammer and saw on old pieces of wood; but having no such pieces about, may start to rip up the living-room furniture. In these cases, you may simply solve the "destructiveness" problem by seeing that a sufficient number of old watches, or hunks of wood, or even old pieces of furniture are around to provide the child with materials that he can less destructively take apart.

Another cause of destructiveness in a child is his ignorance of societal attitudes toward property rights. It takes a long time for him learn, even though his baby sister's toy dog may be great fun to throw against the wall, that (a) she, too, has a right to enjoy playing with it; that (b) she owns it; and that (c) she is likely to become very upset if its stuffing starts pouring out and it loses a leg. Frequently the parent, in lieu of teaching the child that he must not impinge on others' rights, violates the child's *own* rights by failing to respect his toys or the inviolability of his playroom.

The fact remains, however, that some children, and often those who are old enough to know better, are really wreckers of many things in their environment and that they demolish for disturbed reasons: (a) They are hostile and want to wreak vengeance on other people and their possessions. (b) They feel weak and want to compensate for these feelings by showing how "powerful" they can be. (c) They are overly frustrated because they cannot compete well in some fair and aboveboard manner, so they sometimes resort to underhanded or sneaky kinds of destructiveness in order to "win." (d) They are terribly unhappy about something and find that they can divert themselves from their unhappiness, at least temporarily, by being destructive. (e) They want to show off before others and can think of no better way of doing so than by breaking windows, ripping up furniture, or indulging in some other dramatic form of sabotage.

The best way to deal with this kind of behavior on the part of your child is, as ever, first to get at its philosophic roots. The destructive child believes that he is stronger, or more worth-while, or somehow greater if he gives vent to physical force against material objects. Actually, of course, he isn't, since he doesn't change himself one iota even when he radically modifies, by destroying, the objects around him. He therefore has to be disabused of the notion that physical violence against the world will enhance him, release him, or make up for his inner frustration.

As in the case of the angry and temper-tantrum-ridden individual, the destructive child generally sees only two major possibilities of life: (a) feeling upset inwardly and taking out this feeling on his surroundings; or (b) feeling upset and suffocating his feelings until he believes that he is going to burst at the seams. Of these two possible modes of behavior, he finds that the first is better than the second—and often he is quite right about this, because it is the lesser of these two evils.

There is a third path, which you should try to teach a destructive child. Attempt to show him that he is angry and hence destructive because of *what he tells himself* about a given situation, and not because of *the situation itself*. Thus, he becomes angry at school restrictions not because they are restrictive, but because he convinces himself, over and over, that these restrictions are unfair and that he cannot stand unfairness of this sort. After convincing himself of these things—all of which are highly questionable and essentially false—he then feels "irresistibly" impelled to break the school's windows, or take out its light bulbs, or carve up its desks, or to do other destructive acts against its "unfair" and "intolerable" system.

If, therefore, you can show the child that restrictions are not necessarily unfair; that he can stand unfairness even when it does exist; and that he is making a situation really intolerable by lashing out against it, when it will palpably do him no good to do so—there is then a good chance that he will be much less destructive. But not only do you have to convince the child of these points—more importantly, you must finally induce him to *convince himself* of them. For, if you merely brainwash him of his original brainwashing, he can easily reinstitute it and sink back to the old morass. Depropagandization itself, therefore, is not enough; you have to persuade him to keep thinking, to keep depropagandizing himself—practically forever.

At the same time, of course, you can show him the advantages of constructive courses of action. You can show him that not being vandalistic, but instead being cooperative with authorities (even when these authorities are not wholly fair to him) is much more likely to get them on his side, and to induce them to do away with some of the restrictions he deplores. And you can show him that if he makes a concerted, but still creative and unhostile attack on the things that bother him in life, such as unfair restrictions that are placed on him, he is much more likely to correct these bothersome things than if he negativistically and hatefully tries to assail them or the people who are instituting them. By being caught up in constructive efforts, he is likely to have little energy left to expend in fruitless retaliations against the situation.

Don't, in other words, try to prevent the destructive child from taking action against whatever he considers annoying, for that is a healthy, vigorous way of meeting the vicissitudes of life. Try to prevent him, instead, from taking ineffective, unproductive action—the kind that will only get him what he doesn't want out of life, and that will quite possibly help make the world even less fair for him and others than it now is. Sane destructiveness can be a good thing—as when we have to knock down an old, useless building to construct a new, more useful edifice in its place. But insane, wild, shotgun-type destructiveness is the issue; and that is the kind that you should try to win him away from. If this is your goal, then you can truthfully show him, in most instances, that you are out for his own good, and not merely for your own or for that of society; and that by considering others, too, he is most likely to help himself.

Cheating

Cheating, like most other forms of antisocial behavior, is not all to the bad, and is sometimes logical. If all your child's classmates are cheating on an exam, and he refuses to do so but also does not inform on the others, then he will, at least on a short-range basis, be severely handicapped. Or if some crotchety old lady refuses to let your child and his peers play anywhere near her house, and he and the others try to see how near they can play and get away without her noticing them, this kind of cheating is perfectly healthy, and it is probably best to ignore it. Encouraging it is sometimes risky—since the child may then overgeneralize and think that you are condoning all kinds of cheating. But if you make a great issue of minor cheating activities on his part, you will probably also do more harm than good.

Other forms of cheating may by no means be so harmless. If your child routinely cheats on examinations at school, this may well be a sign of his having no confidence that he can pass such exams honestly and may mean that he has an exceptionally low estimation of himself. If he cheats in his transactions with the other boys, or in keeping score in the ball game, or in claiming to have done more of the household chores than he has actually accomplished, this may mean that he is a perennial goofer who thinks that the world is too rough for him, and who is determined to get away with everything he possibly can get away with in life.

These more serious forms of cheating—just like the other kinds of conduct problems that we have been examining in this chapter—have philosophic as well as psychological roots. The youngster who always cheats on examinations usually believes (a) that it is terrible for him to fail on an exam; (b) that he would be a perfect fool if he did fail; (c) that he cannot risk being imperfect and therefore has to succeed beautifully on the exam; and (d) that because he has cheated before and has managed to pass that way, the chances are that he could never succeed without cheating and therefore must resort to this pattern of examination-taking forever. These are all value systems or philosophic hypotheses which the cheater strongly holds—and holds without any confirming evidence. They are essentially definitions that hold water only because the child thinks that they do. But they are very powerful values and motivate human behavior; they literally compel him to keep cheating and therefore never to discover what his true examination-taking ability is.

By the same token, the child who chronically cheats on doing his chores may easily hold certain other values: (a) that it is horrible for him to carry out certain moderately onerous tasks; (b) that it is wise for him to spend more time and energy avoiding than doing such tasks; (c) that life is entirely unfair to him if it forces him to do the same kind of work that others generally do; (d) that he is too weak and inferior to survive in a world of difficulties; and (e) that he is a great person if he outwits his parents and others and successfully goofs. These, again, are all values which he strongly tends to hold, but for which there is, of course, no empirical confirmatory evidence. And they are values which, if he believes in them, will normally get him into much more trouble than they seem, on the surface, to be worth.

These kinds of values, which underlie most serious cheating by children, can be calmly attacked and undermined. You can, for instance, steadily point out to your child, in an objective and dispassionate way, that it is not terrible, though it may be quite inconvenient, for him to fail exams; that even if he does consistently fail, he is still not worthless, but can be a valuable human being to himself (and sometimes to the world as well); that he can risk being imperfect, and be on the same level as the rest of us fallible human beings; and that even if he has cheated many times in the past, there is no evidence that he could not do well on tests if he stopped cheating and buckled down to some active studying. You can also point out to the child who cheats for goofing reasons that it may be onerous but it is hardly horrible for him to carry out various chores; that it is hardly wise for him to exert as much or more energy avoiding life's difficulties as he would have to do in successfully facing them, for failure to acquire tools (such as proper study habits, the ability to solve math problems) may handicap him in the *future* and impel *further* cheating to cover his deficiencies; that things are hardly exceptionally unfair to him when he has to perform certain onerous duties; that he is not too weak to survive in a world of difficulties; and that he is hardly a great person if he does manage to outwit the authorities and to "successfully" goof.

By your own noncheating, nonperfectionistic, and nongoofing actions, as well as by highly verbal attacks on his philosophic assumptions, you can often break the ideological back of your child's cheating propensities.

You can also, if you wish, use penalization techniques, to see that he does not get away with his cheating. But by penalization, I mean just that—and not punishment; for the latter, as we have been showing in this book, include degrading the individual while also penalizing him; and there is no point in your degrading your child if you discover him cheating. One of the main reasons why he does cheat, in fact, is because he would consider himself degraded if he did poorly and if he did not cheat. If, therefore, you depreciate him for cheating, you are only thereby tending to enhance, rather than to alleviate, his deep-seated feelings of inadequacy. So if you want to penalize him for his cheating, you may do so in those cases where he is most persistent in this form of behavior, and where other persuasive methods do not seem to be working. But penalize him in an effort to help rid him of his cheating-creating philosophy and not to get him to live with it, thereby merely squelching the tendencies that he still very much keeps alive underneath the surface of his personality.

Should you inform on your child if he is cheating? Usually, no. In the first place, if you tell the authorities that he is cheating on tests or something of that sort, they may not be as permissive and unpunishing as you are. Secondly, behavior such as cheating should normally be dealt with directly by you, as his parents, and not by other authorities. Thirdly, if you do inform on him, he may well consider you an enemy, and may completely stop confiding in you in the future. Fourthly, there are usually better ways in which you can deal with his cheating other than by "ratting" on him.

Whatever you do about his cheating, the main thing is to try to discover its philosophic core and then to try to make him aware of it. If you and he can discover why he is cheating consistently, then there is a good chance that something can be done about it. The knowledge of the cause itself will not necessarily do away with the symptom, but it may mean that half the battle is won.

Delinquency

About the most antisocial thing your child can do is to be truly delinquent, which usually means to participate in a variety of acts, such as truancy, vandalism, stealing, gang warfare, and even more serious acts such as murder. More often than not, he would be engaging in these acts with several other children, rather than alone; but it is also possible for him to be a loner and still a delinquent.

Is delinquency ever within the normal range? Yes, at least in a few cases. A number of years ago, when I was Chief Psychologist of the New Jersey Department of Institutions and Agencies, I did psychotherapy once a week with the delinquent girls who were incarcerated in the State Home for Girls in Trenton. Most of these girls—and particularly, of course, those that were referred to me—were exceptionally neurotic or psychotic individuals who had first committed delinquent acts and were later caught and convicted mainly because they were seriously disturbed. Thus, they would openly lie, steal, stay home from school, or have promiscuous sex relations, even after they had already been in some amount of difficulty for their previous similar escapades; and it was almost inevitable that they would be caught and apprehended.

I discovered, however, that at least a few of these incarcerated delinquents were in the normal range of both intelligence and emotional stability, and that they were largely victims of circumstances. Thus, there were girls who came from poor neighborhoods, who were often Negro, and who had exceptionally rigid, moralistic parents. When they joined in with other boys and girls and engaged in slightly rowdy activities, they were either quickly pounced upon by the authorities or were actually reported to them by their parents. Where other children, from white middle-class homes, would have been stoutly defended by their parents and protected from being taken to court or adjudged juvenile delinquents, these youngsters were sometimes literally helped into the reformatory by their own families. Ironically, some of them became genuine delinquents after they were incarcerated—since, as everyone seems to know, reformatories and prisons are excellent places for learning better methods of lawbreaking.

The fact remains, however, that most adjudged delinquents are highly disturbed individuals; many of them are outrightly psychotic rather than neurotic. Children who consistently commit armed robbery, or who seriously hurt others, or who go to real extremes and commit murder, are almost always at least in the borderline psychotic range of behavior; and therefore they compulsively rather than volitionally perform their delinquent acts. They are not even, in a psychological sense, responsible for much of their behavior, since they are not very well able to control it; and they certainly should not be condemned for performing their misdeeds. They often have to be put into protective custody—preferably in a mental hospital rather than a reformatory—in order to stop them from committing further antisocial acts; but they should not be excoriated for being institutionalized.

More concretely, juvenile delinquents usually have exceptionally low estimations of themselves and are thoroughly convinced that they cannot compete successfully with others if they stick to normal pursuits. They believe that they are worthless; they feel that they will never be truly accepted by members of respectable society; they frequently view themselves as physically ugly or undesirable; they tend to do poorly in school and to drop out when they are still on a low educational level; and they have serious doubts about their manliness or womanliness. Sometimes they are exceptionally defensive, so that they are not conscious of their underlying feelings of inferiority, and pretend and "feel" that they are actually superior. But very often they are fully conscious of their inadequacies and imagine enormous handicaps to go with the ones that they actually do possess.

Like other disturbed individuals, delinquents are more often than not severe goofers. They find routine tasks, such as attending school or working steadily on a job, monotonous and boring; they shy away from any work that is difficult or requires persistence; and they get great joy out of making a "soft" living. They are consequently, once again, literally driven to occupational pursuits, such as gambling or stealing or strong-arm tactics, which are antisocial and criminal in our society.

Delinquents are also, in many instances, arrant excitement-seekers. They crave momentary thrills and rousing "good times" and therefore they constantly drink, smoke marijuana, take goofballs, or even resort to heroin. Their crimes themselves may seem highly exciting to them; or they may have to resort to crime in order to pay for their excitement-seeking. Similarly, because they rarely are able to attain good, steady heterosexual relationships, they often pay for their sex, in one form or another, if they are males, or resort to prostitution, directly or indirectly, if they are females.

As can again be seen from this description of their character, delinquents are usually as emotionally disturbed as they can possibly be; and it is folly to talk about dealing with delinquency, on either an individual or a social basis, unless we take into account the depth of the disturbance that is present. So if your child happens to be involved in delinquent acts, you would do well to assume that he is probably emotionally unstable, and that his acts are part and parcel of this kind of instability. This means that you'd better look for the philosophic roots of his disturbance: the anxiety- and hostility-creating ideas which encourage and practically drive him to behave in a seriously antisocial way.

Melvin D. was a fifteen-year-old boy who came from an upper-middle-class home and who had been presumably given all the advantages of a respectable upbringing. He had a good allowance; was given a great amount of personal freedom; went to an excellent private school; and had parents who continually went to bat for him whenever he got into trouble—which he had been doing regularly, from the age of eight onward. When I saw him for psychotherapy, he was on probation for two years, mainly because he and one of his older chums had broken into a nearby gas station late one night and robbed it of thirty dollars in cash and whatever else they could lay their hands on.

Melvin's main gripe against the world was that he was very small for his age and looked two or three years younger than he actually was. Because of his height, he could not make any of the school teams, was not popular with the girls in his school or around his neighborhood, and was sometimes considered to be a sissy. He also felt unfairly dealt with by life because although his parents were kind and permissive, they, too, were ridiculously small-statured in his eyes, and he thought that they looked silly, and that the whole family group made an asinine appearance.

When I saw Melvin for treatment, I attempted to show him that he may, indeed, have been somewhat handicapped by his small stature, but that he was really much more handicapped by his own denigrating ideas about himself and his family and by his exaggerated fears of what others might do to him. Even if others did not despise him or overpower him, as he oversuspiciously thought that they might, his own self-deprecatory attitudes were sufficiently overpowering to undermine him; and if he wanted to get along in life, and live up to the potential which he seemed to possess, he would have to give up his inadequacy feelings and try to make it in the world *in spite of* his real, but actually rather minor, handicaps.

At first, Melvin would have none of my arguments. He had already obtained some notoriety in his school for his delinquency; and although he was somewhat ashamed of the fact that he had not got away with the crime he and his associate had attempted, he was rather pleased by the fact that everyone knew about it, and presumably thought him daring. As a tactical measure, I first worked with him on his shame, trying to show him that he had nothing to be ashamed of, either in having tried to rob the store in the first place or in failing in his robbery attempt in the second place. I contended that even if both these things were wrong and stupid—which I, for one, thought that they were—he'd better accept himself as a bright human being who from time to time did very stupid deeds. That was the way of the world, I insisted: the Einsteins and the Oppenheimers, the Leonardos and the Michelangelos, no matter how brilliant and talented they were, all behaved quite moronically at times—because they were human, because they were inevitably fallible.

Moreover, I said to Melvin at one point, "even if you were *generally* idiotic and *kept* doing more crazy than sane things, you still would not have to blame or depreciate yourself; you still wouldn't be a bum."

"Why wouldn't I be?" he asked. "What would be good about me then?"

"*You* would be good about you," I answered. "Your goodness as a person is your you-ness, your aliveness, and not the things that you do."

"But if I don't do anything very well, and nobody thinks I am any good, how could what you call my you-ness be anything but bad?"

"Because what I call your you-ness is not your performances and not what others think about you. These constitute your external value, or your worth to the world. And, under the circumstances that you state, your external value would be low; and that would be sad, since it is nice to know that others value you highly and will give you certain benefits, such as love or money, because they do. But your external value, or your worth to others, is not the same thing as your internal value, or your worth to yourself. You could *still* have a high self-worth, or like yourself distinctly, even when others did not like you and thus awarded you a low external value."

"How *could* I? That sounds like thinking that I'm Napoleon, when everybody else knows that I am not!"

"No, not exactly. Being Napoleon is still an external thing; and if everyone thought that you were Melvin and not Napoleon, you would be Melvin—no matter what you thought. But having self-worth is not an external thing, but is quite within your own control, and does not depend on what others think of you. Isn't it possible, for example, for everyone to think that you're really a great guy and a scholar and for you to think that you're just not great or scholarly enough, and that therefore you're no darned good?"

"Yes, I suppose it is, though that would be rare."

"Would it be? Look at the actual situation of your life, right now. Most people think you are fairly short and so do you—so both you and they are measuring your external measurements fairly accurately. But you think you are *too* short and that you are not a very good person for being so short; while most other people seem to ignore how short you are and think you are all right in spite of your height. So, obviously, your estimation of yourself—how awful you are for being short—is different from theirs."

"But I could be right and they could be wrong—isn't that possible?"

"Yes, it certainly is. But that isn't the point. The point is that *evaluations* of yourself as a person, as a living individual, are never really right or wrong—they just *are*. You are entitled to to think that you are inferior for being short and others are entitled to think that you are all right for being short—although you and they would both have to admit, if a measuring rod were used on you and on other people, that you would definitely be shorter than most of the other boys of your age."

"You seem to mean that everyone would have to agree that they are tall or short, in relation to the measurement of others; but my measurement or evaluation of myself can't really be evaluated in the same kind of objective way."

"That's just what I do mean: that measurements of external things, such as height, weight, and even intelligence are fairly objective and can be legitimately assessed; but that internal values, such as how good or worth-while you are *as a person* cannot really be measured in the same way. Values like these are not objective but subjective, and there is no way of scientifically proving them. You cannot decide whether you are short or tall—for your own height and that of other people decides that for you.

But you can decide whether you are good or bad for being short
—that is your own decision, the personal and subjective value
that you place on your measurements."

"But I could decide, couldn't I, that it is good for me to be
short or tall?"

"Yes, in some degree you could objectively decide—and so
could other people decide for you—that it is beneficial for you
to be tall, for then you could make the basketball team, see better when you were in a crowd, push smaller people around, etc.
But because it is good—meaning, advantageous—for you to be
tall does not mean that you are good for so being. You, and only
you, would still have to decide whether you value yourself for
being tall or whether you think you are a bum for being that
way."

"Then how, or on what basis, should I evaluate myself? The
whole thing seems very slippery!"

"It certainly does! I would say that either you should not
evaluate what you call your *self* at all—but merely *accept* this
process of your being, just because you are alive and therefore
have some kind of a self. Or else, if you must measure this *self*,
I'd say that you would be much better off if you arbitrarily defined it as good rather than as bad—and let it go at that!"

"Why? Because it just works out better that way?"

"Yes, that's exactly why. If you measure your self-worth or
your internal value to yourself at all, and you define this self as
bad, rotten, or no good, then you will get into serious trouble;
while if you define it as good or worth-while, you will not get
into that kind of trouble."

"So if I say, '*I* am no good because I am short or because I
am anything else,' I will feel terrible and will tend to act badly;
while if I say, '*I* am good, whether or not I am short,' I will feel
better and will tend to act well. Seems odd, and yet I think I'm
beginning to get it. But it *is* slippery!"

"It certainly is!"

Melvin continued to get it, and he could soon distinguish quite
accurately between himself, or his self-concept, and his traits and
his deeds. In this respect he did much better than many of my

adult patients do; and it should be understood that I was able to talk to him on this high philosophic level only because he was very bright and sophisticated. If he had been younger or less intelligent, I would have used a much simpler approach. It is surprising, however, how many sharp children of Melvin's age, or even a few years younger, can be approached in this philosophic fashion, in spite of the fact that they are highly disturbed. Using other methods of psychotherapy with them—such as ventilation of feeling or play therapy—often helps them to *feel* considerably better but not necessarily to *get* better; while if the rational-emotive philosophic approach works, it achieves much deeper and more lasting results.

In any event, after a good many more talks with Melvin along the foregoing lines, he was able to accept the fact that even if he was somewhat handicapped because of his small stature, he certainly didn't have to reject himself entirely because of it. When he began to understand this, he began to lose his defensiveness, became much less hostile to others, saw that he didn't need to gain their attention in a boasting, delinquent manner, and buckled down to much more constructive aspects of living. He went on to college and was even able to use his shortness and his slightness to become coxswain of his school's boat-racing team. His conduct became exemplary, and he relinquished, even in his fantasies, his delinquent tendencies.

Similarly, many other delinquents can be handled by showing them that they philosophically believe that they must do perfectly well in their school, sports, social, or other activities, and because, not being able to achieve these high levels, and irrationally hating themselves unless they do, they compensatorily turn to delinquent modes of behavior. They can also often be shown that their hostility toward others is unjustified, even when these others are treating them badly, because they are falsely convincing themselves that the world should be immensely kind and giving to them, when it normally isn't. If these irrational ideas, which underlie their delinquent thoughts and actions are calmly, persistently shown to them, and then dispassionately demolished, many of these delinquents can become self-respecting, unhostile individuals who, at least, keep their delinquency within normal ranges.

Summary

Children who have conduct problems are not merely acting in relation to some outside stimuli, which can then be changed. Sometimes this is true, for most children tend to act badly when they are sufficiently abused or deprived; and we might say that it is their "normal" tendency to do this. Consequently, some problems of conduct may be resolved by your determining what unfortunate factors exist in the child's life, and by your seeing that these are minimized or eliminated. Thus, you can stop being overly critical of a child who has delinquent tendencies; see that he is not unnecessarily put upon by others; do away with exceptional deprivations or frustrations that he now has to bear; and otherwise change his environment to reduce undue pressures on him. Similarly, if you believe that his companions have any unusual influence on him—as when he is delinquent partly or largely because he lives in a neighborhood where delinquency is prestigeful—you may sometimes be able to remove him from these influences by moving to another neighborhood, by sending him to a different school, or by forbidding him to associate with certain children. Along somewhat similar lines, you can also use diversion tactics, so that when the child's environment is too pressuring, you can try to interest him in constructive sports, plan a family program to keep him occupied, praise him for doing what he does do reasonably well, and otherwise try to take his mind off the fact that conditions around him are deplorable.

Changing the child's external environment and diverting him from the unfortunate conditions around him are therapeutic methods, however, that have limited scope and effectiveness. In the main, children are problems to themselves and others largely because they interpret their surroundings poorly and because they view themselves and others in a jaundiced, negativistic light. For a more depth-centered cure of their poor conduct, therefore, you have to try to persuade them to question and challenge their destructive views, both in theory and in practice, until they finally realize that they are self-defeating and then give them up. Moreover, to do a thorough job in this respect, you have to teach these children to acquire a perennial habit of stopping and thinking, when things go wrong in their lives, and of questioning their own philosophies and assumptions about the world and themselves.

Is it easy to rear children, and especially those who have already shown antisocial behavior, in this manner? Indeed it is not! After all, they are children; they do have low mental ages, even when they are intelligent; they have difficulty in stopping to think and find it much easier to let themselves go suggestibly and uncritically through life. So don't expect any miracles in regard to teaching them thoughtful, rational attitudes. Don't, in fact, expect anything—but still try, as hard as you can, for a better solution to the problem than now exists. To some degree, and sometimes to a surprising degree, you will be rewarded. But you can no more be a perfect teacher than a child can be an infallible learner. Human beings, both yourself and others, are invariably error-prone. Always, as you do your best to help malfunctioning children, remember *that!*

9

Helping Children with Personal Behavior Problems

In the previous chapter, we considered what to do to help children who have social behavior problems, that is, those children who act badly with others and are therefore guilty of poor social conduct. Many children, however, have behavior problems in the course of which they hardly bother others at all, even though they do inflict severe penalties on themselves; and this is the kind of personal, self-defeating behavior that we shall consider in the present chapter.

Speech Disorders

Although speech disorders of a serious nature are probably not the most common symptoms of childhood disturbance, they are certainly one of the most visible. If a child is unusually silent; if he continually stammers and stutters; if he mutters under his breath; if he lisps; or if he speaks too rapidly or too slowly, almost everyone soon notices that there is something wrong with his speech, and pretty quickly someone calls this to his attention and makes him highly aware of his disability. This, of course, is unlike what occurs if he has certain other disorders—such as bedwetting or over- or undereating problems—since these may not come to the attention of any but his family members and may consequently not become anything of a social problem.

Are all speech defects caused by emotional disturbances, most especially anxiety? Probably not. Some children speak poorly because they have physiological anomalies, such as a cleft palate, which originally start them in this direction. Some directly learn poor speaking habits from their parents, who themselves may lisp, splutter, or otherwise speak poorly. Some are unwittingly trained to speak oddly early in their lives because they get some original gain—such as the pleased laughter of others—for doing so. Some naturally talk very fast and therefore at times stutter, stammer, or splutter because they have not learned to slow themselves down.

Dr. Isaac Karlin holds that stuttering is basically an organic disorder, even though it may be aggravated and perpetuated by emotional and environmental factors. He believes that boys have more trouble than girls in maturing, as far as their neural structures are concerned, and that therefore they stutter much more frequently. They sometimes outgrow their difficulty because myelinization of their nerve fibers (that is, acquisition of insulation around these fibers) takes place later in their lives. Many other authorities on stuttering have held somewhat similar views.

Although the organic theories of speech defects such as stuttering have not yet been fully validated, there is a good chance that there is something to them. My own observations tend to show that serious stutterers have a trigger-happy kind of nervous system, which makes them more easily liable to certain kind of speech defects than other children. This does not mean that they have to become stutterers or stammerers; because if they were ideally raised, many of them would not reach this stage of maldevelopment. But it may well mean that it is much easier for these children to acquire and to retain speech defects than it would be for neurologically more normal children to do so.

There is also a probability that certain children, as we have noted before in this book, are more liable to acquire almost any kind of an emotional disturbance than are other children because they are born with tendencies to think crookedly, to behave rigidly, and therefore to be unusually anxious and compulsive; and such children, again, may well become upset about their speech and may consequently tend to stutter or have other speech defects. Studies have indicated a significantly higher degree of rigidity, inhibition, and immaturity among stutterers than among nonstutterers. It is difficult to say whether these problems cause the original speech difficulties, result from them, or, which is most likely, are a combination of both.

The point is that speech disorders are probably resultants of a combination of inborn and environmental factors, rather than of emotional factors alone. This may mean that in some instances it is not possible to ward them off entirely, but only to help the child have them in a minimal way; and in other instances they can be completely prevented or eliminated.

A time comes in the lives of many children, however, when they not only fail to overcome their early speech defects, but actually start worsening them. To a large degree, as Dr. Wendell Johnson was fond of pointing out, this is because our society, and the child we raise in it, evaluates and does not merely describe speech difficulties. For if we merely note that a child repeats words and syllables, sometimes prolongs his sounds, and from time to time puts in unnecessary uh-uh-uhs, we are giving an accurate description of the way he talks. But if we say that the child stutters, then we are generally making a judgment on his speech—noting that he is doing something that he should not do and that he presumably is to be blamed for doing.

Because speech disorders are so visible, they are a prime example of a child's acquiring a secondary as well as a primary disturbance, the former often being worse than the latter. Thus, a child may originally stutter because he is overanxious to please others, to answer them quickly, and to get out as many words as he can in a short period of time. However, once his stuttering is noticed and brought to his attention, he may become so ashamed of this symptom that he is much more intent than ever before on pleasing others and more anxious *about* his stuttering —that he consequently stutters much worse than ever. His original, fairly moderate need to please others may become an enormous overconcern with what they think of him; and soon the problem of his stuttering, and his conviction that people look down upon him because he has this speech defect, may overshadow all the aspects of his life and render him exceptionally disturbed.

What can you do if your child does have speech problems? A number of things:

(1) Take the matter calmly and don't catastrophize about it to yourself—let alone aloud, in his presence! Quite possibly, it may be alleviated; and even if it can't be, it is most unlikely to have entirely dire consequences. Millions of human beings have led happy lives in spite of serious speech defects; and, if worse comes to worst in this regard, your child may be one of these millions.

(2) Do not bring the child's stuttering or stammering forcibly to his attention, and certainly never do so in any negative way. Do not call him a "stutterer" or anything like that. If you find that, from time to time, you just have to laugh the way he speaks, do so good-naturedly, and tell him that others will do so in the same manner. If he, on his own, begins to be ashamed of his speech, show him that it is probably not that important, that it will probably improve if he stops worrying about it, and that even if it never improves, he is a worth-while human being who can get along satisfactorily in the world, even if he has this kind of handicap.

One of my patients, after talking over her child's speech difficulties with me and the other patients with whom she was having group therapy, did exactly the right thing with her son. When she saw that he was frequently "stuttering" and "stammering" when he was six years of age, she deliberately did not bring this to his attention, but acted as if he were speaking perfectly well. Not being evaluated as a stutterer, he never came to see himself as one; and consequently, within the next two years, he began to speak more regularly, and soon he was not stuttering or stammering at all.

(3) There are several palliative methods which can be used to help a stutterer, but their use is questionable since they often do more harm than good. Thus, the child can be taught to whistle or snap his fingers, as he starts to speak; to sing instead of talking his words; to stop and think of what he wants to say before he says it; to take a deep breath before speaking; etc. These methods are diversionary, in that they divert the stutterer from focusing on his own stuttering, and are therefore helpful. But they also give him the concept that he *is* a stutterer and that the only thing he can do about this is to use tricks, from time to time, to help himself. They do not tackle his concept of himself, and they thus leave him still essentially afraid of his speech defect.

(4) Let the child alone when he is speaking and do not come to his aid in an impatient manner. In this way, you can give him the idea that he has the ability to get out the words he wants and that he need not worry about your waiting for him to produce them.

(5) Try to be as interested as you can be in the content of what the child is saying. Many of the things he talks about are thoroughly unimportant to you but are supremely important to him; and if you show him that you have no interest in these things, he loses his incentive to talk about them or wants to get them out of the way quickly. He will then tend to speak about them badly.

(6) Watch your own speech when you are talking to him. If you are hurried, hypertense, and agitated when you speak, he will tend to feel under pressure. If you speak fairly slowly, simply, and sometimes briefly, he will tend to follow suit and to speak better himself.

(7) Try not to be anxious *yourself* about his speech. It is certainly too bad if he is a stutterer or stammerer; but that's all it is—too bad. Even if he never overcomes his speech defect, he will not be impossibly handicapped for the rest of his life; and there is nothing for you to be ashamed of if this occurs. If you will take a noncatastrophizing attitude toward his speech trou-

bles, there is a good chance that he will likewise take this kind of attitude; if on the other hand you are woefully upset about his difficulties, he will probably be just as upset himself.

(8) Encourage but do not force the child to participate in speech situations which he finds troublesome. Try to get him to recite publicly, to act in school plays, or to speak up in social groups—but do not insist that he do these things. It is true that the more he does them, the more practice he will get, and the more he will tend to see that the world will not come to an end if he speaks badly. But if he is forced to do so, he will not only dread this, in most instances, but will also resent your forcing him, and may (consciously or unconsciously) deliberately speak badly.

(9) If it is possible to regulate the child's surroundings so that some of the tension and strain of living is at least temporarily removed, this may well be advisable. On the whole, children have to learn to live with the regular routines and difficulties of life; but a stuttering child is usually extremely tense, and then also tense about his speech problems. Therefore, if he can be temporarily relieved to some of the strains of living, he may be able to overcome his speech difficulties—in which case, he may be expected, once again, to face the things that were made somewhat easier for him for a while. But beware lest you shelter a child with speech problems so much that you add social retardation to his difficulties.

(10) In general, do not make unusual demands on the child or try to push him beyond his capacities. If he achieves up to the limits of his abilities, fine; but if he is somewhat underachieving, this may be permissible in his particular case, since demanding that he live up to his full potential may be anxiety-provoking for him. Don't expect him to do things that he cannot readily understand and perform; and don't even expect him to do many things which are well within his theoretical capacity. Show him that he *can* do better than he is doing, if he wishes to work for what he wants in life, but that if he decides not to work, it is hardly a crime.

(11) Especially in view of the fact that stuttering and other

speech defects may be underlain by neurophysiological deficiencies, it is best that you do everything possible to see that your child is in good physical condition. Many individuals with tics and other semineurological disorders exhibit them strongly when they are tired, underweight, or physically ill; and the same may be true of stuttering. Although keeping your diet to a good health regimen will by no means necessarily cure his speech disorders, it may help him keep the kind of psychophysical balance that will enable him to minimize his difficulties in this respect.

(12) If the child becomes overconcerned about his speech problems—because others may draw them rather negatively to his attention—show him that many normal children have similar problems and that it is not necessarily pathological for him to be afflicted. (Actually, it is the rare child or adult who does not have speech defects in some degree. Almost all of us, for example, have some local accent which, because most of the others reared in our neighborhood also have it, we do not consider a defect. Actually, however, it is; and some of us, if we later want to do a good deal of public speaking, or go on the stage, or otherwise present ourselves to audiences, learn to overcome this kind of accent.) Indicate to the child that if he remains calm about his difficulty he way well get over it. Show him that at the very worst he will remain somewhat handicapped; but that this hardly means he is an inadequate person, and certainly does not mean that he cannot excel in various other ways. Do not gloss over the fact that he has a problem or be Pollyannaish about it; but do not give him any indication that he must be irreparably damaged just because he has it.

Tics

A tic is a twitch or a jerk, usually of a specific and limited part of the body, which is compulsive and is beyond the individual's control. A great many children have tics at one time or other; frequently these tics are outgrown if nothing is done to bring them to the attention of the child. In some instances, the tic remains but only erupts on special kinds of occasions: as when the child is tired or overexcited or run-down.

Like virtually all forms of childhood disturbances, it seems likely that tics have both a physiological and a psychological cause. Certain children are probably born with a predisposition to twitch and jerk in various parts of their bodies; and then, as in the case of speech defects, they frequently notice that they do so from time to time, become overconcerned about this fact, and then anxiously develop a *real* tic on a temporary or a permanent basis. Other children, who have exactly the same kind of tendency to exhibit tics, pay no attention to them, and do not have them negatively drawn to their attention by others; and consequently these children tic mildly for a while, and eventually not at all.

It is possible, of course, for tics to be of purely psychogenic origin, since children may twitch and jerk at first solely because they are under some kind of severe psychological stress. Then, once they notice this twitching and think that they should not be so afflicted, they unwittingly focus on it and make it worse and worse. Also, generally disturbed children usually need some form of outlet for their disturbances; and twitching and jerking constitute a "logical" kind of symptom for such children in many instances.

If your child has one or a series of major tics, it is usually best to treat this symptom in much the same way as you might treat speech defects (discussed in the previous section of this chapter). In the main, you should try to ignore the tic as much as possible and try to refrain from showing any annoyance or criticism of him for displaying it. Fortunately, in this respect, you often have the advantage of his tic's being relatively unnoticeable, since children twitch a great deal anyway, and many tics are not readily discernible. What is more, others may well ignore his tic and not make fun of him in the same way they would be tempted to do if he had an audible speech defect. So, in many instances it is quite possible to ignore the tic completely, and to let the child ignore it himself or to believe that it is a normal manifestation of living. If this can be achieved, the tic is very likely to vanish completely or to remain minimal; and no serious emotional harm results.

In those instances where the tic cannot readily be ignored—because it is very pronounced or because others keep bringing it to the attention of your child—the best thing to do is to explain to the child that twitching of some order is rather common among children, that it means nothing, and that it often disappears with advancing age. Since this is true of various other childhood characteristics—such as obesity, in some instances, or other bodily disproportions—it should not be very difficult to convince the child that the same thing occurs with a tic.

Even when it is necessary to admit to yourself and to the child that the tic is a distinct handicap and that it may be a symptom of emotional disturbance, it is still possible to teach him that he need not be terribly ashamed of having it. He can be shown that just as some children have ugly birthmarks, others have unusually tall and short stature, and still others have different kinds of physical anomalies, he happens to be afflicted with this particular tic. It is too bad that he is so afflicted; it is definitely somewhat handicapping. But it is hardly fatal; it does not mean that everyone will hate him; it will not greatly interfere with his interests or the lifework that he chooses in most instances; and therefore he can live with it rather comfortably, and accept it philosophically as his particular physical cross to bear.

It is necessary in this connection that you not be too distressed about your child's tic yourself. Even if it is a sign of emotional disturbance on his part—which it may well not be—and even if you helped create this disturbance—which may only be partly true—you are not a failure for having a child with a pronounced tic. If others wish to condemn you for this, let them; but—please! —forbear from condemning yourself. You can only do your best to bear and rear a child; and if your best has not been enough, you are hardly a villain. The more you bring yourself to realize this, the more your child is likely to be able to bear his own tic with a good measure of equanimity.

You should not assume that your child's tic must be of emotional origin, since it may also be the result of chorea (St. Vitus's dance), epilepsy, and other forms of neurological ailments. See that the child is given a thorough medical examination to determine if there is any physical origin for the tic (without, incidentally, necessarily letting him know why he is having this examination and thus bringing the tic unduly to his attention); and if this proves to be true, follow medical advice in taking the proper prophylactic and curative measures.

If it is ascertained that there is no physical origin of the child's tic but that emotional stress is the real issue, it may sometimes be necessary to reduce some of the strains and responsibilities that are being placed on the child. Some children, for biological and well as sociological reasons, just cannot seem to take the same amount of stress as others easily can; and it is therefore sometimes necessary to place these children on a less strict schedule, to reduce the number of things they have to be concerned about, to prevent them from being overactive physically, or otherwise to minimize the activities that seem to put them under too much stress and to lead to an eruption of tics.

Better yet, of course, is the procedure advocated throughout this book, namely, that of trying to determine exactly what the child is telling himself to make him unduly upset, and trying to convince him to challenge and question his own anxiety-provoking ideas. If he is terribly perfectionistic or if he demands that the world be exactly the way he wants it to be, he is quite likely to place himself under severe psychological pressure, and hence to bring on symptoms like tics. If you can persuade him to surrender some of his perfectionism and to give up his unrealistic demands on the world, you may help him significantly.

The main thing, again, is: Be calm! Look at the problem, the child and his tic, and not at how horrible it is for the problem to exist. Refuse, utterly refuse, to berate either yourself or the child for his predicament, and see if there is not—as there often is under calm circumstances—some reasonably good solution to the difficulty.

Eating Problems

There are a variety of eating problems that children are prey to, including undereating, overeating, dawdling over food, and making a fuss at mealtimes. Some of these are well within the normal range, especially for young children: for they tend, on many occasions, to fuss and fume about practically everything, including something as regular and as important as meals. Moreover, they learn, at an early age, that their parents consider mealtimes unusual events—that their mothers, for instance, are harried during meals, are therefore less attentive, are more concerned with the children's behavior, and want to get the meal over with as quickly and effectively as possible. And they often take advantage of this fact, just as they take advantage of special outings, automobile rides, visits to a department store, and other occasions when the parents particularly want them to act well.

To try to get a child to eat properly, therefore, is something like waving a muleta before a bull. At the very least, it presents him with a challenging kind of game: the game of let's-see-if-I-can-get-their-goat-and-make-them-see-how-important-I-am! For this very reason, and sometimes for no other, he will be a real pain in the neck during meals, while at most other times he is something of a living doll.

Disturbed and unruly children, moreover, have something of a ball during mealtime, since they then have more materials to play with and more leeway to show their symptoms. They have various kinds of food to manipulate; have liquids which they can squish about; have cups, saucers, glasses, cutlery, and bibs to handle; have hot stoves to consider; usually have the close proximity of other members of the family; are somewhat cooped up in a relatively small space; and have various other paraphernalia and people at hand.

For some children all this is great fun. For others it is a miserable problem. For both types it may easily be made into a holy horror for the parents and other adults who are around.

Because so much emotionalism is at times attached to the meal, it may also be attached to the food itself. Thus, a child who wants to get back at his mother for being forced to eat something or for not being given enough of some other food he likes may well, consciously or unconsciously, punish her by refusing to eat all kinds of other foods or by overeating certain things. Or he may use the food largely as play material and therefore show little interest in it as food. A child may sometimes try to please his mother by quietly eating everything in sight, thus acquiring an artificially induced huge appetite.

Children, moreover, have a good many normal reasons for not eating. At times, they are not hungry because they are naturally overtired, ill, or bored with the food they have been getting. Or they may be so focused on other activities that they begrudge eating time and do not bother to make the most of it. Or they may have digestive systems that are better adapted to small rather than to large diets.

On the other side of the fence, children may overeat for a variety of reasonably normal and healthy reasons. They may be growing fast and actually need a lot of food; they may be ailing and not properly digesting the food they do eat; or they may be so focused on other activities while they are eating that they hardly notice how much food they actually consume.

At the same time, of course, both undereating and overeating may result from various emotional problems. Children may eat too much or starve because they feel themselves horribly unloved, are worried about their schoolwork, feel that their peers do not appreciate them, hate their parents, feel jealous of their younger or older siblings, etc. I once, for example, saw a nine-year-old girl for psychotherapy who for several months ate very little because she felt that her baby brother was being overfed, and she wanted dramatically to show how she was being abused while he was being too well taken care of. Then, when she got a great deal of attention by her undereating, she went to the other extreme and began to stuff herself with food, with the idea that she would thus outdo her baby brother and win great additional favor from her mother. Only when she was helped to like herself and to stop comparing herself to her brother and to other children was she able to stop her poor eating habits and to take normal amounts of nourishment.

Assuming that a child is either abnormally undereating or overeating, what can be done to help him? Several things, including these:

(1) Never condemn him for his poor behavior at the table, no matter how deliberately obnoxious he may be making himself. Condemnation is often one of the very things he would like to bring on himself, for he can then be truly convinced that you do not like him and are unfairly against him. Besides, he may actually want you to punish him for various wrongs he thinks he has committed. In any event, he is generally blaming either himself, you, or both himself and you for something or other; and your condemnatory attitudes will only help make him believe all the more that blaming is a sound philosophy of living and that he should be just as nasty as you are when you condemn him. He almost always has enough other influences in this society leading him to be a blamer; and he certainly does not need yours to "help" him in this respect.

(2) Try to discover the philosophic source of his undereating or overeating. Is he mainly, as we implied in the previous paragraph, blaming you or himself? Is he a victim of low frustration tolerance, who is convincing himself either (a) that the food you give him is not quite elegant enough and that he simply can't eat anything that is not most delectable; or (b) that stopping eating, once he has started, is just too difficult, and there is no reason why he should not pleasantly eat and eat and eat? Is his preoccupation with eating or noneating a result of his basic life problems, and is it serving him as some kind of a temporary diversion from these problems? Find out exactly what is bothering him if you possibly can; and then tackle the source of this thing and see if you cannot change it or (more importantly) his attitude toward it.

(3) Be sure you don't make any kind of fetish out of eating. Don't look upon mealtimes as a very special occasion, when your child's behavior has to be remarkably better than it otherwise is. Don't talk endlessly about food, or be a victim of peculiar food faddism yourself. Set him, if you possibly can, a good example of one who neither overeats nor undereats, but who is well and nutritiously nourished with a minimum of idiosyncrasy and taboo.

(4) See if you can arrange a proper atmosphere for eating. Quarters that are not too large or too small, that are reasonably

well ventilated, that are not too noisy, that do not put him in physical jeopardy, that do not include too many people eating at one time, that are bright and cheery to eat in, that are not filled with expensive, easily damaged furniture—these are some of the things you can watch out for when you arrange for his eating facilities. Avoid letting the dinner table become, as it is in so many homes, the place where all the day's tensions are noisily discharged.

(5) Be definite but in some ways minimal about the eating rules that you set for the child. It is all very well to encourage him not to waste food; but forcing him to eat every scrap on his plate may be too onerous for him to take. To let him eat or not eat anything he wants may be rather disastrous; but to rigidly force him to eat everything that the other members of your family eat may also result in a holocaust. Usually, he should be required to start and finish his meal within reasonable time limits; to eat most of the main dishes that the rest of the family eats; and to do minimal table-setting and table-cleaning chores if he is old enough to do so. But each child is an individual in this respect, and the fewer rules that are set, the better it usually is. Avoid making mealtime a miniature totalitarianism—with precise rules, diet, manners—when it should be a relaxed and satisfying occasion.

(6) Try to provide a fairly wide variety of foods, especially over the period of a week, so that he has many things to pick from and does not become bored with the selection. Within limits, let him make some of his own choices over the period of a week or two; experiments show that most children will choose wisely during this kind of period. Let him have certain snacks in between meals, as long as they do not truly disrupt his eating habits, and as long as the snacks themselves are fairly nutritious. Don't think that three rigorously timed meals a day are necessarily good for all individuals; in fact, most people would probably benefit from four or five smaller meals, spread out more evenly over the day. Provide sweets and other nonessentials in small amounts; and sometimes use them as rewards for generally good eating habits.

(7) Some children who are overeaters can be induced to improve their eating habits if attention is paid to aspects of eating such as the appearance of the food, the setting of the table, the linking up of the food with certain games, etc. Ingenuity in these respects, especially when it is adapted to the likes and dislikes of a particular child, may pay off.

(8) Sometimes a child's interest in food may be enhanced if he is encouraged to cooperate in its purchase, its preparation, the cleaning-up process, and the planning of future meals. Children with small appetites may eat much more if they prepare some of the food themselves. Children with overeating habits may sometimes be discouraged if they are made to do some of the perpetual shopping, cooking, and cleaning that goes with satiating their immense appetites.

(9) The teaching of table manners is generally a good thing, since the child to some degree has to eat in other homes and in public places, and should be taught to do so adequately so that others are not unduly annoyed by him. But the teaching of rigid table manners may make meals quite unenjoyable and help make the child rebellious against the parents who have such rigid customs.

Sibling Rivalry

Not all children are jealous of their siblings—in spite of what many of the psychoanalysts would have you believe. Many of them are exceptionally loving and cooperative, right from the start, when a baby brother or sister is brought into the family, and rarely, from then on, show undue distrust or distaste for their siblings. Accepting of themselves, they are not constantly seeking proof of their parents' love and approval; hence, they are sufficiently absorbed in enjoying life that a baby simply becomes a nice new toy. Probably the majority of children, however, are more or less competitive with the other children in their family, and a sizable minority of them are exceptionally rivalrous.

Not that this form of competition is abnormal. Competition itself is a healthy component of human behavior and gives us the motivation for many of our most constructive accomplishments. A number of talented statesmen and artists have achieved more than they otherwise would have done because they wanted to be *better* practitioners than some of their rivals.

Competition becomes invidious when the individual feels that he *has* to be more successful than others, and that he is a total bust if he is not. If Johnny, aged seven, wants to be a better reader, writer, or baseball player than his eight-year-old brother, Tom, his desire in this regard need cause neither him nor Tom any emotional difficulty. But if Johnny must be more proficient than Tom in any or all these respects, disaster is likely to ensue.

For one thing, Johnny will then tend to hate Tom, try to sabotage some of Tom's efforts, try to impress others with his superiority over Tom even when there is no evidence of this superiority, to become obsessed with beating out Tom rather than with doing many other enjoyable things he might do, to gain more attention from his parents than Tom does, etc. Johnny's goals and subgoals in this regard will tend to cause family bickering, increase his own anxiety and depression, and result in a considerable waste of time and energy for everyone.

To make matters still worse, Johnny's dire need to outdo his brother Tom may well result in *underachievement* on his own part, since he may easily conclude (especially since he is younger than Tom) that he simply cannot perform better than his brother, that it would be disgraceful for him to try and fail, and that therefore he'd better stay out of various fields of endeavor in which Tom does fairly well. Or he may focus on being outstanding in some field, such as music, which he does not particularly enjoy, but in which he knows that Tom has little inclination or talent.

Sibling rivalry, in other words, becomes harmful when it turns into the essential game of life. We all, to enjoy a happy existence, seem to have to pick some particular game—whether it be that of accounting, politics, composing, social climbing, or psychotherapy—and to center a good deal of our life around it. For we are thereby able to give ourselves a concerted goal which will keep us occupied and absorbed for a good part of our life, and around which we can structure a good deal of the rest of our existence.

Ideally, however, we should pick this game out of our own natural bents, and after a considerable amount of experimentation with alternative games which we might also enjoy playing to a considerable degree.

When Johnny picks the game of sibling rivalry and notably competes with his brother Tom in various ways, he hardly does so "voluntarily," on the basis of choosing out of many possible games the one he would truly enjoy more or most. Rather, he does so *compulsively,* fixatedly—and once he does so, he allows himself virtually no choice or bent. Moreover, he frequently plays this compulsive game as if his very life, and certainly his intrinsic worth, depended on it; and although he thereby distinctly enhances his level of absorption (and thus enjoys *some* distinct benefits from the game), he also puts too much of himself at stake and consequently plays the game in a kind of desperate, anxious, often angry manner. He rarely relaxes enough to enjoy it; and, as noted above, he frequently dooms himself to playing it in a losing manner.

For several important reasons, then, the game of sibling rivalry is not a good game for anyone. The main participants do not reap great benefits from it, and the immediate onlookers, the parents, often suffer much pain. Society rarely benefits; and nobody, all told, derives much good or enjoyment.

What can be done to combat intense sibling rivalry that tends to lead to poor results? Here are some points that may be useful in this connection:

(1) Parents should usually forbear from deliberately pitting children in the same family against each other. This does not mean that Johnny should be taught that under no circumstances can he compete with his brother Tom; nor that he should be made to feel guilty if he doesn't love Tom enormously and always go out of his way to cooperate with him in different games and ventures. But it does mean that parental comparisons between the two boys should be minimized, and rarely mentioned in the presence of either child—nor even openly made to friends and relatives who themselves are likely to repeat these comparisons to the brothers. And Johnny should definitely not be

told. "Why can't you do as well as your brother did in school (or in sports or in social affairs), dear?"

Each child should be treated as an entity in his own right and in some ways be handled as if he were the only child in the family. Whether he does as well as or better than his siblings should be made to seem of little consequence. If comparative notes on his performances must be made, they should be as much as possible the comparison of his performance with *his own* other performances or potential achievements.

If inevitable comparisons are made, by teachers, friends, or anyone else, and Johnny knows full well that he is inferior to Tom in some area, great pains should be taken to let him see that he is fully acceptable to you, his parent, in spite of this acknowledged inferiority in this area. He should be shown that it is only to be expected that he will do worse than Tom in some areas (and better than he in others); that it would be nice if he could be universally successful in relation to others, including his brother, Tom; but it is distinctly not necessary that he be that successful; and that he can lead a fine, happy life whether he is or not.

(2) Although it is not essential that Johnny like Tom, and vice versa, it is certainly desirable; and if they do like each other, some of their intense sibling rivalry will probably tend to become subdued. When Johnny, the younger child, is born, therefore, some effort should be made to let Tom know that he is coming and to have Tom look forward to his arrival as a happy event. When Johnny is young, Tom should preferably be called upon to help with his care, to get pleasure from observing him, to play with him in various feasible ways, and to take a little responsibility for him. At the same time, Tom should definitely not be saddled with considerable, onerous responsibility for Johnny and his welfare, since Tom will thereby often become resentful and feel that he is overburdened with the care of Johnny. Nor should Johnny be favored over Tom just because he is younger and weaker.

On Johnny's side, he should be taught that having a bigger brother has clear-cut advantages, that he should not take advantage of Tom's age and bigness, that he can easily do return favors for Tom from time to time when Tom is helpful to him, that it is only to be expected that Tom will be given favors and an amount of freedom that he, Johnny, is not ready for yet, and so on. Games can be encouraged in which the brothers, though of different ages, can both actively and enjoyably participate; items can be purchased which they both can advantageously use; and other things can be done to encourage them to see the mutual benefits of having a sibling.

(3) When two siblings fight with each other, little cognizance should usually be taken of their squabbles and even their fist-fights, unless it becomes apparent that one is abusing the other unusually or taunting the other into doing the abusing. Siblings, whether boys or girls, inevitably do fight with each other, and much of their fighting is experiential and enjoyable. If kept within ordinary bounds, it is actually useful as part of their experience in handling somewhat difficult situations.

When the fighting between two siblings goes beyond ordinary bounds, something should be done to stop it. First, the causes should be ascertained—such as one sibling's bullying the other and forcing the other to respond with combative behavior. Such a cause should be dealt with promptly, with firm kindness. If six-year-old Mickey is discovered bullying and pummeling her three-year-old brother Adam, she should clearly and calmly be shown that its continuation will simply not be tolerated. She should be dealt with not as if she is a vicious, villainous child, but as if she is a disturbed or easily upsettable one; and her underlying disturbance, rather than his "villainy," should be ferreted out and attacked. Distinct penalties for continued fighting should be laid down; but these should not be accompanied by anger and moralism on the part of the penalizer.

(4) Children should not be made to feel guilty when they do not happen to like other children in the family or to get along with these others well. Blood may be technically thicker than water, but there is no reason why each sibling must like or love his brothers and sisters. Some children, for various reasons, are little monsters; and it is most difficult for anyone, including their

own parents, to love them. Many children, moreover, have quite different basic interests from those of their siblings and therefore cannot be expected to be too close to these siblings. If Johnny finds that his brother Tom is cold and harsh and teasing, or if he sees that Tom is only interested in sports while his own interests run mainly to reading and chess, he should not be made to feel that he has to like Tom and have a great deal to do with him. Perhaps the two, if not forced to "love" each other when they are young, will find more in common when they are older, even helping each other with their deficiencies. At worst, they will miss some of the potential joys of brotherhood; but they will be even more deprived, in most instances, if they are forced to associate with each other continually and told that there is something radically wrong with them just because they are not lovey-dovey as all good brothers "should" be.

(5) Much sibling rivalry stems from the parents favoring one child over another for one reason or another. If Tom is palpably favored, because of his good looks, his charm, his intelligence, the fact that he was first-born, or his tractability, his brother Johnny is soon going to discern that discrimination exists, and is going to resent both his parents and Tom. He may then either try to emulate Tom in those traits for which he thinks he is favored; or, failing to do this successfully, may give up and go to opposite extremes. He may attempt to ingratiate himself with Tom, in an effort to identify with him and magically have some of the favoritism rub off on himself; or he may treat Tom with hostility, cruelty, bitterness, or studied indifference. Unfortunately, too, there is a strong tendency for parents to be less patient with an older child when he misbehaves. And often, frenzied by a harassing afternoon with five-year-old Peter, a mother will then turn about and slap Jerry at the first peep. This does little to promote feelings of love for the little brother.

The point is, of course, that siblings are sufficiently likely to get into rivalrous situations with each other without any favoritism occurring on the part of their parents; and when such discrimination does occur, the rivalry is likely to be intensified. This does not mean that you, as a parent, must equally love all your children, for it is improbable that you will. One will naturally tend to be more lovable to you than another. Nonetheless, you should lean over backward not to manifest your favorable prejudices in overt action that the nonfavored children can clearly diagnose. If one of your children is difficult or disturbed, it will sometimes be necessary for you to outwardly favor him, even though he may least deserve it. But on the whole you should try to treat your offspring equally and to ascertain that one does not feel that the others are given unusual attention or privileges. If you have difficulty in treating them that way, then it is probable that you have some kind of emotional problem yourself; and it might well be proper for you to seek psychological help for this problem.

Sleep Disturbances

Some children are naturally good sleepers—especially when they are very young—but others are poor sleepers, and will remain so all their lives. Inborn physiological factors are very often the cause of sleep disturbances, and there may be nothing that can be done about these factors except to accept the fact that they are there and to try to compensate for them in some ways. Thus, the child who has trouble sleeping for any length of time during the night may have to be given a nap period during the day, even when most other children are no longer taking this kind of a daytime nap. Or a child who tends to sleep too much, especially during the day, may have to be forcibly wakened and kept awake for a while, until he gets out of his sleeping groove.

Emotional causes of a child's sleeping disorder tend to be more common than purely physiological reasons. For one thing, the child may have become too excited during the day, and especially just before bedtime, and may therefore have great difficulty falling asleep. Or he may be too afraid of something—such as darkness or of being alone—to sleep well. Or he may use sleep, just as he may use eating or playing or anything else, as an occasion to work out his poor relations with his parents. Thus, he may deliberately refuse to go to sleep, in order to annoy his parents;

or may lie awake nights in an injustice-collecting mood, as he ruminates on the unfair ways they have treated him during the day; or may keep interrupting his sleep with bad dreams and nightmares, which originate in his hostility to them or in his dire need of love from them.

When poor sleeping is caused by any kind of emotional upset on the part of your child, the first thing to do, of course, is to try to determine exactly what is leading to his poor sleeping; that is, what kind of anxiety-creating or hostility-inciting sentences he is telling himself during the day, or just before it is time to sleep, to make himself upset. Generally, he will be convincing himself that something is or would be terrible. For example, it would be terrible if the bogeyman got him while he was sleeping, or if he died in his sleep, or if he had to face the harsh things that he expects to happen to him the next day when he wakes, or if he had a bad nightmare tonight along the lines of the one that scared him on previous nights.

Try to get your child to verbalize some of these disturbance-creating beliefs that he is telling himself. If he cannot at first do so, assume that some such belief does exist, try to guess what it could possibly be, and ask him if your guess could be right. Don't nag him to look at his internalized sentences; but at the same time don't give up too easily and assume that they don't exist or that he cannot find them. They are invariably there, when he is disturbed, and with a little persistence, he can almost always dig them up and explain to you what they are.

When you start to discover what anxiety- and hostility-provoking attitudes your sleep-disordered child is telling himself, figure out the philosophic core of these sentences yourself and then show him what this core is and how to challenge and question it. As noted above, the core generally is that something is terrible, awful, horrible. When you see what this something is, try to convince him that it is not as horrendous as he thinks, even though it may well be inconvenient, annoying, frustrating, or overexciting. Teach him, over and over, how to anticatastrophize and how to unangrily accept grim reality when it cannot be changed. Teach him, more specifically, that there are no bogeymen; that worrying about dying in one's sleep will probably be far more painful than such a death, if it did occur, would actually be; that the realities he has to face on waking tomorrow may be unfortunate but they are hardly too rough for him to handle; that even if he has a bad nightmare, nothing will actually happen to him and its effects will shortly pass. Attempt to restrict such discussions to the less demon-filled daytime, as verbalization during the fearsome night hours may only double his anxieties.

Try, at the same time, to get your child relatively unconcerned about sleeping. If you harp on the fact that he is a poor sleeper, he will begin to see himself as such and will become more and more certain that he cannot sleep well. Insomnia, of course, is often caused or exacerbated by the fact that the individual incessantly worries about his sleeping, and keeps himself awake by this very worrying. People who believe that they are light sleepers tend to wake more often at the slightest sound than those who believe that they sleep soundly. Children (and adults) who have an image of themselves as individuals who are not able to wake easily in the morning tend to actualize this image and make it true. For the most part, therefore, do not emphasize the child's poor sleeping tendencies. Try to convince him, instead, that he can sleep well and that he probably is going to do so on this particular night, even though he may have recently been sleeping poorly.

Sometimes gimmicks are desirable to put a child to sleep or to keep him sleeping. Drugs are dangerous in this respect and should be used with great caution, only under a physician's advice. But various other kinds of devices can often be employed with good effect. Many children can be lulled to sleep with a steady, humming sound such as the sound of a fan, or the ticking of a loud grandfather clock, or the playing of a musical selection. Similar sounds can sometimes also be used to drown out street and other noises and to keep a light sleeper from waking.

Children can often be put to sleep by reading or telling them stories; by stroking various parts of their bodies (such as their forehead, arms); by allowing them to go through certain rituals (such as cuddling up with a doll or teddy bear); by having them exercise vigorously before going to bed; by giving them a light meal just before bedtime; by removing them from the presence of exciting stimuli (such as TV shows) for an hour or two before they go to bed; and by various other devices which can be experimentally determined with an individual child. By the same token, children can be fully awakened in the morning by baths or showers; by food; by exercise; by cold; by forcing them to respond to conversation; and by various other methods which may be individually discovered.

As a general rule, it is best to allow your child, as he reaches the age of nine or ten years, to assume responsibility for his own getting up in the morning; for if you pamper him in this respect, you will not be preparing him for getting up later on in life, when you are not around to assist him. Therefore, it is best that he have and set his own alarm clock; and that on a few occasions, if necessary, you allow him to be late for school, for appointments with his peers, or for other things, so that he finally learns that he must exert himself more in order to get up on time. If, however, your child has exceptional difficulty arousing himself in the morning—which may be the result of peculiar physiology on his part and not an outcome of emotional disturbance—you may just have to keep getting him up and getting him up, or otherwise he may never make his classes and other appointments. If this is the case, don't make a big thing about his difficulty, but accept it calmly as one of the unfortunate facts of life, and see that he is not made to feel guilty about it—you might even adopt a policy of humor about it.

In the case of an older child who has sleep problems, you may be able to discuss these with him openly and to suggest various methods that he can use to help himself sleep better or wake more easily. For instance, you can show him that people often do keep themselves up by worrying about their going to sleep and can teach him not to worry too much about his sleep habits. You can also show him several methods of putting himself to sleep that he can consciously employ—such as counting sheep, listening to the ticking of a clock, focusing on pleasant fantasies, reading just before going to sleep, etc. In teaching him these methods, as long as you do not catastrophize about his poor sleeping, you may be able to help him to help himself and may provide him with information that he can usefully employ for the rest of his life.

Bed-Wetting

A special kind of sleep problem is that involved with enuresis or bed-wetting. Enuresis technically means any involuntary urination after the age of self-control has supposedly set in for a child. Most children are able to control their urination by about the age of three; but many are not able to do so until they are five or six years old; and about 5 per cent wet the bed occasionally after this age. For some reason which is not too well understood, boys are afflicted about twice as often as are girls with persistent bed-wetting.

There are many theories about why a child suffers from enuresis, and many psychologists are coming to favor the hypothesis that enuresis results from a *combination* of causes—in other words, stems from both organic and psychogenic factors. First, there are the physiological theories, according to which it is believed that some children have trigger-happy or defective nervous systems and that they therefore have much more difficulty than do other children in controlling urination. Some of these neurologically different children may have retarded maturation, and may later develop proper control; but some of them go on into their teens or adulthood and still, at least on occasion, have bed-wetting problems.

On the physical side, it is thought that improper bladder training may also be the cause of enuresis. Thus, a child may not be duly impressed with the importance of controlling himself during sleep or may even be unwittingly encouraged by his parents to forgo this kind of control; and therefore he may wet the bed. Continence, in such cases, may be achieved by some amount of disciplining the child and by teaching him bladder control.

On the psychological side, there may be many reasons why a child is enuretic. He can be generally anxious and may take his anxieties to bed with him. He may use bed-wetting as a symbolic means of expressing himself—of letting himself go, having his own way, controlling the reactions of his parents. He may be quite hostile to his parents and may deliberately—consciously or unconsciously—urinate in his bed. He may occasionally find some kind of sexual or semisexual gratification in bed-wetting and may tie it up with masturbatory or other sexual practices. He may worry so much about his original enuretic symptoms, and loathe himself so mightily for having them, that he may then unwittingly bring on further symptoms by his worrying. He may occasionally wish to punish himself for his misdeeds during the day and may therefore resort to this unpleasant kind of activity. He may have some objection to sleeping through all night and may use his enuresis as a method of waking himself from time to time.

Because enuresis may result from so many different causes, it is important that the particular cause be discovered in each case. This is sometimes difficult to do without drawing the child's attention unduly to his bed-wetting problem. For, as in the case of stuttering, tics, and various other symptoms of emotional disturbance, it is usually better to take the child's enuresis in a calm, almost ignoring manner, so that he does not harp on it himself, become thoroughly ashamed that he is afflicted with it, and thereby make it worse. On the other hand, it is a symptom that is impossible to ignore completely, since the child will tend to learn that not everyone wets his bed at night and that he is therefore different from other children.

Probably the best plan is to call the enuresis to the child's attention but only as a moderate problem which it is desirable—but not absolutely necessary—to solve. If he is made to feel that it would be nice and convenient if he did not wet the bed at night, but that it would hardly be a terrible thing if he did keep wetting it, his unexcited cooperation may be gained in dealing with this problem. He can then be asked about things that may be upsetting him (including the bed-wetting itself); and if it is thereby determined that he is catastrophizing or angering himself about something, his basic philosophies in regard to it may be further explored, and he can be shown how it is possible for him to change his views and think differently about himself and the world.

In this respect, I frequently cite the case of an eight-year-old boy whom I saw some years ago who was not only wetting his bed frequently during the night, but who was so ashamed of what he was doing that he usually hid the wet sheets in the morning, so that his mother would have difficulty in finding them. As a result of his bed-wetting and his other behavior connected with it, he was teased rather unmercifully by his siblings and by some of his peers; and he was terribly upset about this teasing.

Since this boy was quite bright, I used with him exactly the same kind of rational-emotive psychotherapy that I would have employed with an older individual, and in much the same manner. I kept showing him that it was not awful and horrible for him to be teased by others, although it was admittedly annoying. I insisted that he could well stand this teasing, and could teach himself that "Sticks and stones will break my bones, but names will never hurt me." I also showed him that some of those who were teasing him obviously had their own problems, and that they were delightedly after him in order to convince themselves that they were superior to him and in order to avoid facing their own difficulties. I convinced him that he could understand and pity these others and that he by no means had to take their teasing seriously.

After first deindoctrinating this boy as far as the horrors of being teased were concerned, I then got back to the problem of the bed-wetting itself. I informed him that many children wet their beds and that this was a bothersome but hardly disgusting or revolting habit. I got him to see that he was not a "baby" just because others thought that he was, or because his behavior was, in one tiny respect, not appropriate to his age. Much to my surprise, he was soon repeating back to me my own statements and obviously understood that there was nothing shameful about bed-wetting unless, as he said to me during our fourth session, "I *think* that it is shameful . . . and I don't *have* to think that way, do I?" No, I said again, he didn't have to think that way; and after a while, he no longer seemed to be. When he did wet the bed at night, he made no more attempts to hide the sheets; and when his parents showed anger or disgust at his bed-wetting, he was able to see that they had problems of their own and that he did not have to take their views too seriously either.

After I had seen this boy for only seven sessions, spread out over a period of about twenty weeks, his bed-wetting almost entirely stopped. Moreover, he was also getting along better in his social relations with others, in his contacts with his teachers, and in his family associations. His mother, who had been convinced when she first brought him around to see me, that very little could be done to help him, was most surprised by his improvement and insisted that I have some talks with her other children, who were not as seriously disturbed. Although this child's situation, in his home and at school, was far from ideal, and although there were very real pressures placed on him that I could not eliminate, my talking to him about his philosophy of life, and how he could like himself even when others teased him and when his behavior was inefficient, apparently helped him enormously; and I would say that a real emotional disaster was averted in his case.

Other children are often not as easy to talk to as this particular enuretic boy was, but still something can be done to show them that they are not horrible creatures for being enuretic and that they need not despise themselves even when their symptoms continue.

For children who are younger or not as receptive to verbal therapy, various other kinds of deconditioning treatments can be employed. The main device which has been found effective is this respect is a pad which is placed in the child's bed, attached to which are electric wires and a bell. As soon as the child wets the pad, a signal is transmitted to the bell, which rings and wakes him. As originally invented by Pfaundler, and later modified by several others, this device has proved to be effective with a large number of children, ranging from three to seventeen years of age. A version of it is marketed today by the Enurtone Company, 40-03 National Street, Corona 68, N.Y.; and, as long as it is used with professional consultation, it appears to do much good in helping some enuretic children control themselves. Others, however, simply become annoyed, and may even take to sleeping on the floor to avoid it.

This does not mean that bed-wetting is always a problem of emotional upset or faulty conditioning, for there are various other physical as well as psychological factors involved. Consequently, good physical routines are often desirable or necessary to stop a child from frequent enuresis. To this end, the following steps may be tried:

(1) Restrict the child's intake of fluids, particularly in the later afternoon and evening. Real fluids, such as water and milk, should be plentifully given during the day but not after four in the afternoon; semifluids, such as applesauce and watermelon, should also be omitted at suppertime and before going to bed.

(2) If your child's doctor permits, giving him plenty of salt at his last meal may cause temporary retention of his body fluids and cut down his urinating at night.

(3) Sweating may eliminate or cut down the tendency to be enuretic, and therefore the child may be given extra blankets at night to help him sweat.

(4) You may routinely wake the child during his sleep—especially when you yourself are going to bed late or getting up for something during the night—and let him go to the bathroom when he is awake, so that he will not have a full bladder when he is sleeping.

(5) Encourage the child to go for longer and longer periods of time throughout the day without urinating. This can stretch the bladder, helping to increase its capacity (and with it the child's ability to control urination).

(6) Be sure to provide positive reinforcement for the child after he has kept dry on several nights; this aids in diminishing the anxiety often responsible for wetting. Do not, however, imply that the child is a better person because he has stayed dry; rather, indicate how very nice it is that his bed stayed nice and dry all night.

(7) If the child persistently bed-wets, have him examined by

your family physician to see if there is any special physical cause involved. He may possibly have a bladder infection, urethritis, or some other ailment that induces him to urinate frequently and to be unable to retain his urine for any long period of time. If so, care should be taken to correct this ailment.

By combining emotional and physical attacks on the problem of enuresis, you will usually be able to help your child overcome or reduce this problem. If any unusual difficulties in this respect continue to persist, be sure to get professional aid from your family physician and from a psychologist or a psychiatrist. Most of the time, enuresis is not a terribly serious problem and does disappear as the child chronologically matures; but it should be faced and tackled in those cases where it does persist.

Physical Ailments

It has been observed that anxious children, being fearful and unsure of themselves, appear to be more susceptible to both mental and physical ills. As Mary B. Hoover states, "they are apt to suffer from listlessness, poor coordination, and accident-proneness, and they seem to be quick to 'catch' things, from the common cold to more serious communicable diseases."

They frequently suffer from headaches, nausea, vomiting, dizziness, gastrointestinal disorders, rapid heart beating, and many other complaints that result from their emotional upsets. There is a good chance, in most of these cases, that the child also has a basic predisposition to the kind of physical ailment with which he is afflicted, that is to say, that there really is something weak, deficient, or wrong with his intestines, heart, respiratory system, or other parts of his anatomy in which he is most seriously ailing. If, however, he were not emotionally disturbed, he might rarely or never turn up with the severe kind of disorder that he does exhibit—so that it is a combination of physical and mental factors that sets him off.

Moreover, many individuals—and here we can easily talk of adults as well as of children—become legitimately plagued with some physical symptom, such as earache, bronchitis, indigestion, or what you will; and then, once they realize that they are afflicted, they become so worried about their symptom or about some disability in connection with it, that they then manage to exacerbate and prolong it mightily with their overconcern. Children in this class may have a childhood illness of a fairly serious nature, may have to stay in bed for a while and picture themselves as being isolated from the world, and may wittingly or unwittingly play up their illness to such a degree that they hardly ever fully recover from it. Years later they may still be playing the invalid—either because they are genuinely fearful that they cannot cope with the world in a healthy manner or because they have begun using their ailment as an excuse for getting out of such onerous activities as attending school or competing on the playing field with other children.

When, therefore, emotional distress does not literally cause physical illness, it can easily contribute to its prolongation and intensification. This means that if you would help a child minimize his physical disabilities, you must not only see to it that he has a sane attitude toward himself and the world, but also see that he does not unduly catastrophize about illness and see himself as being unable to cope with it.

It is of prime importance that you be generally nonanxious yourself—by following the aforementioned rules that no matter how badly your child or anyone acts, they are no less valuable as human beings; and by teaching these rules to your child, you can rear a child who will be able to face life's difficulties with minimum disturbance. Such a child will have a low probability of inducing psychosomatic ills, or of taking to his bed for days at the onset of a brief tummyache.

Secondly, you should rear your child so that he is fully aware of the fact that he may have pains and aches, and that he may become physically handicapped on a temporary or permanent basis, but that this is not utterly shattering or happiness-destroying, and that he can take whatever life dishes out to him in these respects. You can let him know that, at the very worst, he is eventually going to die from some physical cause; and even that will hardly be catastrophic, since death need not be painful or horrible, but is a natural and expectable extension of the living process. So there is no need for him to exaggerate the significance of death—just as there is no need for him to deny that it is unfortunate that he has to die someday.

While he lives, the worst that can happen to him through physical malfunctioning is some kind of pain or handicap. This, if it occurs, will certainly not be fortuitous or great. It will be just what it actually is—a bad handicap. But he can live, and I mean *live,* successfully with various handicaps, and can find numerous ways of enjoying himself in spite of them. His job, therefore, if he becomes physically ill, is to accept this illness with equanimity, to do everything in his power to minimize its effects and help himself get rid of it as soon as possible, and to refrain from catastrophizing about it and thereby aggravating it.

Thirdly, when a child actually does become afflicted with a serious ailment, such as epilepsy, you can enable him to live fairly comfortably with it by reacting calmly to his attacks, doing what must be done to assist him while making it clear to him that, aside from these sporadic periods of unpleasantness stemming from his ailment, there is good deal of richness and enjoyment in life to be derived despite his handicap. Do not try to pull the wool over a handicapped (or ill) child's eyes by pretending that he is perfectly normal. By acknowledging his problem, you help root out a sense of uneasiness and self-consciousness that can stem from other people's strained and ill-guided attempts to ignore an obvious problem.

10

How to Live with a Neurotic Child and Like It

You don't *have* to live with a neurotic child—at least, not very much. There are various ways in which you can get rid of him. You can, for example, palm him off to maids and baby-sitters. Or send him away, even at an early age, to school. Or manage to work day and night, yourself, so that you are practically never at home with him. Or turn him over to kind friends or relatives—such as his grandparents or your ex-spouse—if they are foolish enough to want to keep him. Or, in extreme cases, institutionalize him in a setting where there are specialists in raising severely disturbed children.

All these kinds of plans are at least to be seriously considered —especially after you have tried all the other methods in this book and find that you just can't live happily with a child who remains exceptionally aberrated and who may be, because of his neurosis or psychosis, eminently unlovable. Normally, you would be expected to live with and rear your neurotic offspring yourself. Since you unquestionably are responsible for bringing him into the world, you are likely to take care of him better than anyone else is, and you are the one who is the best candidate to put up with the inconveniences he creates.

At the same time, there may be several good reasons why you should not assume the full or even the main responsibility for rearing your highly disturbed son or daughter. You may be too neurotic yourself and therefore be unable to help even a "normal" and healthy child, let alone a terribly difficult child. You may be exceptionally busy and simply not have the time or energy to devote to him. You may have already done too many wrong things with the child, so that your poor relationships with him are well-nigh impossible to untangle. You may be so prejudiced against him already that you are likely to do him more harm than good by being in his company very often. You may not be able to get along very well with your spouse and may create a worse atmosphere for the child by living with him or her than would be created if you left home and continued to see the child on a regular-visitation basis.

On one or more major counts, then, you may not truly want to raise a disturbed child or may not be able to do so adequately in spite of your ardent desire to do so. Under such conditions, it is most dubious whether you should live under the same roof with such a child, even though you are its biological parent and legal guardian. If for example, your child were mentally deficient, or if you were severely crippled, it might not be advisable for you to be around the child constantly; and other kinds of living and child-rearing arrangements might well have to be made. Why, therefore, should it seem shocking, if you and/or the child is distinctly emotionally handicapped, that mutual living arrangements consequently become impractical or undesirable?

Give serious thought, then, to the question of whether you should live under the same roof with and spend a good deal of time rearing your neurotic or psychotic child. If you soberly decide, after much consideration and after professional consultation with a psychologist, psychiatrist, or psychiatric social worker, that conditions might be better if either you or the child were living away from your present home, experiment with this kind of a possible solution—and don't berate yourself in any way for adopting such a radical step. Obviously, you will not be a perfect parent if your child is disturbed in the first place and if you decide to leave him in the second place; but you will also not be a rotten person for so deciding. You have a right, as a human being, to your own happiness and to your own (good or bad) decisions; and even if you should irresponsibly and immorally desert your neurotic child, you will still only, at worst, be a wrongdoer. Your *acts,* in such circumstances, will be bad; but *you* will not be totally worthless for committing these unfortunate acts.

It is most likely that you will decide, after due consideration, to stay with and to take an active part in rearing your child if he is neurotic. How, if this is the case, will you be able to live with this child and like it? In *How to Live with a Neurotic,* I give several important rules for staying with a person who remains emotionally disturbed; let me now adapt these rules to the problem of living with a disturbed child.

First of all, you must *fully* and *unequivocally* accept the fact that your child is disturbed and that disturbed children act in a distinctly aberrated manner. It is far from enough to tell yourself. "Oh, yes. I know that my son is neurotic; that's the way he is." Knowing is *not* accepting! You know that you have a cold or that your mate is quarrelsome. But you can easily gripe all all day about your cold or feel utterly surprised when your mate picks another fight. In these cases, you have not truly accepted the grim reality of your cold or your mate's quarrelsomeness— even though you know the facts.

This important distinction, or the lack of it, seems to be at the bottom of most neurotic manifestations. To know you made a mistake means to admit the fact that you were in error. To accept your mistake (or, better, to accept yourself with the mistake) means (a) to admit the fact that you were in error; (b) to realize that being in error is undesirable, but that perhaps something can be done about correcting it in the future; and (c) to acknowledge that you can be a worth-while person who is deserving of happiness, even though you have made this error and even though you may not be able to correct it.

Similarly, to know that you have a cold (or some other un-pleasant condition) means to admit the fact that the cold exists. To accept the cold (or yourself with the cold) means (a) to admit the fact that the cold exists; (b) to realize that having it is undesirable, but that perhaps something can be done about ameliorating or curing it; and (c) to acknowledge that your life can be worth-while even though you have this cold and may have to keep suffering with it. Obviously, therefore, accepting one of life's grim realities goes far beyond knowing that it exists. Knowledge in itself is potentially useful; knowledge without ac-ceptance is often less than useful and results in neurosis; knowl-edge with acceptance is truly useful and results in a healthy attitude toward oneself and life and in a sane effort to minimize your own errors and the harshness of the world.

To return to our main theme, then: In living with a neurotic child, it is best to fully and unequivocally accept the fact that he is the way he is; that it is doubtless most unfortunate that he is that way; but that that's the way things are, and no amount of wishing on your part will by itself change the way they are. A neurotic child is exactly that—a *neurotic* individual. He is not, nor can he reasonably be expected to be, nice, well-disciplined, mature, well-behaved, responsible, or consistent. If he were all these things, he would hardly be disturbed!

Accepting a neurotic child for what he is means, of course, not blaming or condemning him for his characteristics and symp-toms. This is all-important in handling emotionally disturbed children, for the more you blame them, the more disturbed they will usually tend to be. It is also most important for you if you choose to live with an easily upsettable son or daughter. For blaming your child for displaying unpleasant characteristics will almost certainly give you an additional, gratuitous pain in your own insides; and then you will have two pains for the price of one: first, that of the child and his or her annoying behavior; and second, that of your own unrealistic reaction to this annoyance.

Anger at your neurotic offspring may, admittedly, make you feel good temporarily, since it "proves" how great you are in comparison to the upset child. But how long-lasting and meaningful is this kind of good feeling? In the longer run, you will still have your own negativism, your annoyance at being annoyed; and this is likely to upset you and depress you far more than is the child's original poor behavior. So the more you tolerate your child in spite of his neurotic manifestations, the happier you will be in living with him and the more you will probably be able to help him become somewhat less disturbed.

Don't *personalize* your child's disorganized and disordered activities. If he gets into fights with other children, or shirks his schoolwork, or is anxious about almost everything he does, this does not mean anything about *you*. Perhaps his poor behavior indicates that you have raised him poorly; or perhaps it doesn't, since he can easily manage to act pretty badly even if you have done your very best and have reared him rather well. But even if his disturbances do indicate that you have made mistakes in rearing him, they do not mean that you yourself are a failure; they merely show that you, like the rest of us, are human and fallible—and maybe a little more fallible than most. All right: You are fallible. What is so highly personal about that?

You may, indeed, be a unique individual—for who of us, in various ways, isn't? But you are hardly the sole error-prone person in the world. If your child is irresponsible, this hardly proves that *you* are; and, even if you are, you are not an undesirable person for being so. So try to view his neurotic behavior objectively and not as something that must be your fault, and that must show your ineffable reprehensibility if it does turn out to be partly your doing.

Don't assume, moreover, that when your disturbed child acts badly, or even when he reacts poorly to you, that his actions are necessarily directed against you. For the most part, he is compulsively driven rather than voluntarily led to his negative actions; so that, even if they are specifically pointed in your direction, this does not mean that you should take them personally. He basically, in almost all instances, hates himself and feels that he is not able to be happy in this difficult world; and it is his self-hatred and low frustration tolerance which force him to strike out against others, including you. As I note in *How to Live With a Neurotic,* "A man who is panic-stricken when caught in a fire will ruthlessly knock down others in order to escape. But this does not mean that he hates these others in particular, or wishes them any harm. Similarly, a neurotic frequently is quite different, sometimes even friendly, to a person even while he is panic-strickenly pushing that person out of his way. It is not that he necessarily wants to do so; he is literally forced to be antagonistic, and he himself often regrets this."

After accepting the fact that living with a neurotic child is no party, you can do several things to minimize the difficulties involved in this kind of domestic arrangement. For example:

(1) Work on your own frustration tolerance! Try to see that you are minimally *annoyed at being annoyed.* When your child rips up the furniture, or bangs needlessly on the piano, or trips you in the hallway, remember that it is terribly bothersome to have him acting in these ways, but that it is not necessarily horrible, awful, or catastrophic. You can survive under these thankless conditions; and however unfair he may be to you and other members of your household, there is no reason why he should not be that unfair. The more you keep convincing yourself that he shouldn't be annoying, the more frustrated and bothered you will make yourself. You certainly will never enjoy frustration; but you can stand it.

(2) Do your best to see that the other members of your family fully understand your neurotic child's condition and that they do not expect too much from him. Let your spouse and even your other children know that the child is seriously disturbed and in all probability is going to remain so for some time to come. Consequently, you should help them see that he will behave badly in a number of ways, and there is no point in anyone's becoming upset about his behavior. Your family members need not like your neurotic child's actions; but they can, along with you, learn to accept his doings gracefully. The better example you set them in this regard, the better it will be. Also, in most instances, you have to convince them, by words as well as deeds, that it is silly to expect the neurotic child to behave differently, and that life

can be livable, if not thoroughly enjoyable, when he is the way he is.

(3) Convince yourself, particularly, and try to convince the other members of your family that the words, gestures, and attitudes of your disturbed child can easily be accepted, edited out, and largely ignored. If he spits his food in your face or urinates on the living-room rug, that is one thing, and something will have to be done about it. But if he calls you a goon, makes fun of your ways, and thumbs his nose at you, these are only symbolic gestures which you need not take in the least seriously. You can easily say to yourself, whenever he calls you a name or gestures his dislike of you, "There goes my disturbed child again, acting the way he feels impelled to act. It is too bad that he is behaving this way; and I wish he weren't! But the sorry truth is that he is behaving badly; and, fortunately, he is just calling me names. So, as long as I don't take his names seriously, don't sharpen them up and stick them in my own breast, there is nothing about them that can hurt me."

As long, then, as you don't believe your child's invectives against you—don't agree that you are a goon because he says that you are—his words, gestures, and attitudes cannot possibly hurt you; and you can live with him very successfully. Similarly, you can teach your other children and your spouse not to take his words and gestures too seriously and not to hurt themselves by exaggerating their significance.

(4) When your neurotic child keeps doing things that are truly harmful—such as physically hurting you or others or inciting your neighbors or the police to take punitive measures against him—you will of course have to try to stop him. Again, however, you should keep calm in the face of his harmful acts and convince yourself that it is too bad that he is behaving in this manner but that he's not utterly reprehensible for doing so and that there is no reason why he should not do so. Once you have calmly accepted the fact of his harmful activity, you can then plan a campaign to get him to reduce or stop it.

As noted above, the best plan in this respect is one of kind firmness, meaning that you should get the child to see that physical injury will definitely not be tolerated, but also show him that you do not consider him to be vermin for having resorted to this kind of injury. He should distinctly and consistently be penalized every time he tries to injure you or anyone else, and he should be shown that just as soon as he desists, the penalties will stop. But as long as he persists in harming other human beings, he will be deprived of things that he wants, restricted in his movements, or even physically harmed himself. In this manner, he can be taught that physically injuring others is pernicious and that there is no possibility of his really getting away with it.

(5) Although it will not work in all or even perhaps in most cases, it is worth trying to continually show love to annoying and injurious neurotic children. When they keep behaving badly, show them that their deeds are misdeeds and indicate to them why they are mistaken in their conduct; but then, in spite of your calm lectures, continue to show them that you love them as human beings and that you can do many loving things for them. When they are behaving well, be exceptionally kind to them— even though they have previously acted very badly. But when they are not behaving well, you can also show them that although you disapprove of their deeds, you do not disapprove of them, and that you can be forgiving and loving in a demonstrative way.

When disturbed children are loved in spite of their shortcomings, they frequently will learn, at the very least, to be annoying to others rather than to you. As long as they continue to be neurotic or psychotic, we may expect them to perform poorly. But they can still often be selective in their performances—and become, for example, hellions at school while remaining near-angels at home. This selective performance on their part will hardly itself be curative; but it will at least make them a lot better for you, personally, to live with. In the long run, moreover, some disturbed children who are accepted and loved in the face of their disruptive activity become so grateful to their parents that they try harder to curb their poor behavior, and sometimes succeed in doing so.

(6) If you would live most successfully with a neurotic child, you would do well to acquire a highly stoic philosophy of life.

Stoicism is often misinterpreted to mean that the individual should accept anything that life brings him and be as happy as he can be with it. Actually, it means that one should try to change the things in the world that are unpleasant and changeable and that one should accept only those undesirable things which are clearly unchangeable—and learn, of course, to know the difference between the two!

If, then, your child is exceptionally neurotic or psychotic, and you still want to live with him and be as happy as you can be under such conditions, you have to stoically accept those aspects of his personality which are unpleasant and which, at least for the time being, you cannot help change. It would be nice, very nice, if he were otherwise; but he isn't! So you'd better give up the idea that he's got to change; that you can't stand the way he is; and that he should be much better than he actually is. A romantic, idealistic attitude toward life has many advantages and is not to be sneered at. But as the parent of a neurotic, annoying child, a more realistic, stoical attitude is by far the better part of valor!

(7) Normally, it is best to try to live in a democratic, equalized kind of way with other members of your family, including your children. But the fact has to be faced that a neurotic child is not only a youngster, who for that reason cannot be treated with full equality, but that he is also an anxiety-ridden, compulsively driven youngster, who is therefore not able to cooperate fully with others. Consequently, you will usually have to treat him, in some respects, as a nonequal, and particularly as a weaker and sicker individual than you are.

Can you actually act as a therapist to your own neurotic child? Not only can you, but in many ways you must if you are to live well with him and he is to be helped to keep his head above water emotionally. As a neurotic, he will have a hard time helping himself get better; and as a child, he will have an even more difficult time attacking and minimizing his disturbances. You, on the other hand, are older than he, are presumably wiser and more educated, and are hopefully not as severely disturbed as the child is. Therefore, even though you are hardly a trained therapist, and may have much to learn yourself in that respect, it behooves you to try to be as therapeutic as possible with your difficult child.

This means that, like the trained psychotherapist, you should try to accept your child fully, in a noncondemning fashion; try to understand things from his distorted frame of reference, rather than merely from your own view of the world; do the best you can to diagnose the source of his disturbances—meaning, the irrational philosophies he believes and which he uses to upset himself with; and calmly and persistently, in an active-directive manner, fight, fight, fight against his self-deprecating and frustration-intolerant tendencies. The content of the therapy you try to give your child can largely be derived from the material we have been examining in the previous chapters of this book; but to this content must be added your great determination to adopt a therapeutic attitude and to use it with your own disturbed youngster. For unless you want to be therapeutic and will back up your desire with concerted action, your pious resolutions to this effect will surely go for naught.

The choice, then, is yours. If you want to live with your neurotic child and help him, the chances are that you definitely can do so, and often help him to a considerable degree. Not that you will ever be able to cure him completely of his underlying emotional disturbances—for that is doubtless too difficult a task for parents, no matter how competent and active they are, to accomplish. Children are both born and raised to be easily upsettable; their entire culture, as well as their heredity, contributes to make them and keep them overly anxious and hostile. The only complete attack on the problem of childhood neurosis, therefore, would have to be a parental-societal attack, using many institutional and other approaches.

One necessary approach, for example, would be the educational one. Our schools, at the present time, are somewhat proficient in teaching children how to read, write, do arithmetic, and comprehend various other subjects. But they as yet do little to help them in their emotional growth and development. At the Institute for Rational Living, Inc., where I am now Executive Director, we take the position that children *can* be taught, in the regular classroom situation, to think clearly about themselves and others, as well as to think about external reality. We teach children how to go through life without unduly upsetting themselves about anything and how to maximally enjoy themselves.

Similarly, other schools and agencies, such as clinics, hospitals, community centers, libraries, films, TV presentations, and theatrical shows, have to be employed if a concerted, large-scale attack on emotional disturbance in children is to be effectively made. You, as a parent, can probably help with some of these efforts; but obviously you cannot produce and direct them by yourself. No matter what you directly and indirectly do in regard to the emotional education of your child, it still will not be enough, and complete success is most unlikely.

Nonetheless, there is much that you can do, if you will willingly take and persist at some of the lines that have been outlined in this book. First, do your best to help yourself become as mature and tolerant as you can be. Read pertinent psychological books; take courses in self-improvement; if necessary, go for psychological guidance on an individual- or group-therapy basis. Second, firmly and kindly try to apply your knowledge to the understanding and guidance of your child. Try to help him be minimally disturbed, if that is possible; and to become maximally undisturbed if he is already seriously neurotic. You won't be, nor should you ever demand that you be, totally successful in these respects. But you can at least try your very best.

Bibliography

Andreev, B. V. *Sleep therapy in the neuroses.* New York. Consultants Bureau, 1960.

Andrews, Gavin, and Mary Harris. The syndrome of stuttering. London Spastics Society, 1964.

Arlitt, A. *The child from one to twelve.* New York: McGraw-Hill, 1931.

Arnold, Magda. *Emotion and personality.* 2 vols. New York: Columbia University Press, 1960.

Barnett, L. The Kibbutz as a child-rearing system: a review of the literature. *Journal of marriage and the family,* 1965, pp. 348–349.

Baruch, Dorothy. *New ways in discipline: you and your child today.* New York: Whittlesey House, 1949.

Beck, Aaron T. Thinking and depression. *Arch. Gen. Psychiat.* 1963 (9), 324–333.

Beigel, Hugo. *Sex from a to z.* New York: Ungar, 1962.

Bergler, Edmund. *Parents not guilty! of their children's neuroses.* New York: Liveright, 1964.

————. *Tensions can be reduced to nuisances.* New York: Liveright, 1960.

Berne, Eric. *Games people play.* New York: Grove Press, 1964.

Bettelheim, Bruno. Dialogue with mothers. *Ladies' Home Journal*, Oct., 1965, 62–65.

————. *Love is not enough*. New York: Collier, 1964.

————. When children lie or steal. *Redbook*, Oct., 1965 (74), 139–142.

Bowlby, John. *Child care and the growth of love*. Baltimore: Penguin, 1953.

Bronfenbrenner, Urie. The changing American child—a speculative analysis. *Merrill-Palmer Quarterly*, 1961 (7), 73–84.

Buxbaum, Edith. *Understanding your child*. New York: Grove Press, 1962.

Calderone, Mary S. Quoted in Bob Lardine, What *not* to tell your child about sex. New York *Sunday News,* July 3, 1966, 6–7.

Camper, Shirley. *How to get along with your child*. New York: Belmont, 1962.

Cattell, R. B. Discussion in *Canadian Psychiatric Assoc. Journal,* Special Supplement, Discussion IV, 1962, 7.

Chess, Stella, Alexander Thomas, and Herbert G. Birch. *Your child is a person*. New York: Viking, 1965.

Davitz, Joel R. Contributions of research with children to a theory of maladjustment. *Child Development*, 1958, 29, 1–7.

Dollard, John, and Neal Miller. *Personality and psychotherapy*. New York: McGraw-Hill, 1950.

Duvall, Evelyn M. *Why wait till marriage?* New York: Association Press, 1965.

Edwards, Morton. *Your child today*. New York: Pocket Books, 1965.

Ellis, Albert. *How to live with a neurotic*. New York: Crown Publishers, 1957.

————. The psychology of sex offenders. In Albert Ellis and Albert Abarbanel (eds.), *The encyclopedia of sexual behavior*. New York: Hawthorne Books, 1961.

————. *The American sexual tragedy*. New York: Lyle Stuart, 1962.

————. *Reason and emotion in psychotherapy*. New York: Lyle Stuart, 1962.

————. *If this be sexual heresy*. New York: Lyle Stuart, 1963.

————. *The intelligent woman's guide to man-hunting*. New York: Lyle Stuart, 1963.

————. *The origins and the development of the incest taboo*. New York: Lyle Stuart, 1963.

————. *Sex and the single man*. New York: Lyle Stuart, 1963.

————. *Homosexuality: its causes and cure.* New York: Lyle Stuart, 1965.

————. *Sex without guilt.* New York: Lyle Stuart, 1965.

————. *Suppressed: 7 key essays publishers dared not print.* Chicago: New Classics House, 1965.

————. *The art and science of love.* New York: Lyle Stuart, 1965.

————. *The case for sexual liberty.* Tucson: Seymour Press, 1965.

————. *The search for sexual enjoyment.* New York: Macfadden-Bartell, 1966.

————, and Robert A. Harper. *A guide to rational living.* Englewood Cliffs, N.J.: Prentice-Hall, 1961.

English, O. Spurgeon, and Constance J. Foster. *Fathers are parents too.* New York: Belmont, 1962.

Faegre, Marion L., and John E. Anderson. *Child care and training.* Minneapolis: University of Minnesota Press, 1958.

Fenichel, Otto. *Psychoanalytic theory of neurosis.* New York: Norton, 1945.

Fine, Reuben. *Freud: a critical re-evaluation of his theories.* New York: David McKay Co., 1962.

Finger, Frank W. Sex beliefs and practices among male college students. *Journal of Abnormal Soc. Psychol.,* 1947 (42), 57–67.

Fraiberg, Selma H. *The magic years.* New York: Charles Scribner's Sons, 1959.

Frank, Lawrence K. *Feelings and emotions.* Garden City: Doubleday, 1954.

Frank, Mary and Lawrence. *How to help your child in school.* New York: Viking, 1950.

Franks, Cyril and Violet. *Questions and answers concerning bed-wetting (enuresis).* New York: Enurtone Co., 1963.

Freud, Anna. *The ego and the mechanisms of defense.* London: Hogarth, 1937.

Freud, Sigmund. *Basic writings.* New York: Modern Library, 1938.

————. *Collected papers.* New York: Collier Books, 1963–64.

Fromme, Allan. *The parents' handbook.* New York: Simon & Schuster, 1956.

Gardner, John. *Excellence; can we be equal and excellent too?* New York: Harper, 1961.

————. *Self-renewal.* New York: Harper, 1965.

Garvey, Wm. P., and Jack R. Hegrenes. Treatment of school phobia. *Am. Journal of Orthopsychiatry,* 1966 (36), 147–157.

Gebhard, Paul H., John H. Gagnon, Wardell B. Pomeroy, and Cornelia V. Christenson. *Sex offenders.* New York: Harper, 1965.

Geis, H. Jon. Unpublished Ph.D. dissertation, New York University, 1966.

Genne, William H. Are the churches changing sex? *Sexol.,* 1965 (32), 312–315.

Gerard, R. The scope of science. *The Scientific Monthly,* 1947, (64), 496–513.

Ginott, Haim G. *Between parent and child.* New York: Macmillan, 1965.

Glasser, William. *Reality therapy.* New York: Harper, 1965.

Good Housekeeping. If a child is a bed wetter. *Good Housekeeping.* Oct., 1965, 174.

Gottlieb, Bernard S. *What a boy should know about sex.* Indianapolis: Bobbs-Merrill, 1960.

Gratch, Gerald. An exploratory study of the relative dependence upon adult approval and age to children's risk-taking. *Child Dev.,* 1964 (35), 1155–1167.

Gregg, Alan. Character building in children. In Sidonie Matsner Gruenberg (ed.), *Our children today.* New York: Viking, 1952.

Gross, Leonard. Sex education comes of age. *Look,* March 8, 1966, 21–25.

Guttmacher, Alan F., with B. Winfield and F. Jaffe. *The complete book of birth control.* New York: Ballantine, 1961.

Guyon, René. *The ethics of sexual acts.* New York: Knopf, 1934.

———. *Sexual freedom.* New York: Knopf, 1950. Hollywood: France International, 1963.

Hadfield, J. A. *What is neurosis, childhood and adolescence.* Baltimore, Penguin, 1960.

Halpern, Howard M. *A parent's guide to child psychotherapy.* New York: Barnes, 1963.

Hartman, Robert. *The measurement of value.* Crotonville, New York: General Electric Co., 1959.

———. *The individual in management.* Chicago: Nationwide Insurance Co., 1962.

Hicks, Granville. Asphalt is better soil. *Sat. Review,* Oct. 13, 1962, 20, 37.

Hoffer, Eric. *The passionate state of mind.* New York: Harper, 1955.

Holt, L. Emmett. *The* Good Housekeeping *book of baby and child care.* New York: Popular Library, 1957.

Hoover, Mary Bidgood. Anxiety . . . hidden threat to children's health. *Parents' Mag.,* Nov., 1965, 74–76, 156.

Hymes, James L., Jr. *How to tell your child about sex.* New York: Public Affairs Pamphlets, 1965.

Ilg, Frances, and Louise Bates Ames. *Gesell Institute's child behavior.* New York: Harper, 1955.

Johnson, Adelaide M. The adolescent and his problems. *Amer. Journal Occup. Ther.,* 1957 (11), 255–261.

————, and David B. Robinson. The sexual deviant. *Journal Amer. Med. Assn.,* 1957 (164), 1559–1565.

Johnson, Warren and Julia Ann. *Human sex and sex education.* Philadelphia: Lea and Febiger, 1963.

Johnson, Wendell. *Stuttering and what you can do about it.* University of Minnesota Press, 1961.

————. *Diagnostic methods in speech pathology.* New York: Harper, 1963.

————. *People in quandaries.* New York: Harper, 1946.

Kinsey, Alfred C., Wardell B. Pomeroy, and Clyde E. Martin. *Sexual behavior in the human male.* Philadelphia: Saunders, 1948.

Kirkendall, Lester A. *Helping children understand sex.* Chicago: Science Research Associates, 1952.

————, with Elizabeth Ogg. *Sex and our society.* New York: Public Affairs Pamphlets, 1964.

Langmuir, Mary F. Discipline: means and ends. In Sidonie M. Gruenberg (Ed.), *Our children today.* New York: Viking, 1952.

Lardine, Bob. What *not* to tell your child about sex. *New York Sunday News,* July 3, 1966, 6–7.

Levin, Phyllis Lee. There are babies and babies. *New York Times Magazine,* May 12, 1965, 132–134.

Lipton, Lawrence. *The erotic revolution.* Los Angeles: Sherbourne, 1965.

London, Perry. *The modes and morals of psychotherapy.* New York: Holt, 1964.

Lovibond, S. H. *Conditioning and enuresis.* New York: Macmillan, 1964.

McClelland, D. C., and others. *The achievement motive.* New York: Appleton, 1953.

McCord, William, *The origins of crime.* New York: Columbia University Press, 1959.

MacIntyre, Alasdair. The psychoanalysts: the future of an illusion. *Encounter,* 1965.

Malinowski, Bronislaw. *The sexual life of savages.* New York: Halcyon House, 1941.

————. *Sex and repression in savage society.* London: Routledge, 1949.

Malone, Charles A. Safety first: comments on the influence of external danger in the lives of children of disorganized families. *Am. Journal of Orthopsychiatry*, 1966 (36), 3–12.

Martin, Irene. *Handbook of abnormal psychology*, Eysenck, H. J. (Ed.). New York: Basic Books, 1960.

Martin, William E. Rediscovering the mind of the child: a significant trend in research in child development. *Merrill-Palmer Quarterly*, 1960 (6), 67–76.

Maslow, Abraham H. *Motivation and personality*. New York: Harper, 1954.

—————. *Toward a psychology of being*. Princeton: Van Nostrand, 1962.

Medinnus, Gene R., and Floyd J. Curtis. The relationship between maternal self-acceptance and child acceptance. *Journal of Consulting Psychol.* 1963 (27), 542–554.

Menninger, Karl. *Theory of psychoanalytic technique*. New York: Basic Books, 1958.

—————, Judith Porta, and Joan McCord. The familial genesis of psychoses. *Psychiatry*, 1962 (25), 60–71.

Miller, J. G. Review of joint commission on mental illness and health: action for mental health. *Contemporary Psy.* 1961 (6), 293–296.

Moll, Albert. *Sexual life of the child*. New York: Macmillan, 1912.

Money, John. *Sex research—new developments*. New York: Holt, 1965.

Moore, Brian. *See* Hicks, Granville.

Mowrer, O. Hobart. *The new group therapy*. Princeton: Van Nostrand, 1964.

—————, and W. M. Mowrer. Enuresis: a method for its study and treatment. *Amer. Journal of Orthopsychiatry*, 1938 (8), 436.

Murphy, Lois, and others. *The widening world of childhood*. New York: Basic Books, 1962.

Neill, A. S. *Summerhill*. New York: Hart, 1964.

Newcomb, Theodore M. Inside the family today. *Social Order*, May, 1956, 195.

Pastore, Nicholas. A neglected factor in the frustration-aggression hypothesis. *Journal of Psychol.*, 1950 (29), 271–279.

—————. The role of arbitrariness in the frustration-aggression hypothesis. *Journal of Abnor. Soc. Psychol.* 1952 (47), 728–731.

Pfaundler, M. Demonstration eines Apparates zur selbstätigen Signalisierun stattfehabter Bettnassung. *Verhandl. d. deutsch. Gesselsch. f. Kinderheilk*, 1904 (21), 219.

Phillips, E. Lakin. Logical analysis of childhood behavior problems and their treatment. *Psychol. Reports,* 1961 (9), 705–712.

Piers, G., and M. G. Singer. *Shame and guilt,* Springfield, Ill.: Charles C Thomas, 1953.

Podolsky, E. The logotherapy of Viktor Frankl. *Indian Journal of Psychiat.,* 1962 (4), 9–11.

Potter, Stephen. *One-upmanship.* New York: Holt, 1952.

Powell, Marvin. Is free will really necessary? *Amer. Psychologist,* 1960 (15), 217–219.

Ramsey, Glenn V. *Factors in the sex life of 291 boys.* Madison, N.J.: Author, 1950.

Redlich, Fritz, and Jane Bingham. *The inside story—psychiatry and everyday life.* New York: Knopf, 1953.

Reik, Theodor. *Listening with the third ear.* New York: Rinehart, 1948.

Remy-Roux. Nouvel appareil électrique contre l'incontinence nocturne d'urine. *Bulletins et mémoires de la Société de médecine de Vaucluse,* 1908–1909 (2), 337.

Renaud, Harold, and Floyd Estess. Life history with one hundred normal American males: Pathogenicity of childhood. *Amer. Journal of Orthopsychiatry,* 1961 (31), 786–802.

Ringness, Thomas A. Affective differences between successful and nonsuccessful bright ninth grade boys. *Personnel and Guidance Journal,* 1965 (43), 600–606.

Rosenthal, M. The syndrome of the inconsistent mother. *Amer. Journal of Orthopsychiatry.* 1962 (32), 637–644.

Rubin, Isadore. Stop worrying about masturbation. *Sexol.,* May, 1963, 707–710.

Schaefer, Roy. Review of D. W. Winnicott, *Collected papers. Contemp. Psychol.,* 1959 (4), 282–283.

Science News Letter. Parents' maladjustments reflected in children. *Science News Letter,* Feb. 12, 1966, 105.

———. T.V. good life spurs delinquency. *Science News Letter,* June 9, 1962, 362–363.

Scott, D. H. *Thirty-three troublesome children.* London: Natl. Children's Home, 1964.

Sears, Robert R. Relationship of early socialization experiences to aggression in middle childhood. *Journal of Abnorm. Psychol.,* 1961 (63), 466–492.

Seiger, H. W. Record U.S. Patent Office. Washington, D.C., 1936.

———. A practical urine or wet diaper signal. *Journal of Pediat.,* 1946 (28), 733.

———. Treatment of essential nocturnal enuresis. *Journal Pediat.,* 1952 (40), 738–749.

Seipt, Irene. *Your child's happiness.* Cleveland: World Pub., 1955.

Shafer, Nathaniel. False gonorrhea. *Sexol.,* 1965 (32), 338–340.

Skard, Aase Gruda. Maternal deprivation: the research and its implications. *Journal of Marriage and Family,* 1965, 333–342.

Smart, Mollie. How does a conscience grow? *Parents' Mag.,* Aug., 1965 (59), 127–130.

Spock, Benjamin. *Baby and child care.* New York: Pocket Books, 1961.

Stokes, Walter R. How to handle children's masturbation. *Sexol.,* 1965 (32), 297–300.

Sullivan, Harry Stack. *Conceptions of modern psychiatry.* Washington: William Alanson White Foundation, 1947.

———. *The interpersonal theory of psychiatry.* New York: Norton, 1953.

Symonds, Percival M. *Dynamics of psychotherapy.* 3 vols. New York: Grune & Stratton, 1956–1959.

Taylor, G. Rattray. *Sex in history.* New York: Ballantine, 1962.

Thomson, Helen. Anger in children. *Parents' Mag.,* April, 1952.

Unger, Sanford M. Antecedents of personality differences in guilt responsivity. *Psychol. Reports,* 1962 (10), 357–358.

United States Dept. of Health, Education, and Welfare. *Behavior problems and fears.* Washington: Government Printing Office, 1962.

———. *Your child, six to twelve.* Washington: Government Printing Office, 1962.

Wahler, Robert G., Gary H. Winkel, Robert F. Peterson, and Delmont C. D. Morrison. Mothers as behavior therapists for their own children. *Behav. Res. Ther.,* 1965 (3), 113–124.

White, Robert W. Motivation reconsidered: the concept of competence. *Psychol. Rev.,* 1959 (66), 297–333.

Wolf, Anna W. *The parents' manual.* New York: Simon & Schuster, 1941.

Wolpe, Joseph. *Psychotherapy by reciprocal inhibition.* Stanford: Stanford University Press, 1958.

———. The systematic desensitization treatment of neurosis. *Journal of Nerv. Mental Dis.,* 1961 (132), 189–203.

Yolles, Stanley F. Giant steps in baby research. *New York Times Magazine,* April 17, 1966, 91–94.

Young, Gordon C. Personality factors and the treatment of enuresis. *Behav. Res. Ther.,* 1965 (3), 103–105.

————, and R. K. Turner. CNS stimulant drugs and conditioning treatment of nocturnal enuresis. *Behav. Res. Ther.,* 1965 (3), 93–101.

Young, Leontine R. The truth about children's lying. *McCall's Magazine,* Nov., 1965, 186–222.

Young, Wayland. *Eros denied.* New York: Grove Press, 1964.

Index

...If you feel as though you are on a runaway emotional roller coaster with your partner at the controls, this book is for you! It can save you years of torment, tumult, and tears.

The Powerful, Life-Changing Secret of Overcoming Verbal Abuse

If you are being mistreated by your partner, *The Secret of Overcoming Verbal Abuse* can dramatically change your life. You will learn an entirely new way of perceiving and coping with your relationship and your feelings.

The time-tested, proven secret contained in this book will wrap itself around you like a thick, warm, protective blanket, insulating you from your pain. And the next time your "Prince Charming" takes aim and tries to pierce your heart with his unkind words, you will be ready. You will feel strong and be in charge of your own reaction.

Whether you want to stay, need to stay, or plan to leave, this book can help you to

- Set yourself free from confusion, anxiety, frustration, self-doubt, guilt, anger, and depression
- Restore your dignity, self-respect, self-love, and personal power
- Create the inner peace and happiness you have wanted, wished for, and in tearful private moments prayed for—perhaps for years

Now get ready to begin an exciting journey of enlightenment and empowerment that will help you regain control of your life. Your guides will be one of the most famous and influential psychologists in the world, **Dr. Albert Ellis,** and **Marcia Grad Powers,** accredited psychological educator and bestselling author.

Available at bookstores or send $12.00 (CA res. $12.96) plus $2.00 S/H to Wilshire Book Co., 12015 Sherman Road No. Hollywood, CA 91605.

For our complete catalog, visit our Web site at www.mpowers.com.

For every man who wants to shed his armor—and for the women who care about them...

KNIGHTS WITHOUT ARMOR

If you are struggling to get rid of heavy old restrictive armor that limits pleasure and joy in your life, hurts your relationships, damages your health, causes you to do destructive things to yourself and others—or if someone you care about is engaged in this struggle—*Knights Without Armor* is just what you need.

For centuries men have been taught from childhood that encasing themselves in armor is an integral part of being a man. And some men are further trapped by roles and jobs that demand they be tough and cold and hard as steel. They use psychological armor to forge ahead and to protect themselves from the potential ravages of what they confront day after day.

For many, maintaining their armor results in their walling themselves off from their feelings and from other people, which comes at a very high cost—isolation, confusion, frustration, anger, depression, addictions, troubled relationships, stress-related illnesses. But they fear that if they remove their armor, they may lose their strength, their power—even their masculinity.

Not so! says *Knights Without Armor*. Living the myth of the lone hero, who conquers all through the force of his will, is not the *only* way—or the *best* way—to be strong and powerful. This book is an adventure of self-discovery for male readers. The "Twelve Tasks of Men" guides them past the major problems they have in opening up their lives, and the "Male Manifesto" clarifies what it means to be a man. The adventure for women is in gaining insight into their man's quest to find a new way to live in the world.

For a beautiful, 294-page hardcover edition of *Knights Without Armor: A Practical Guide for Men in Quest of the Masculine Soul* by Aaron R. Kipnis, Ph.D.—psychotherapist, leader of men's groups, and expert in modern man's quest to live a new masculine role—send $10.00 (CA res. $10.80) plus $2.00 S/H to Wilshire Book Company, 12015 Sherman Road, North Hollywood, CA 91605 or order online at www.mpowers.com.

A Personal Invitation from the Publisher, Melvin Powers...

I would like to introduce you to a wonderful, unique book guaranteed to captivate your imagination as it helps you discover the secret of what is most important in life. It is *The Knight in Rusty Armor*, a delightful tale of a desperate knight in search of his true self.

Since first publishing this book we have received an unprecedented number of calls and letters from readers praising its powerful insights and entertaining style. Readers say that this memorable story, rich in wit and humor, has changed their lives in important ways. *The Knight* is one of our most popular titles. It has been published in numerous languages and has become a well-known favorite in many countries. I feel so strongly about this book that I am personally inviting you to read it.

The Knight in Rusty Armor

Join the knight as he faces a life-changing dilemma upon discovering that he is trapped in his armor, just as *we* may be trapped in *our* armor—an invisible one that we use to protect ourselves from others and from various aspects of life.

As the knight searches for a way to free himself, he receives guidance from the wise sage Merlin the Magician, who encourages him to embark on the most difficult crusade of his life. The knight takes up the challenge and travels the Path of Truth, where he meets his real self for the first time and confronts the Universal Truths that govern his life—and ours.

The knight's journey reflects our own, filled with hope and despair, belief and disillusionment, laughter and tears. His insights become our insights as we follow along on his intriguing adventure of self-discovery. Anyone who has ever struggled with the meaning of life and love will discover profound wisdom and truth as this unique fantasy unfolds. *The Knight in Rusty Armor* is an experience that will expand your mind, touch your heart, and nourish your soul.

Available at all bookstores. Or send $5.00 (CA res. $5.41) plus $2.00 S/H to Wilshire Book Company, 12015 Sherman Road, No. Hollywood, CA 91605.

For our complete catalog, visit our Web site at www.mpowers.com.

THE LAW OF SUCCESS IN SIXTEEN LESSONS

By Napoleon Hill

Over the years, Wilshire Book Company has sold more than seven million copies of *Think and Grow Rich* and has had thousands of requests from enthusiastic readers for Napoleon Hill's original eight-book series, *The Law of Success in Sixteen Lessons.*

After many years of intensive and extensive research, we found a set of the books in mint condition. We are excited to finally be republishing this original, unabridged, classic edition of the world famous series, reproduced just as it first appeared, and compiled into a convenient, beautiful two-volume set.

If your life has been enriched by Napoleon Hill's *Think and Grow Rich,* you'll love *The Law of Success in Sixteen Lessons.* It teaches the life-changing philosophy upon which *Think and Grow Rich* and most modern motivational books are based.

We have received accolades from all over the world for making Napoleon Hill's timeless words of wisdom available to enhance the lives of new generations. We know you'll be delighted with this two-volume treasure. It is a blueprint for success in any field of endeavor. You will learn how to think like a winner . . . be a winner . . . and reap the rewards of a winner. Now get ready for Napoleon Hill to help make your most cherished dreams come true.

Two-Volume Set...$30.00

THE PRINCESS WHO BELIEVED
IN
FAIRY TALES
By Marcia Grad

"Here is a very special book that will guide you lovingly into a new way of thinking about yourself and your life so that the future will be filled with hope and love and song."

OG MANDINO
Author, *The Greatest Salesman in the World*

The Princess Who Believed in Fairy Tales is a personal growth book of the rarest kind. It is a delightful, humor-filled story you will experience so deeply that it can literally change your feelings about yourself, your relationships, and your life.

The princess' journey of self-discovery on the Path of Truth is an eye-opening, inspiring, empowering psychological and spiritual journey that symbolizes the one we all take through life as we sort out illusion from reality, come to terms with our childhood dreams and pain, and discover who we really are and how life works.

If you have struggled with childhood pain, with feelings of not being good enough, with the loss of your dreams, or if you have been disappointed in your relationships, *The Princess Who Believed in Fairy Tales* will prove to you that happy endings—and new beginnings—are always possible. Or if you simply want to get closer to your own truth, the princess will guide you.

You will experience the princess' journey as your own. You will laugh with her and cry with her, learn with her and grow with her, and if you are in pain, you will begin to heal with her.

The universal appeal to both men and women of *The Princess Who Believed in Fairy Tales* has resulted in its translation into numerous languages.

Excerpts from Readers' Heartfelt Letters

"*The Princess* is truly a gem! Though I've read a zillion self-help and spiritual books, I got more out of this one than from any other one I've ever read. It is just too illuminating and full of wisdom to ever be able to thank you enough."

"Your loving story tells my story and many other women's so beautifully. I related to each page for different reasons. Thank you for putting my experience into words for me.... I've been waiting to read this book my entire life."

Available at bookstores. Or send $10.00 (CA res. $10.83) plus $2.00 S/H to

Wilshire Book Company
12015 Sherman Road, No. Hollywood, California 91605

For our complete catalog, visit our Web site at www.mpowers.com.

Books by Melvin Powers

HOW TO GET RICH IN MAIL ORDER

1. How to Develop Your Mail Order Expertise 2. How to Find a Unique Product or Service to Sell 3. How to Make Money with Classified Ads 4. How to Make Money with Display Ads 5. The Unlimited Potential for Making Money with Direct Mail 6. How to Copycat Successful Mail Order Operations 7. How I Created a Bestseller Using the Copycat Technique 8. How to Start and Run a Profitable Mail Order Special Interest Book Business 9. I Enjoy Selling Books by Mail—Some of My Successful Ads 10. Five of My Most Successful Direct Mail Pieces That Sold and Are Selling Millions of Dollars' Worth of Books 11. Melvin Powers's Mail Order Success Strategy—Follow it and You'll Become a Millionaire 12. How to Sell Your Products to Mail Order Companies, Retail Outlets, Jobbers, and Fund Raisers for Maximum Distribution and Profit 13. How to Get Free Display Ads and Publicity that Will Put You on the Road to Riches 14. How to Make Your Advertising Copy Sizzle 15. Questions and Answers to Help You Get Started Making Money 16. A Personal Word from Melvin Powers 17. How to Get Started 18. Selling Products on Television   8½" x 11½" — 352 Pages . . . $20.00

MAKING MONEY WITH CLASSIFIED ADS

1. Getting Started with Classified Ads 2. Everyone Loves to Read Classified Ads 3. How to Find a Money-Making Product 4. How to Write Classified Ads that Make Money 5. What I've Learned from Running Thousands of Classified Ads 6. Classified Ads Can Help You Make Big Money in Multi-Level Programs 7. Two-Step Classified Ads Made Me a Multi-Millionaire—They Can Do the Same for You! 8. One-Inch Display Ads Can Work Wonders 9. Display Ads Can Make You a Fortune Overnight 10. Although I Live in California, I Buy My Grapefruit from Florida 11. Nuts and Bolts of Mail Order Success 12. What if You Can't Get Your Business Running Successfully? What's Wrong? How to Correct it 13. Strategy for Mail Order Success   8½" x 11½" — 240 Pages . . . $20.00

HOW TO SELF-PUBLISH YOUR BOOK AND HAVE THE FUN AND EXCITEMENT OF BEING A BEST-SELLING AUTHOR

1. Who is Melvin Powers? 2. What is the Motivation Behind Your Decision to Publish Your Book? 3. Why You Should Read This Chapter Even if You Already Have an Idea for a Book 4. How to Test the Salability of Your Book Before You Write One Word 5. How I Achieved Sales Totaling $2,000,000 on My Book *How to Get Rich in Mail Order* 6. How to Develop a Second Career by Using Your Expertise 7. How to Choose an Enticing Book Title 8. Marketing Strategy 9. Success Stories 10. How to Copyright Your Book 11. How to Write a Winning Advertisement 12. Advertising that Money Can't Buy 13. Questions and Answers to Help You Get Started 14. Self-Publishing and the Midas Touch
8½" x 11½" — 240 Pages . . . $20.00

A PRACTICAL GUIDE TO SELF-HYPNOSIS

1. What You Should Know about Self-Hypnosis 2. What about the Dangers of Hypnosis? 3. Is Hypnosis the Answer? 4. How Does Self-Hypnosis Work? 5. How to Arouse Yourself From the Self-Hypnotic State 6. How to Attain Self-Hypnosis 7. Deepening the Self-Hypnotic State 8. What You Should Know about Becoming an Excellent Subject 9. Techniques for Reaching the Somnambulistic State 10. A New Approach to Self-Hypnosis 11. Psychological Aids and Their Function 12. Practical Applications of Self-Hypnosis
144 Pages . . . $10.00

Available at your bookstore or directly from Wilshire Book Company.
Please add $2.00 shipping and handling for each book ordered.

Wilshire Book Company
12015 Sherman Road, No. Hollywood, California 91605

For our complete catalog, visit our Web site at www.mpowers.com.